Everything You Always Wanted to Know about Lacan (But Were Afraid to Ask Hitchcock)

Edited by
SLAVOJ ŽIŽEK

VERSO

London · New York

First published by Verso 1992
© in the collection Verso 1992
Individual chapters © contributors 1992
All rights reserved

Reprinted 1993, 1995, 1996, 1997, 1999, 2000, 2002

Verso
UK: 6 Meard Street, London W1F 0EG
USA: 180 Varick Street, New York NY 10014-4606

Verso is the imprint of New Left Books

ISBN 0-86091-394-5
ISBN 0-86091-592-1 (pbk)

British Library Cataloguing in Publication Data
A catalogue record for this book is available from the British Library

Library of Congress Cataloging-in-Publication Data
A catalog record for this book is available from the Library of Congress

Typeset in Baskerville by Leaper & Gard Ltd
Printed and bound in Great Britain by Biddles Ltd
www.biddles.co.uk

Contents

INTRODUCTION   **Alfred Hitchcock, or, The Form and its Historical Mediation**   *Slavoj Žižek*   1

PART I   **The Universal: Themes**

1   Hitchcockian Suspense   *Pascal Bonitzer*   15
2   Hitchcock's Objects   *Mladen Dolar*   31
3   Spatial Systems in *North by Northwest*   *Fredric Jameson*   47
4   A Perfect Place to Die: Theatre in Hitchcock's Films   *Alenka Zupančič*   73
5   *Punctum Caecum*, or, Of Insight and Blindness   *Stojan Pelko*   106

PART II   **The Particular: Films**

1   Hitchcockian *Sinthoms*   *Slavoj Žižek*   125
2   The Spectator Who Knew Too Much   *Mladen Dolar*   129
3   The Cipher of Destiny   *Michel Chion*   137
4   A Father Who Is Not Quite Dead   *Mladen Dolar*   143
5   *Notorious*   *Pascal Bonitzer*   151
6   The Fourth Side   *Michel Chion*   155
7   The Man Behind His Own Retina   *Miran Božovič*   161
8   The Skin and the Straw   *Pascal Bonitzer*   178

does not want see himself in the picture. In the end in the picture from nature.   *change.*

9   The Right Man and the Wrong Woman   *Renata Salecl*   185

10   The Impossible Embodiment   *Michel Chion*   195

PART III   **The Individual: Hitchcock's Universe**

'In His Bold Gaze My Ruin Is Writ Large' *Slavoj Žižek*   211

What's wrong with *The Wrong Man*? · The
Hitchcockian allegory · From I to *a* · *Psycho*'s
Moebius band · Aristophanes reversed · 'A triumph
of the gaze over the eye' · The narrative closure and
its vortex · The gaze of the Thing · 'Subjective
destitution' · The collapse of intersubjectivity

Notes on the Contributors   273

Index   275

Sources

Pascal Bonitzer's 'Hitchcockian Suspense' was first published in *Cahiers du cinéma* no. 8 hors-série; Michel Chion's 'The Cipher of Destiny' was first published in *Cahiers du cinéma*, no. 358, April 1984; Pascal Bonitzer's '*Notorious*' was first published in *Cahiers du cinéma* no. 309, 1980; Michel Chion's 'The Fourth Side' was first published in *Cahiers du cinéma*, no. 356, February 1984; Pascal Bonitzer's 'The Skin and the Straw' was first published in *L'Ane*, no. 17, July–August 1984; Michel Chion's 'The Impossible Embodiment' was first published in his *La Voix au cinéma*, Cahiers du cinéma/Etoile 1982. Thanks are due to the copyright holders for permission to reproduce them here. All appear for the first time in English and are here translated by Martin Thom.

INTRODUCTION

Alfred Hitchcock, or, The Form and its Historical Mediation

SLAVOJ ŽIŽEK

What is usually left unnoticed in the multitude of attempts to inter-pret the break between modernism and postmodernism is the way this break affects *the very status of interpretation*. Both modernism and postmodernism conceive of interpretation as inherent to its object: without it we do not have access to the work of art – the traditional paradise where, irrespective of his/her versatility in the artifice of interpreting, everybody can enjoy the work of art, is irreparably lost. The break between modernism and postmodernism is thus to be located within this inherent relationship between the text and its commentary. A modernist work of art is by definition 'incompre-hensible'; it functions as a shock, as the irruption of a trauma which undermines the complacency of our daily routine and resists being integrated into the symbolic universe of the prevailing ideology; thereupon, after this first encounter, interpretation enters the stage and enables us to integrate this shock – it informs us, say, that this trauma registers and points towards the shocking depravity of our very 'normal' everyday lives.... In this sense, interpretation is the conclusive moment of the very act of reception: T.S. Eliot was quite astute when he supplemented his *Waste Land* with notes on literary references such as one would expect from an academic commentary.

What postmodernism does, however, is the very opposite: its objects *par excellence* are products with a distinctive mass appeal (films like *Blade Runner*, *Terminator* or *Blue Velvet*) – it is for the

1

interpreter to detect in them an exemplification of the most esoteric theoretical finesses of Lacan, Derrida or Foucault. If, then, the pleasure of the modernist interpretation consists in the effect of recognition which 'gentrifies' the disquieting uncanniness of its object ('Aha, now I see the point of this apparent mess!'), the aim of the postmodernist treatment is to estrange its very initial homeliness: 'You think what you see is a simple melodrama even your senile granny would have no difficulties in following? Yet without taking into account ... /the difference between symptom and *sinthom*; the structure of the Borromean knot; the fact that Woman is one of the Names-of-the-Father; etc., etc./ you've totally missed the point!'

If there is an author whose name epitomizes this interpretive pleasure of 'estranging' the most banal content, it is Alfred Hitchcock. Hitchcock as the theoretical phenomenon that we have witnessed in recent decades – the endless flow of books, articles, university courses, conference panels – is a 'postmodern' phenomenon *par excellence*. It relies on the extraordinary transference his work sets in motion: for true Hitchcock *aficionados, everything has meaning* in his films, the seemingly simplest plot conceals unexpected philosophical delicacies (and – useless to deny it – this book partakes unrestrainedly in such madness). Yet is Hitchcock, for all that, a 'postmodernist' *avant la lettre*? How should one locate him with reference to the triad realism–modernism–postmodernism elaborated by Fredric Jameson with a special view to the history of cinema, where 'realism' stands for the classic Hollywood – that is, the narrative code established in the 1930s and 1940s, 'modernism' for the great *auteurs* of the 1950s and 1960s, and 'postmodernism' for the mess we are in today – that is, for the obsession with the traumatic Thing which reduces every narrative grid to a particular failed attempt to 'gentrify' the Thing?[1]

For a dialectical approach, Hitchcock is of special interest precisely in so far as he dwells on the borders of this classificatory triad[2] – any attempt at classification brings us sooner or later to a paradoxical result according to which Hitchcock is in a way *all three of them at the same time*: 'realist' (from the old Leftist critics and historians in whose eyes his name epitomizes the Hollywood ideological narrative closure, up to Raymond Bellour, for whom his films vary the Oedipal trajectory and are as such 'both an eccentric and exemplary version' of the classic Hollywood narrative[3]), 'modernist' (i.e. a forerunner and at the same time one in the line of the great *auteurs* who, at the margins of Hollywood or outside it, subverted its narrative codes – Welles, Renoir, Bergman . . .), 'postmodernist' (if for no other reason, then for the above-mentioned transference his films set in motion among the interpreters).

What, then, *is* Hitchcock, 'in truth'? That is to say, one is tempted to take the easy way out by affirming that he is 'truly a realist', firmly embedded in the Hollywood machinery, and only later appropriated first by modernists around *Cahiers du cinéma*, and then by postmodernists – yet such a solution relies on the difference between the 'Thing-in-itself' and its secondary interpretations, a difference which is epistemologically deeply suspect in so far as an interpretation is never simply 'external' to its object. It is therefore far more productive to *transpose this dilemma into Hitchcock's opus itself* and conceive the triad realism–modernism–postmodernism as a classificatory principle that enables us to introduce order into it by means of differentiating its five periods:

● Films before *The Thirty-Nine Steps*: Hitchcock before his 'epistemological break', before what Elizabeth Weis appropriately called 'consolidation of [Hitchcock's] classical style',[4] or – to put it in Hegelese – before he became his own notion. Of course, one can play here the game 'the entire Hitchcock is already there', in the films before the break (Rothman, for example, discerned in *The Lodger* the ingredients of the entire Hitchcock up to *Psycho*[5]) – on condition that one does not overlook the *retroactive* nature of such a procedure: the place from which it speaks is the already-actualized notion of 'Hitchcock's universe'.

● English films of the second half of the 1930s – from *The Thirty-Nine Steps* to *The Lady Vanishes*: 'realism' (clearly the reason why even a hardline Marxist like Georges Sadoul, generally very critical towards Hitchcock, finds them likeable), formally within the confines of the classic narrative, thematically centred on the *Oedipal story of the couple's initiatory journey*. That is to say, the animated action in these films should not deceive us for a minute – its function is ultimately just to put the love couple to the test and thus render possible their final reunion. They are all stories of a couple tied (sometimes literally: note the role of handcuffs in *The Thirty-Nine Steps*) by accident and then maturing through a series of ordeals – that is, variations on the fundamental motif of the bourgeois ideology of marriage, which gained its first and perhaps noblest expression in Mozart's *Magic Flute*.[6] The couples tied by chance and reunited through ordeal are Hannay and Pamela in *The Thirty-Nine Steps*, Ashenden and Elsa in *The Secret Agent*, Robert and Erica in *Young and Innocent*, Gilbert and Iris in *The Lady Vanishes* – with the notable exception of *Sabotage*, where the triangle of Sylvia, her criminal husband Verloc, and the detective Ted foreshadows the conjuncture characteristic of Hitchcock's next stage.

• The 'Selznick period' – films from *Rebecca* to *Under Capricorn*: 'modernism', formally epitomized by the prevalence of long, ana-morphically distorted tracking shots, thematically centred on the perspective of the *female heroine, traumatized by an ambiguous (evil, impotent, obscene, broken . . .) paternal figure.* That is to say, the story is, as a rule, narrated from the point of view of a woman divided between two men: the elderly figure of a villain (her father or her aged husband, embodying one of the typical Hitchcockian figures, that of a villain who is aware of the evil in himself and strives after his own destruction) and the younger, somewhat insipid 'good guy' whom she chooses in the end. In addition to Sylvia, Verloc and Ted in *Sabotage*, the main examples of such triangles are Carol Fisher, divided between loyalty to her pro-Nazi father and love for the young American journalist, in *Foreign Correspondent*; Charlie, divided between her murderous uncle of the same name and the detective Jack, in *Shadow of a Doubt*; and, of course, Alicia, divided between her aged husband Sebastian and Devlin, in *Notorious*.[7] The ambiguous apogee of this period is, of course, *Rope*: instead of the female heroine, we get here the 'passive' member of the homosexual couple (Farley Granger) divided between his charmingly evil companion and their teacher, the Professor (James Stewart), who is not prepared to recognize in their crime the realization of his own teaching.

• The big films of the 1950s and early 1960s – from *Strangers on a Train* to *Birds*: 'postmodernism', formally epitomized by the accentuated allegorical dimension (the indexing, within the film's diegetic content, of its own process of enunciation and consumption: references to 'voyeurism' from *Rear Window* to *Psycho*, etc.), thematically centred on the perspective of the *male hero to whom the maternal superego blocks access to a 'normal' sexual relation* (Bruno in *Strangers on a Train*, Jeff in *Rear Window*, Roger Thornhill in *North by Northwest*, Norman in *Psycho*, Mitch in *The Birds*, up to the 'necktie-murderer' in *Frenzy*).

• Films from *Marnie* onwards: in spite of isolated touches of brilliance (the hulk at the end of the street in *Marnie*, Gromek's murder in *Torn Curtain*, the backward tracking shot in *Frenzy*, the use of parallel narration in *Family Plot*, etc.) these are 'post'-films, films of disintegration; their principal theoretical interest lies in the fact that – precisely because of this disintegration; because of the breaking apart of Hitchcock's universe into its particular ingredients – they enable us to isolate these ingredients and grasp them clearly.

The feature which is crucial for an analysis of 'social mediation' in Hitchcock's films here is the coincidence of the dominant type of subjectivity in each of the three central periods with the form of subjectivity that pertains to the three stages of capitalism (liberal capitalism; imperialist state-capitalism; 'post-industrial' late capitalism): the couple's initiatory voyage, with its obstacles stirring the desire for reunification, is firmly grounded in the classic ideology of the 'autonomous' subject strengthened through ordeal; the resigned paternal figure of the second stage evokes the decline of this 'autonomous' subject to whom is opposed the victorious, insipid 'heteronomous' hero; finally, it is not difficult to recognize, in the typical Hitchcockian hero of the 1950s and early 1960s, the features of the 'pathological narcissist', the form of subjectivity that characterizes the so-called 'society of consumption'.[8] This in itself is a sufficient answer to the question of the 'social mediation' of Hitchcock's universe: the inherent logic of his development is immediately social. Hitchcock's films articulate these three types of subjectivity in a clear – one could say distilled – form: as the three distinct modalities of desire. One can delineate these modalities with reference to the predominant form of the subject's opposite pole, the *object*, in each of the three periods. When we say 'Hitchcockian object', the first – one could say automatic – association is, of course, the McGuffin – yet the McGuffin is just one of the three types of object in Hitchcock's films:

- First, then, the McGuffin itself, 'nothing at all', an empty place, a pure pretext whose sole role is to set the story in motion: the formula of the warplane engines in *The Thirty-Nine Steps*, the secret clause of the naval treaty in *The Foreign Correspondent*, the coded melody in *The Lady Vanishes*, the uranium bottles in *Notorious*, and so on. It is a pure semblance: in itself it is totally indifferent and, by structural necessity, absent; its signification is purely auto-reflexive, it consists in the fact that it has some signification for others, for the principal characters of the story, that it is of vital importance to them.

- But in a series of Hitchcock's films, we find another type of object which is decidedly *not* indifferent, *not* pure absence: what matters here is precisely its presence, the material presence of a fragment of reality – it is a leftover, remnants which cannot be reduced to a network of formal relations proper to the symbolic structure. We can define this object as an object of exchange circulating among subjects, serving as a kind of guarantee, pawn, on their symbolic relationship. It is the role of the key in *Notorious* and *Dial M for Murder*, the role of the wedding ring in *Shadow of a Doubt* and *Rear Window*, the role of the lighter in *Strangers on a Train*, and even the role of the child circulating between the two couples, in *The Man Who Knew Too Much*. It is unique, non-specular – that is, it has no double, it escapes the dual mirror-relation, which is why it plays a crucial role in those very films that are built on a whole series of dual relations, each element having its mirror-counterpart (*Strangers on a Train*; *Shadow of a Doubt*, where the name of the central character is already redoubled – uncle Charlie, niece Charlie): it is the one which *has no* counterpart, and that is why it must circulate between the opposite elements, as if in search of its proper place, lost from the very beginning.

The paradox of its role is that although it is a leftover of the Real, an 'excrement' (what psychoanalysis would call the 'anal object'), it functions as a positive condition of the restoration of a symbolic structure: the structure of symbolic exchanges between the subjects can take place only in so far as it is embodied in this pure material element which acts as its guarantee – for example, in *Strangers on a Train* the murderous pact between Bruno and Guy holds only in so far as the object (the cigarette lighter) is circulating between them.

This is the basic situation in a whole series of Hitchcock's films: at the beginning we have a non-structured, pre-symbolic, imaginary homeostatic state of things, an indifferent balance in which the relations between subjects are not yet structured in a strict sense – that is, through the lack circulating between them. And the paradox is that this symbolic pact, this structural network of relations, can establish itself only in so far as it is embodied in a totally contingent material element, a little-bit-of-Real which, by its sudden irruption, disrupts the homeostatic indifference of relations between subjects. In other words, the imaginary balance changes into a symbolically structured network through a shock of the Real.[9]

• Finally, we have a third kind of object: the birds in *The Birds*, for example (we could also add, in *Marnie*, the hulk of a giant ship at the end of the street where Marnie's mother lives, not to mention the giant statues in a whole series of his films, from the Egyptian statue in *Blackmail* through the Statue of Liberty in *Saboteur* to Mount Rushmore in *North by Northwest*). This object has a massive, oppressive material presence; it is not an indifferent void like the McGuffin, but at the same time it does not circulate between the subjects, it is not an object of exchange, it is just a mute embodiment of an impossible *jouissance*.

How can we explain the logic, the consistency – that is, the structural interdependence – of these three objects? In his Seminar *Encore*, Lacan proposes a schema of it:[10]

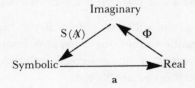

Here, we must interpret the vector not as indicating a relation of determination ('the Imaginary determines the Symbolic', and so on) but more in the sense of the 'symbolization of the Imaginary'. So:

• The McGuffin is clearly the *objet petit a*, a gap in the centre of the symbolic order – the lack, the void of the Real setting in motion the symbolic movement of interpretation, a pure semblance of the Mystery to be explained, interpreted;

• the circulating object of exchange is S($\cancel{A}$), the symbolic object which, in so far as it cannot be reduced to imaginary mirror-play, registers the impossibility around which the symbolic order is structured – the tiny element which sets in motion the crystallization of the symbolic structure;

• and finally, the birds are Phi, the impassive, imaginary objectification of the Real – an image which gives body to the impossible *jouissance*.[11]

It is not difficult to see how these three types of the object are disposed in accordance with the three central periods of Hitchcock's work:

• the first period stands clearly under the sign of *a*, i.e. McGuffin: a pure semblance which lures the hero into the Oedipal journey (it is not by accident that in this period, the role of the McGuffin is most exposed: from the design of the warplane engines in *The Thirty-Nine Steps* to the coded melody in *The Lady Vanishes*);

• the second period is marked by the predominance of S($\cancel{A}$) – the insignia, the index of the father's impotence: a fragment of reality which functions as the signifier of the fact that the 'big Other' is barred, that the father is not able to live up to his Name, to his symbolic Mandate, in so far as he is caught in an obscene enjoyment (the ring in *Shadow of a Doubt*, the key in *Notorious*, etc.);

• in the third period, the different forms of the big Phi become predominant: the gigantic statues, the birds and other 'stains' which materialize the enjoyment of the maternal superego and thereby blur the picture, make it non-transparent.

The predominance of a certain type of object thus determines the modality of desire – its transmutation from the unproblematic chasing of an elusive lure to the ambiguous fascination with the Thing. One is even tempted to say that these three periods gradually render visible the impossibility of the sexual relationship: this impossibility is registered in Hitchcock's universe by means of a growing discordance between the two levels of the relationship between woman and man: the love-relationship and that of a part-nership:[12]

• The films of the 1930s rely on a kind of pre-established harmony between these two levels: the investigative partnership itself, into which the hero and the heroine are thrown by means of an external necessity, begets the 'inner' link, love (*The Thirty-Nine Steps*, *Secret Agent*, *Young and Innocent*, *The Lady Vanishes*). So, even if the couple is produced here, the standard ideological frame of this production is undermined: the couple is produced so to speak 'from outside', love is not an affair of deep feelings but a result of external, contingent encounters – the couple is first thrown together, sometimes even literally chained together (as in *The Thirty-Nine Steps*). This is what we might call the Pascalean side of Hitchcock: act as if you were in love and love will emerge by itself.

• The films of the second (Selznick) period introduce a note of irreducible disharmony and renunciation: at the end, partnership does prevail, the couple are happily united, yet the price to be paid for this is the sacrifice of a third, truly fascinating person. This sacrifice confers on the happy ending a subterranean bitter taste: implicitly at least, the happy ending is conceived as a resigned acceptance of bourgeois everyday life (as a rule, this third person is an ambiguous paternal figure – Herbert Marshall in *Foreign Corres-pondent*, Joseph Cotten in *Shadow of a Doubt*, Claude Rains in *Notor-ious* – yet it can also be a fatal Other Woman – *Rebecca* – or simply the imagined murderous reverse of the hero himself – as in *Suspicion*, where Cary Grant turns out to be a rather childish common fraud).

• In the films of the third period, every relation of partnership is either doomed to fail or totally void of libidinal content – that is to say, partnership and love-relations are mutually exclusive (from Jane Wyman and Richard Todd in *Stage Fright*, through James Stewart and Barbara del Geddes in *Vertigo*, up to Sam and Lila in *Psycho*). The overall logic of this development is that the more we progress from the outside towards the inside, i.e. the more a love-relationship loses its support in the external symbolic texture, the more it is doomed to fail and even acquires a lethal dimension.

The pages which follow may from time to time appear as a Hitchcockian version of what, in Holmesiana, is called 'Higher Criticism': one plays seriously the game whose ground rule is acceptance that Hitchcock is a 'serious artist' (a rule which is no less incredible to many than the affirmation that Sherlock Holmes really existed). Yet from what we have already said, it should be clear how one should answer those who reproach Hitchcockian *aficionados* with the 'divinization' of their interpretive object – with the elevation of Hitchcock into a God-like demiurge who masters even the smallest details of his work: such an attitude is simply a sign of transferential relationship where Hitchcock functions as the 'subject supposed to know [*sujet supposé savoir*]' – and is it necessary to add that there is more truth in it, that it is theoretically far more productive, than the attitude of those who lay stress on Hitchcock's fallibility, inconsistencies, etc.? In short, here, more than ever, the Lacanian motto *les non-dupes errent* is in force: the only way to produce something real in theory is to pursue the transferential fiction to the end.

Notes

1. See Fredric Jameson, 'The Existence of Italy', in *Signatures of the Visible*, New York: Routledge 1990. The applicability of the Jamesonian triad realism–modernism–postmodernism is further confirmed by the way it enables us to introduce *ordre raisonné* into a series of contemporary films. It is thus not difficult to perceive how, in the series of three *Godfather* films, the first is 'realist' (in the sense of Hollywood-realism: the narrative closure, etc.), the second 'modernist' (the redoubling of a unique narrative line: the entire film is a kind of double appendix to *Godfather I*, a prequel and a sequel to the already-told main story), and the third 'postmodernist' (a *bricolage* of narrative fragments which are no longer held together by an organic link or by a formal mythical frame). The diminishing quality of each

subsequent unit attests that the dominant of the entire trilogy is 'realist', which cannot be said of the three other films from the mid 1980s which also form a kind of trilogy: *Fatal Attraction, Something Wild, Blue Velvet.* The triad realism–modernism–postmodernism is here epitomized by the three different attitudes towards the Other Woman as the point of 'fatal attraction' through which the Real invades everyday reality and perturbs its circuit: *Fatal Attraction* remains within the confines of the standard family ideology where the Other Woman (Glenn Close) personifies the Evil to be rejected or killed; in *Something Wild*, on the contrary, Melanie Griffith is represented as the one who disengages Jeff Daniels from the fake yuppie world and forces him to confront real life; in *Blue Velvet*, Isabella Rossellini eludes this simple opposition and appears as the Thing in all its ambiguity, simultaneously attracting and repelling the hero.... The ascending quality proves how the dominant is here on 'postmodernism'.

2. It was Deleuze who located Hitchcock at the very border of '*image–mouvement*', at the point at which '*image–mouvement*' passed over into '*image–temps*': 'le dernier des classiques, ou le premier des modernes' (Gilles Deleuze, *Pourparlers*, Paris: Editions de Minuit 1990, p. 79).

3. Raymond Bellour, 'Psychosis, Neurosis, Perversion', in Marshall Deutelbaum and Leland Poague, eds, *A Hitchcock Reader*, Ames: Iowa State University Press 1986, p. 312. If, moreover, one accepts Bellour's definition of the fundamental Hollywood matrix as a 'machine for the production of the couple', then one has to look for the continuous functioning of this machine not in Hitchcock but in a great number of recent films which, ostensibly, have nothing in common with classic Hollywood.

Let us just mention two films from 1990 which appear to have nothing whatsoever in common: *Awakenings* and *Dances with Wolves* – there is none the less a crucial feature which unites them. In terms of its 'official' content, *Awakenings* is a story of a doctor (Robin Williams) who, by using new chemical remedies, awakens patients from their decades-long comatose state and enables them to return briefly into normal life; yet the key to the film lies in the fact that the doctor himself is shy, reserved, sexually 'non-awakened' – the film ends with *his* awakening: i.e. when he asks his helpful nurse for a date. Ultimately the patients awaken only to deliver to the doctor the message that concerns him: the film's turning point occurs when Robert de Niro, one of the awakened patients, just before his relapse, tells the doctor to his face that the one truly 'non-awakened' is none other than himself, unable as he is to appreciate the little things that give meaning to our lives.... The denouement of the film thus relies on a kind of unspoken symbolic exchange: as if the patients are sacrificed (allowed to relapse into the coma, i.e. to 'fall asleep' again) so that the doctor can awaken and get a sexual partner – in short, so that a couple is produced. In *Dances with Wolves*, the role of the group of patients is taken over by the Sioux tribe which is also allowed to disappear in an implicit symbolic exchange, so that the couple of Kevin Costner and the white woman who has lived among the Indians since childhood can be produced.

4. Elizabeth Weis, *The Silent Scream*, London: Associated University Presses 1982, p. 77.

5. See Chapter 1 of William Rothman, *The Murderous Gaze*, Cambridge, MA: Harvard University Press 1982.

6. The parallel could be expanded to details: the mysterious woman who charges the hero with his mission (the stranger killed in Hannay's apartment in *The*

Thirty-Nine Steps; the nice old lady who vanishes in the film of the same title) – is she not a kind of reincarnation of the 'Queen of the Night'? Is not the black Monostatos reincarnated in the murderous drummer with blackened face in *Young and Innocent?* In *The Lady Vanishes*, the hero attracts the attention of his future love by playing what? – a flute, of course!

7. The notable exception here is *Under Capricorn*, where the heroine resists the superficial charm of a young seducer and returns to her aged, criminal husband after confessing that the crime her husband was convicted of was her own – in short, the condition of possibility for this exception is the *transference of guilt* which announces the next period.

8. For a more detailed account of this periodization of Hitchcock's work, see Chapter 5 of Slavoj Žižek, *Looking Awry: An Introduction to Jacques Lacan through Popular Culture*, Cambridge, MA: MIT Press 1991.

9. As to this second type of object, see Mladen Dolar's chapter 'Hitchcock's Objects' in this book, pp. 31–46. Another aspect of this object is that it is what remains the same in the change from one narrative space to another, like the necklace in *Vertigo*, the one and only detail that links the common redheaded Judy to the sublime Madeleine (thereby enabling Scottie to recognize their identity). One is tempted to say that S($\cancel{A}$) figures here as a kind of 'rigid designator' (to borrow the term from Saul Kripke, *Naming and Necessity*, Oxford: Blackwell 1980): the kernel which remains the same in all possible (narrative) universes.

10. See Jacques Lacan, *Le Séminaire, livre XX: Encore*, Paris: Editions du Seuil 1975, p. 83.

11. For an elaboration of the theoretical context and further consequences of this Lacanian scheme, see Chapter 5 of Slavoj Žižek, *The Sublime Object of Ideology*, London: Verso 1989; for another reading of it apropos of the stories of Patricia Highsmith, see Chapter 7 of Slavoj Žižek, *Looking Awry*.

12. On this dialectical tension between love-relationship and partnership in Hitchcock's films, see Fredric Jameson, *Signatures of the Visible*, New York: Routledge 1990, pp. 215–16.

PART I

The Universal:

Themes

1

Hitchcockian Suspense

PASCAL BONITZER

Asked to name the inventor of suspense in the cinema, many people would choose D.W. Griffith. Suspense is in fact produced by editing, but it is also probably one of its immediate causes. Consider, for example, the editing of chases, which are as much a feature of large-scale, ambitious frescoes (such as *Intolerance* or *The Birth of a Nation*) as of comedies and melodramas (for example, *Sally of the Sawdust*). The editing of chases is a parallel editing, in which the images of pursuer and pursued alternate – either with the scale of the shot being varied so as to increase the emotional impact, or, as in *Intolerance*, with actions running parallel to, and so by contrast intensifying, each other. Griffith thus dismantled the primitive races and chases of the early Mack Sennett shorts, and replaced a merely mechanical diet of gags with an emotional register, built up through the interplay of close-up shots of the protagonists' faces.

If one shows an image of a knife approaching a bared throat, against one of a car racing along a road in a cloud of dust, the audience may wonder whether the latter will arrive in time to prevent the crime. This is, however, generally what happens, through the editing of parallel actions, whether it is in fact logically feasible or merely dictated by the morality of the drama. To a great extent, the cinema of terror or of anxiety still depends upon the principle of editing.

How is one to distinguish Hitchcockian suspense, or 'Hitchcock's

15

touch', from the mechanical suspense described above? What are the characteristic features of each?

A good part of Hitchcock's work in cinema could in fact be summarized in terms of the editing of chases, with the proviso that the chase, which is precipitated by a token object – which Hitchcock himself calls, as is well known, a McGuffin – is so weighed down with incidents, diversions, events, details and people that it ends up being confused with the film as a whole. Hitchcock would appear to have 'hollowed out' the cinematic chase that he had inherited from Griffith, much as Mallarmé claimed to have 'hollowed out' Baudelaire's verse. What, then, is the object that this anxiety or suspense releases, revives and sets going? I would hazard the response that this object, which emerged at the same time as the close-up was discovered, is, because of its characteristic malice, the gaze.

We ought therefore to return to the source, to Griffith's films, for the gaze is a feature of his work. The gaze, as it functions in Griffith, doubtless issued from cinematography to be born of cinema, yet it was not originally in cinematography. For the first fifteen or twenty years, cinematographers allowed themselves to be captivated by things, by movement and by life, by the animated spectacle of the world. Nowadays, the first films, whether by the Lumière brothers, by Méliès, Zecca and the others, or by Mack Sennett, Charlie Chaplin and Fatty Arbuckle, seem to us to be the fruits of a cinematographic Eden, in which anxiety, and the editing of the gaze, were as yet unknown. This is why we talk about the freshness and innocence of such works. One simply put the camera on its tripod, in front of whatever was to be filmed, and on one went with the comic turns and the wild gesticulations. Early acted cinema was, whether intentionally or not, burlesque in character, a cinema based upon an uninterrupted flow of gestures, with pumping legs, flailing arms and rolling eyes.

According to Edgar Morin (*Les Stars*), it was around 1915–20 that actors, instead of gesticulating wildly, began to stay more or less still. The turning point came with Griffith, whose films ushered in the age of close-ups and editing. The Japanese critic Tadao Sato has argued that this reversal is attributable in large part to the runaway success of Sessue Hayakawa in Cecil B. DeMille's *The Cheat*.[1] Hayakawa, a Japanese actor, was so still and impassive that, notwithstanding the hackneyed, racist nature of the character he was portraying (the disquieting 'inscrutability' of the Yellow men), he achieved an intensity of expression that audiences found very moving. His approach, Sato notes, depended upon the gaze, and was rendered yet more intense by a technique known as *haragei*, which means literally 'art of the stomach'. The Japanese actor's technique was thus one of holding back, by contrast with the theatrical expressivity of Western acting in that period, and with the heightened gestures then in fashion.

It is not irrelevant to note that it was during approximately the same period, give or take two or three years (1918–19), that Kouleshov made the most famous of his experiments, the Moszhukin experiment, which is habitually confused with the so-called 'Koulechov effect'. Its impact depended upon the immobility of the actor's face, upon its 'expressive neutrality' when seen in close-up. What was involved was in some way a third stage, a reduction of acting to its zero degree, so that its powers might be delegated to editing alone, to the *auteur*. Gesture, concentration [*haragei*] and neutrality would thus represent three stages in a progressive domestication of the actor's body, 'through the top', through the face, which benefited staging and editing and was crucial to establishing the laws of suspense. Hitchcock often recalled that he would keep the face neutral.[2]

There was in fact a revolution in the cinema. The triumph of editing, the close-up, immobility, the gaze and the corresponding repression of the gestural caused a wide range of cinematic elements to disappear, never to be restored to their original exuberance. I have in mind the excremental carnivalesque of the burlesque. The cinema, which had been innocent, joyful and dirty, was to become obsessional, fetishistic and frozen. The dirtiness did not disappear but was interiorized and moralized, and passed over into the gaze — that is, into the register of desire. Characters were no longer pelted with cream buns; revenge was no longer had by bespattering one's enemies with mud or by destroying anything and everything. Once the body had been rendered immobile and attention had become focused upon the face or the gaze, the law, desire and perversion

17

made their entrance into the cinema. Sessue Hayakawa is the proto-type 'villain'. Hitchcock always used to say that the more successful the villain, the better the film. Moszhukin's experiment, it should be remembered, depends upon the interpretation of desires.

Hitchcock is undoubtedly the filmmaker who has drawn the most logical conclusions from this signifying revolution, beside which the advent of the talkies may be reckoned a relatively unimportant affair (since it merely represented the continuation of an already-existing programme). It was indeed a revolution and, like all revolutions, it was based upon death and upon a staging of death (a revolution whose symbol in this case too was a severed head, the close-up). Neither death nor crime existed in the polymorphous world of the burlesque, in which everyone deals and takes blows as best he can, in which cream buns fly and buildings collapse in a burst of collec-tive laughter. In a world of pure gesture, such as the animated cartoon (itself a substitute for slapstick), the protagonists are in prin-ciple immortal and indestructible – except in the rare and provo-cative case of figures such as Tex Avery – violence is universal and inconsequential, and guilt does not exist. The weight of death, murder and crime have meaning only through the proximity of a gaze. All Hitchcock has done in his films is to make the best possible use, where staging is concerned, of the function of the gaze laid bare by crime. The dictum that 'there is crime only where there is a gaze' also means that the positing of a crime causes the gaze to function quite nakedly, and delivers up its essential obscenity, as the case of *Rear Window* proves.

For Hitchcockian suspense to arise, very little is required, at least as far as narrative is concerned. It is sufficient to announce, by means of some artifice or other, a catastrophic event affecting the lives of the characters in the film, the assumption being that they do not question it. (This might be described, in Bachelardian terms, as the 'Cassandra complex'.) From this point of view, even one of the Lumière brothers' films could be 'Hitchcockized'.[3]

I would go still further, and argue that it is because every film functions a priori like a film by the Lumière brothers that Hitch-cockian suspense is possible, and that Hitchcockian staging works by reacting provocatively to their kind of cinema. Let me explain.

I mentioned above a sort of cinematographic Eden, characteristic of the first years, the first gestures and the first games. Thus, in some of the first films by the Lumière brothers, a soldier courts a nanny who is pushing a pram in a park, something which is not so much a fiction as a sketch. At this level, cinema makes do with life – indeed, a cinema of this sort *is* life. The Lumière brothers' cinema does not in fact see death.

One could perhaps say that the recording of this scene in the park is innocent, that the spectacle is innocent also, as are the protagonists. Finally, the audience too shares in this innocence. However, while the cinema may originally be innocently recording life in all its innocence, it may be held guilty of adding something, through the simple fact of recording it. Why film the soldier and the nanny, why choose precisely this scene, why opt for this cutting, this framing or this gaze? Once such questions arise, everything has changed, the original innocence has become suspect and is in effect already lost. The soldier and the nanny are already playing an ambiguous and guilty game, and the audience's interest has already changed its meaning. Smut is none too far off, and even if the smut is still frank and innocent, a short step will suffice to render it filthy. This is how fiction is introduced, for, as Godard has observed – actually with reference to Hitchcock – it is the gaze which creates fiction.[4]

What was required to turn a Lumière brothers' sketch into a Hitchcockian fiction? One merely had to interpose a crime, for example, to state a priori that the nanny has decided to drown the baby. Even if everything is filmed as it was before, the meaning of the sequence is overturned. When one sees the baby babbling in its pram, the soldier clowning around in an attempt to seduce the nanny, and the latter simpering and shaking her rear, an underlying sense of horror serves to destroy the apparent meaning – what semiologists would call the 'denotated' meaning – of the scene, and distorts all its signs. The audience, which is thus no longer able to cling naively to the apparent reality of the image, and knows what is being woven below the surface, has suffered a loss of innocence. The baby that is seen making the soldier laugh is under threat of death, and the audience is struck by the silliness of the latter, and by his 'failure to come to the assistance of a person in danger'.

The 'impression of reality' shifts to a secondary level, that of connotation. For the camera is no longer saying to us: 'Look at this baby, how sweet it is', but rather: 'Look at this baby, how sweet it is, it has only a few minutes to live, unless the soldier understands what is going on.' None the less, the camera is able to say these things with precisely the same images. The 'innocent' meaning is not wholly lost, for the baby is still sweet, the soldier weak and the nanny saucy; however, it has become troubled, doubled, distorted and 'hollowed out' by a second signification, which is cruel and casts back every gesture on to a face marked by derision and the spirit of the comic and the macabre, which brings out the hidden face of simple gestures, the face of nothingness. Suspense is an anamorphosis of cinematographic time, which shifts the audience towards that point of the picture where, in the oblong form of which the characters are unaware, it will recognize the death's-head.

Such is the function of crime in Hitchcock's films. For crime drives both the natural order of things and the natural order of cinema off course, by introducing a *stain* which precipitates a gaze and so brings about a fiction. Evil itself is a stain.[5]

Hitchcock's films can therefore work only if a natural order is presupposed. Everything is proceeding normally, according to routines that are ordinary, even humdrum and unthinking, until someone notices that an element in the whole, because of its in-explicable behaviour, is a stain. The entire sequence of events unfolds from that point.

The most characteristically Hitchcockian staging effects are always organized around such a stain. However, anything whatso-ever may function as the stain inducing the gaze – the blood on the dress in *Stage Fright*; the glass of milk in *Suspicion*, 'intensified' by placing a small light bulb inside it; the black rectangle of the window in *Rear Window* and, within that black rectangle, the red tip of the murderer's cigarette or, indeed, the plane in *North by Northwest*, which is at first no more than a speck in the sky.

Let me explain how fiction works. Consider some man or other – for example, Cary Grant, who has arranged to meet an unknown person ('Kaplan') at a bus stop, in open country. There is no one and nothing about. After a few moments, a vehicle sets down an individual at this same bus stop. It turns out not to be Kaplan *because*, says the man in answer to Cary Grant's question, *that's not what I am called.* The bus arrives. Just as he is getting on, the man without a name gazes at the horizon and observes: 'That's strange, there's a plane spraying crops but there's no crops there.' The bus departs with the unnamed man on board, leaving Cary Grant, faced with this distant, tiny, almost imperceptible anomaly – a plane spraying nonexistent crops – which, as we already know, will come closer, grow larger and ultimately fill the whole frame.

This famous scene illustrates the function of the anomaly or the stain in Hitchcock's cinema, for by means of the empty plain, it verges upon abstraction. Cary Grant is looking for someone, he is on the look-out for the slightest sign of recognition, but this recognition, which would restore things to their rightful place, does not occur. Everything remains overhanging, and finally it is he, Cary Grant, who is a stain in the picture, and whom others, as we learn, are trying to 'eliminate'.[6]

In *Rear Window*, James Stewart locates something abnormal going on in one of the windows opposite, until the succession of small anomalies assumes the configuration of a crime, and the criminal in his turn locates the observer.

We also know that the whole fiction of *Foreign Correspondent* was based upon the idea of a windmill whose sails turned in the opposite direction to the wind.[7] The-object-which-makes-a-stain is thus, literally speaking, an object which goes against nature. The object in question invariably shows up against the background of a natural nature – of a nature that is, as it were, too natural. The framework and set of Hitchcock's films often consists, as is well known, of a conventional, picture-postcard nature, so that if the action is set in Switzerland, there must be mountains and chocolate; if in Holland umbrellas, windmills and fields of tulips are required. If *Foreign Correspondent* had been shot in colour, Hitchcock has said:

> I would have used an idea of which I have long dreamed, that of staging a murder in a field of tulips.... The camera approaches a tulip, goes into the tulip. The noise of a struggle can still be heard on the sound-track. We home in on a petal, which fills the whole screen and, blam, ... a drop of blood falls on to the petal.[8]

The same idea is used in *The Trouble with Harry*: 'It is as if I were showing a murder beside a singing stream, and I would spread a drop of blood into its clear waters.'[9]

There is invariably the same point of departure – namely, nature, a Lumière approach in the parodic and silly form of a touristic travelogue, then the stain which 'throws the whole system off course', the perverse or inverted element (such as the windmill sails turning against the wind) which serves to overturn our sense of reality. This element, this stain, is therefore often, logically enough, a bloodstain – for example, the red stain by which Marnie is haunted, and hallucinates; but blood may still be too 'natural', and must itself be perverted. Thus, speaking of *The Man Who Knew Too Much*, Hitchcock describes a scene which he never managed to complete, in which Daniel Gelin, before dying, was to have walked in some blue dye: 'It was a variant of the old idea of following a trail of blood, but in this case one was following blue instead of red.'[10] (This blue would then, as a complementary colour, have matched the walnut stain which is left on James Stewart's hands when the victim's face eludes them: here too, a 'natural' forgery, the 'native' brown, is perverted by a stain.)

The problem of convention, of a nature that is false – or, if you like, of façade – touches directly upon an aspect of Hitchcock's films which is generally misunderstood or despised: namely, politics. Hitchcock is a great political filmmaker. A number of his films are explicitly political – for example, the anti-Nazi films of the 1940s (from *The Lady Vanishes* to *Notorious*) and the anti-Communist films of the 1960s. It was not merely that the conventions of the genre required that secret agents should indeed have a political and national identity. One has only to see a police comedy like *The Lady Vanishes* to appreciate that no other film of the period laid bare in this fashion the face of the European democracies when confronted with pressure from the new dictatorships. The point is that a filmmaker interested to this extent in what, beneath the superficially benign appearance of things, was not working, could not help but encounter what was in turmoil beneath the falsely reassuring mask of the bourgeois world, as also beneath the more rigid mask worn by the dictatorships. We should take seriously the motif of 'the drop of blood in a singing stream'. As a poet has said, 'No bird has the heart to sing in a bush of questions'. But if a bush of birds were to rise up in the midst of singing children, there would be some questions asked and some voices raised. Consider the unforgettable cry uttered by the old lady in *Rear Window* after her little dog has been found strangled: 'Everyone lies! Why can't we love one another?' So much for the charge that Hitchcock is merely a formalist filmmaker, preoccupied solely with technique and trickery.

Hitchcock's films are full of decent, ordinary petty-bourgeois people. These are masks. Thus, in *The Lady Vanishes*, the good Miss Froy, with her tea and her meaningless chatter, is really a spy. All the others have something else to hide, a concealed point of abjection, which the perverse element, the visible but barely perceptible stain of the crime, will reveal. *Rear Window* is a cruel picture of the American way of life.

Hitchcockian narrative obeys the law that the more a situation is somewhat a priori, familiar or conventional, the more it is liable to become disturbing or uncanny, once one of its constituent elements begins to 'turn against the wind'. Scenario and staging consist merely in constructing a natural landscape with its perverse element, and in then charting the outcome. Suspense, by contrast with the accelerated editing of races and chases, depends upon the emphasis which the staging places upon the progressive contamination, the progressive or sudden perversion of the original landscape. The staging and editing of the suspense serve to draw the audience's attention to the perverse element. The film's movement invariably proceeds from landscape to stain, from overall shot to close-up, and this movement invariably prepares the spectator for the event. Hitchcock systematically opposes suspense to surprise. He prides himself not so much on directing the actors – since he asks of his actors merely that they remain 'neutral', so that he can then edit a scene, a neutrality which he in fact takes some pleasure in testing by introducing postures which are frequently difficult, if not acrobatic – as on directing the audience.[11]

It is worth noting that this concern is contrary to all the generally accepted rules of staging. If one were to believe, for example, Jean Mitry, it is in fact 'surprise [which] constantly arouses the spectator's attention', as a consequence of which

a shot ... must never 'prepare' an event. If, for example, the frame presents the interior of a café with, in the first shot, a table and two empty chairs and if, a little later, a couple (who are expected) enter the frame and come and sit down in this spot, the director has obviously blundered. It is as if one were telling one's audience: 'Watch out! This is where they'll come.' In thus allowing the audience to anticipate, one is by the same token letting it be known that the director is in control of events.[12]

Yet this is precisely what Hitchcock does claim, and suspense consists precisely in this sort of warning. In *Sabotage*, for example, there is a sequence in which a child carries a parcel into a bus, without ever suspecting that it contains a bomb. Hitchcock explains:

> If I had constantly shown the bomb from the same angle, the audience would have grown used to the parcel and would have thought 'Fine, so it is only a parcel after all', but I wished to tell it: 'No, no, that's precisely the point! Watch out! You're making a blunder!'[13]

It is significant that Mitry immediately goes on, as if to correct the judgement quoted above, to describe a scene from *Shadow of a Doubt*.

The perverse element, the anomaly and the stain which preci-pitate and justify the marvels of staging, do not function only in the domain of crime and politics, but also in that of eroticism. The essence of Hitchcockian suspense is eroticism, and Hitchcockian editing is an erotic editing. As is well known, Hitchcock makes films about the couple, and what interests him in couples is, more speci-fically, coupling, or what he terms love 'at work'. How is one to show love 'at work'? In what way can one show coupling? Critics have emphasized how, in spite of the censor, Hitchcock often repre-sented sex on the screen, by employing such procedures as metaphor (the famous shot at the end of *North by Northwest*), inver-sion (the 'dressing' of Kim Novack by James Stewart in *Vertigo*) or fragmentation (the shower-murder in *Psycho*), and so on.[14] Yet one does not represent sex by representing coupling. Sex is indeed the object of suspense – in Hitchcock's best films, we invariably want to know when, at what precise moment (at the end, of course, for that is what is meant by a 'happy ending') the hero and heroine can at last be 'reunited' – but coupling is one of suspense's main modal-ities.

When the male and female protagonists in a Hitchcock film are coupled together, there is always something fundamentally uneasy about their situation, and they are always in some way forced into it by an outside object, a perverse element. The example that springs to mind is that of the handcuffs attaching hero and heroine in *The Thirty-Nine Steps*, but the same structure recurs in the majority of Hitchcock's films. There is, as François Regnault has observed, a sort of *fatal promiscuity* 'either between two men (*Strangers on a Train*, perhaps *The Wrong Man*, *Frenzy*), or between a man and a woman (*The Thirty-Nine Steps*), where they are chained together by handcuffs, *Notorious*, by the detective's mission and by a kiss, *Suspicion*, *Marnie*, by marriage, *Young and Innocent*, *Saboteur*, by an encounter, etc.'

A couple is stuck together to this degree only when something is there to divide it or to put it in the wrong. This was true of the scene in *Notorious* with the kiss, where the awkwardness was wholly shifted from the characters on to the actors,[15] and it was the telephone which caused the lovers to turn together. This was also true of *Rear Window*, where James Stewart's camera may be regarded as an object which serves both to unite and to divide the couple, a reporter and a model, but which, through the crime in the flat opposite, sets love 'to work', gets it 'going'. In *Blackmail*, too, a man goes into a tobacconist's and asks for a cigar. The two lovers, the innocent murderess and her policeman accomplice, are in the shop too, and because they, like the audience, know what is happening, they are petrified with fear. Yet for all their terror, we see them hold each other increasingly tightly, and so improbable does this seem that the effect actually becomes in some way comic.

We have here a perfect diagram of the Hitchcockian system, featuring the function of the natural, of the crime and of the perverse object. What could be more natural – indeed, more normal – than to buy a cigar at a tobacconist's? Now, the suspense derives here from the fact that the man – who, as both the couple and the audience know, was a witness to the murder committed by the young woman to save her honour – is going to take his time paying for his cigar. If he takes his time, it is because it is natural to take one's time savouring a cigar; he therefore removes the ring, rolls it between his fingers, draws on it voluptuously, and finally lights it from the pipe on the counter, while the policeman and his fiancée are glued to each other as if they wished to be melted into a single block. Then, as one might expect, the smoker realizes that he has no money on him, and cheerily asks for a note from the young policeman, who naturally ends up by complying. So the blackmailing begins, and the fiction with it. The whole scene is thus polarized around the cigar, which becomes an object of terror, a perverse, almost obscene object. The cigar represents here the point upon which the gaze settles, the *fascinum*, and the blackmailer, like Hitchcock with his tricks, directs the audience. At the same time, he welds the couple together in unease and a sense of instability and anxiety. This magisterial effect recurs, in a wholly stylized form, in *Rear Window*, when, to the astonishment of James Stewart and Grace Kelly, the red tip of the murderer's cigarette, seen against the black screen of the window – like a sign flashing at intervals on a road at night, warning of a detour – instantly betrays the fact that a crime has been committed, just as irrefutably as the 'strawberry' betrays Charlus's homosexuality in the eyes of Proust's narrator.

There is thus always a third party in a couple, a gaze welding it together. A couple implies a third, and functions only in 'a kind of temporary *ménage à trois*', as Hitchcock remarked of the kiss in *Notorious*, in spite of the fact that the third would seem initially to be absent from that sequence. In *Notorious*, however, the same function is fulfilled by the camera, and subsequently by the audience:

I felt that it was crucial not to separate them and not to break their embrace; I also felt that the camera, in representing the audience, should be allowed in, as if it were a third person joining in with this extended embrace. I granted the audience the great privilege of embracing Cary Grant and Ingrid Bergman at once. It was a kind of temporary *ménage à trois*.[16]

In order to explain why he 'felt' that it was necessary, for the expression of love, to show the couple actually bound together, physically welded together, even at the risk of throwing the actors off balance, Hitchcock told a curious anecdote:

I was in the Boulogne to Paris train and we were travelling through

Etaples at a fairly leisurely pace ... through the window I saw a large factory with a red-brick building and, against the wall, were a young couple; the girl and boy were arm in arm, and the boy was pissing against the wall; the girl never once let go of his arm; she was looking at what he was doing, looking at the train as it passed by and then once more she looked at the boy. I have found that that was, really, genuine love 'at work', a genuine love which 'functions'.[17]

We find here a combination of all the elements of Hitchcockian eroticism – the convention of the landscape, the 'façade', the couple as natural, the stain in the form of a jet of urine against the wall, the gaze welding the couple into a 'temporary *ménage à trois*'; finally, the substance in the strict sense of the suspense, an intimate mixture of movement and immobility, a viscosity and slow motion that are characteristic of Hitchcock's editing. We know that in *North by Northwest* Hitchcock shot a remake of the famous kiss in *Notorious*, this time integrating the train into the sequence (the scene of the kiss in Eva-Marie Saint's compartment).

If I were to hazard a biographical interpretation of this recurrent erotic motif, featuring a couple hanging on to each other, off balance and welded together by a gaze, I would say that the memory recounted by Hitchcock to Truffaut has all the characteristics of a 'screen-memory', and that some deeper circumstance in his life must lie behind it. We now know – thanks to Odette Ferry, a personal friend of Hitchcock – what this crucial circumstance was. When he asked for the hand in marriage of Alma Reville, the quintessential Hitchcockian heroine, as Odette Ferry somewhat oddly observes:

> the two of them had to be on a boat in the middle of a storm before he could pluck up enough courage to knock on her cabin door and ask her to marry him.... 'The wind was gusty,' he told me, '... the boat was pitching so violently that I had to lean against the door, the hinges of which were creaking (as in certain horror films made by my colleagues!), so as not to lose my balance. I thought that it was a bad omen, and I was about to withdraw when Alma smiled at me. I realised then that she was accepting me.'[18]

The unease, the instability, the couple clinging on to each other

27

though off balance in what is an immobile movement, the lovers' hands reaching out to each other as if suspended over a gulf (the abandoned mine in *Young and Innocent*, Mount Rushmore and the couchette in *North by Northwest*, or – in an unhappy, masculine version – the Statue of Liberty in *Saboteur*), the happy ending which arrives *in extremis*, with the two hands linking and clasping at the last possible moment, and, finally, the viscous durée, the slow motion, virtually all feature in this episode of the 'proposal of marriage'.

We are now in a better position to understand why Hitchcock should have insisted so often upon the paradoxical use of sloweddown time in suspense, as in the scene with the cigar in *Blackmail* where, if the behaviour had been natural rather than perverse, it would have seemed extremely drawn-out and boring. This subjective stretching, this viscosity of time, is related to eroticism, and it concerns the eroticized time in the prolonged, necessarily disturbing undecidability of an event. Suspense is the erotic prolongation of the trajectory of a coin thrown up into the air, before it falls on one side (tails: yes) or the other (heads: no). In real time, an event may be extremely short, like the shower-murder of Janet Leigh in *Psycho*, but it will then be broken up into as many parts as possible (seventy shots, the majority of which were filmed in slow motion, lasting a full forty-five seconds of film time).

Suspense is thus indeed achieved through editing, but Hitchcock, in contrast to the Griffithian acceleration of parallel actions, employs an editing of convergent actions in a homogeneous space, which presupposes slow motion and is sustained by the gaze, itself evoked by a third element, a perverse object or a stain. The remarkable formal invention precipitated and polarized by this structure, in the admitted absence of any real emotional depth in Hitchcock's films (a shortcoming for which he has been much criticized), makes his staging of inestimable importance.

We are now better equipped to understand why the laws of suspense – laid out so calmly by the master and expounded by him in a mechanical, behaviourist and Pavlovian fashion – have always failed when applied by other filmmakers, and why it is that he still has, in his own words, a 'monopoly'. 'Hitchcock's touch' can at best only be parodied or pastiched (sometimes intelligently, as in the case of Brian de Palma), and is necessarily inimitable, since it presupposes the form, substance and content of Hitchcockian fiction – in other words, its actual singularity.

Notes

1. Tadao Sato, 'Le point de regard', *Cahiers du cinéma*, 310.

2. François Regnault, 'Système formel d'Hitchcock (fascicule de résultats'), *Cahiers du cinéma*, special issue on Alfred Hitchcock, 1980. Hitchcock thus rebuked Paul Newman in *Torn Curtain*, for not knowing how to 'be satisfied to give merely neutral looks, such as allow me to edit a scene' (François Truffaut, *Hitchcock*, London: Panther 1969, p. 390). Hitchcock makes a direct reference to Koulechov and Mosz-hukin's experiment in relation to the editing of James Stewart's looks in *Rear Window* (Truffaut, p. 265).

3. The very first suspense effect would surely be *The sprinkler sprinkled*. This situation frequently occurs in Hitchcock, generally in the form of the hunter hunted or, more radically still, as Raymond Bellour has shown in relation to *The Birds*, the *watcher watched*. *Rear Window* is a good example of such a reversal.

4. Jean Luc Godard, *Introduction à une (véritable) histoire du cinéma*.

5. Gilles Deleuze, *Francis Bacon, logique de la sensation*, Paris: Minuit 1981, p. 24. The Germanic root *Mal* derives from the Latin *macula*, a stain; hence *malen*, to paint, and *Maler*, a painter.

6. Truffaut, pp. 151 (the nothingness of the McGuffin); 280–87, the obsession with 'nothing' which permeates the entire film, the development of the scene which was never shot, in which a corpse, in an edited sequence, was to have fallen from nowhere, etc., 'nothing' whose symbol is the name of Kaplan. In the course of the film, Roger O. Thornhill (Cary Grant) is seen asking Eva-Marie Saint what the O in the middle of his name means. He answers 'zero'. (Elsewhere, Hitchcock divides humanity into two: those people who are 1 and those people who are 0, and he says that he himself belongs, of course, to the second category.)

7. Truffaut, p. 151.

8. Ibid., p. 152.

9. Ibid., p. 255.

10. Ibid., p. 259.

11. Ibid., p. 303.

12. Jean Mitry, *Esthétique et psychologie du cinéma*, Paris: Editions universitaires 1965, p. 399.

13. Truffaut, pp. 297–8.

14. Jean Narboni, 'Visages d'Hitchcock', in *Cahiers du cinéma*, hors-série 8: *Alfred Hitchcock*, Paris 1980.

15. Truffaut, p. 292: 'The actors obviously hated doing this. They felt terribly ill at ease and they disliked having to cling to each other.' A specifically Hitchcockian situation, the meaning of which I shall try to elucidate below.

16. Truffaut, p. 293.

17. Ibid., pp. 293–4.

18. Odette Ferry, 'Hitchcock, mon ami', *Cahiers du cinéma*, special issue on Alfred Hitchcock. One cannot help but wonder whether the situation described

here is not perhaps typically British – indeed, Anglo-Catholic – by which I mean 'love rewarded, after unease, in a boat on the high seas'. This theme also features in the most British of Joseph Conrad's novels, *Fortune*, which is full of Hitchcockian characters and situations (including sexual suspense), or again in Evelyn Waugh's *Brideshead Revisited* (where a storm forces the characters to cling to the rigging), which is itself concerned with Anglo-Catholicism. Marriage at sea would thus be a sort of contraction (metaphor or crasis) of Victorian Britain (a tying up, a pitching which renders actions difficult to perform but, by the same token, liberates them by means of this same unease) and of Marian desire, with the sea itself bringing the Virgin Mary to mind. Alma's own name may itself be of some significance here.

In the episode recounted by Odette Ferry, the third party would be the pitching of the boat and so, at a deeper level, a pitching God – a God who is, according to Hitchcock, the sole author of documentaries, whereas, in fiction films, it is the director who must become God (Truffaut, p. 111).

2

Hitchcock's Objects

MLADEN DOLAR

Hitchcock often said that *Shadow of a Doubt* was his favourite film – the one he would take to a desert island, if he had to choose just one. Perhaps we should take him seriously and seek in this film the clue (or one of the clues) to the fundamental Hitchcockian fantasy.

The classical formal analysis of the film, to which all the subsequent interpretations are indebted, has been given by François Truffaut in the famous issue of *Cahiers du cinéma*[1] which marked the pathbreaking first step into the prolific history of Hitchcockian studies. According to this analysis, *Shadow of a Doubt* is a film about the dual relationship. The doubling seems to be the very principle of its formal construction.

The axis of duality is the dual relationship between Uncle Charlie and his niece Charlie, who has been named after him. Their connection is immediately introduced by the mirror-presentation in the opening sequences, undoubtedly one of Hitchcock's master-pieces:

- in a Philadelphia suburb, Uncle Charlie is lying on his bed, fully clothed, with his head to the right, with the door in the back to the right;

- in Santa Rosa in California, his niece Charlie is lying on her bed, fully clothed, her head to the left and the door in the back to the left, as a mirror-reflection;

- Uncle Charlie goes to the post office to send a telegram to his niece, to inform her that he is coming to Santa Rosa;

- the niece goes to the post office to send a telegram to her uncle, with an invitation for a visit, but his telegram is already waiting for her;

- Uncle Charlie hums a melody which, as by telepathy, jumps over to his niece (it is the *Merry Widow* waltz – let us leave aside for the moment its first occurrence during the credits on the background of dancing couples).

The niece Charlie will later reflect on this dual bond between them: 'We are like twins; we are both alike.'

Around this central axis Charlie–Charlie, there is a duplication of other participants:

- Uncle Charlie is sought by two detectives in Philadelphia;

- there are two detectives disguised as journalists who visit the Santa Rosa home to check up on Uncle Charlie;

- we find out that there is another suspect, on the east coast, chased by two other detectives;

- the other suspect, who has been in the same places of crime, is eventually caught and, trying to escape, he is crushed by a propeller;

- Uncle Charlie, in the end, is crushed by a train, in a sort of mirror-correspondence;

- there are two younger children, two doctors, two amateur sleuths (the father and the neighbour Herbie) engaged in two conversations about murder;

- there is a duplication of scenes: two scenes at the railway station, two scenes in the garage, two murder attempts on Charlie, two family dinners, two church scenes, two visits by detectives; and, as a kind of ironical commentary on this universal doubling, the key scene takes place in a bar called 'Till Two' (with a sign outside showing a clock with hands at two to two); in the bar, Uncle Charlie orders two double brandies.

These dualities were first pointed out by Truffaut (especially those in the opening shots), and the list was later completed by Donald Spoto.[2]

So all the elements in the film seem to fall into two; they have their double or mirror-image, a structural necessity that has to be assumed even by elements we do not see in the film (the absent suspect).

It is obvious that all the dualities hinge upon the central one, that between the uncle and his niece, and in the nature of their dual relationship. Some interpreters (for example Gavin Millar[3]) have suggested that the duality is nothing but the dichotomy of good and evil, the 'good' and the 'bad' side, which makes it possible to get rid of the bad side and wind up in a Hollywoodian happy ending. The evil is personified by Uncle Charlie, who came into the small town from outside as a kind of 'natural catastrophe', a foreign body, not its inner product. The link between good and evil remains an external one, the idyllic small-town life has no inner connection with its 'dark side', the nightmare comes from some other place (the big cities?).[4]

Yet the structure presented by Hitchcock is much more complex than this superficial account. There is a thesis implied on the structural level – not simply an obsession with duplication, but quite the contrary: *every duality is based on a third.* The third element is both excluded and introduced as a stain in this mirror-relationship, the object around which it turns and which fills the gap of the exclusion, makes the absence present.

First we have to concentrate on the element which is not doubled in the mirror-image and which presents the hinge of the duplication. Already in the opening shots, the element which is not repeated is *money*. Uncle Charlie lies apathetically on his bed with large sums of money spread around. It doesn't seem to evoke his interest, he doesn't try to count it or to hide it; it seems like a surplus he doesn't know what to do with. Since it becomes clear that this is the money he got from his victims, it also appears that he didn't kill them primarily for money. His later justification of his murders is that he wanted to clean the world of this filth (the widows who take advantage of their late husbands' fortunes) – he sees his mission as ethical, not as profiteering. He murders to improve the world, he sees himself as the executor of certain principles and, consequently, he doesn't know what to do with the money. As for him the murdered widows are just rubbish to get rid of, so the money is the surplus he can dispose of only in the bank in Santa Rosa. In the corresponding shot, his niece Charlie is woken from her reveries on her bed by a conversation about the lack of money. So here the money is the non-specular entity that binds the two together.

The *melody*, the *Merry Widow* waltz, is the next element which seems to circulate among the protagonists. We first hear it during the opening credits on the background of dancing couples in somewhat outdated sumptuous costumes, and it is rather difficult to establish what it has to do with a crime story set in mid-century America. The solution to the puzzle is that one has to consider the couples as the images in a rebus: if we concentrate on the images, on the ornate visual presentation, we will never find the answer, which lies only in words – here in the title of the operetta from which the waltz is taken. It looks as if this melody is simply the melody of initiation binding together a couple (this device has become trivial; examples range from *The Magic Flute* to *The Lady Vanishes*[5]). But as in *The Lady Vanishes*, the melody bears a lethal message, hidden where one would not think to look for it: in its title. Everybody starts humming the melody at dinner – it has become contagious, presenting the tie of the whole family – but nobody can remember the title in a kind of collective amnesia; when somebody suddenly remembers and starts saying the first word, 'Merry ...', Uncle Charlie tips over his glass to cover the sequel. What appeared to be the bond of the couple and the family turns into a blot, an agent of disruption.

But by far the most important and central to the film is the *ring*. *Shadow of a Doubt* could be schematically summarized as the journey of a privileged object, the circulation of the ring. It goes back and forth between the two specular protagonists, and their dual relationship can ultimately be seen as the background for this circuit of the object. The journey can be summed up in four stages:

1. The ring is a present from the uncle to his niece which links them as a couple, a pledge – but a poisoned present, since it bears the wrong initials. It arouses the first suspicions in the niece; the first shadow of a doubt is cast on their relationship.

2. It is by the initials that the niece obtains the first proof of her uncle's guilt – they match the initials of a murdered woman. Charlie learns this in the library when she is checking on the newspaper report that Uncle Charlie tried to hide from her. The ring provides the moment of recognition. This is underlined in a beautiful backward tracking shot when the camera recedes higher and higher under the ceiling, losing sight of the ring, and we see Charlie small and alone in the dark library.

3. The third moment is when Charlie returns the ring to her uncle in the bar. Up to that point in their conversation, Uncle Charlie tries to bluff his way, but when she responds only by silently returning the ring, placing it on the table, he knows that she knows. He stops bluffing; the dual relationship falls apart; it is disrupted by the very object that constitutes its bond; the imaginary crumbles ('Do you know that the world is a foul sty? Do you know if you ripped the fronts off houses you'd find swine? The world is a hell!')

4. When another suspect is apprehended for the murders, Uncle Charlie is safe and the only one who knows about his guilt and presents a danger to him is his niece. Now she steals the ring from her uncle while everybody is at a party, thus getting back the only piece of evidence against him and showing her determination to go on to the end. Her possession of the ring is disclosed in another beautiful tracking shot: Teresa Wright slowly descends the stairs, her hand on the rail; the camera slowly approaches, this time to single out the ring on her hand – only the uncle can realize its significance. The ring is again a pledge, but of another kind: she won't betray him if he goes away (because of her mother), but she will use it if he doesn't.

At every stage of this progression, the ring becomes more fascinating – as the lethal object of exchange between the two sides of the mirror, as the object, both sublime and uncanny, that serves both as the link of the dual relationship and as its destruction.

In *Shadow of a Doubt*, all the murders have taken place before the beginning of the film – we see only the rather gallant Joseph Cotten – and their only representative is the circulating lethal object, the stand-in for the absent murders. The mirror-relationship is based on the blot that has no mirror-correspondence. But this is only one part of this mechanism.

Niece Charlie goes to the post office to send a message to her beloved uncle, her hero, the object of family worship – the message to come and save her from her uneventful and boring small-town life. The miracle happens, and the message about his arrival is already waiting for her. This is indeed a case of a successful communication: the sender receives literally her/his own message from the receiver, as the Lacanian formula of communication goes, though not in an inverted but in the same form. Yet the successful encounter, as psychoanalysis has taught us, is much more fatal than the failed one. Niece Charlie elaborates on this happy union:

> 'I'm glad that she [her mother] named me after you and that she thinks we're both alike. I think we are, too. I *know* it. . . . We're not just an uncle and a niece. It's something else. I know you. I know that you don't tell people a lot of things. I don't either. I have a feeling that inside you somewhere there is something nobody knows about ... something secret and wonderful. I'll find it out. . . . We are like twins, don't you see?'

This text points very precisely to the conditions of dual relationships, to what transcends the duality and makes it possible:

1. The object hidden in Uncle Charlie, somewhere deep, something secret and wonderful, like a treasure, the *agalma*, the most precious part of him, that which, in him, is more than himself.[6] But the *agalma* turns lethal as soon as she touches it.

2. The secret object is mediated through *Mother's desire*, it is the object of the desire of the Other. The mother appears as the agent of naming; she is the one who gives names. She has named her

daughter after her beloved brother, the one marked by fate (as a child, he miraculously recovered from a fateful accident). The mother's desire is now delegated to her daughter marked by his name. If, for her, Uncle Charlie carries in him the secret object, it is so only because he carried it already for her mother; her own desire could be constituted only through her mother's desire. The mother is thus in position of the third in the relationship Charlie–Charlie.

It may come as a surprise that we find the mother where one would expect the father-figure, but Hitchcock's universe is a maternal universe. Mother's desire makes law – Father is presented as incompetent: he can't drive a car, he engages in rather comical conversations about murders with the neighbour Herbie, who is even more inept than himself; they both seem rather like well-disposed idiots, both dependent on woman figures larger than themselves. Spoto remarks that in *Shadow of a Doubt* we find the last 'good mother' in Hitchcock's films, not presaging the disasters to come (compare the mother figures in *Notorious*, *Psycho*, *The Birds*, *Marnie*, etc., etc.). But even this 'good mother' has her counterpart in Herbie's mother, who is sick and possessive and whom we never see, like the first sketch of the 'acousmatic' mother in *Psycho*. So on closer inspection there is nothing idyllic about this small-town life and the 'good ordinary people'.

What simultaneously holds together and disrupts the dual relationship, then, is the link between the desire of the Other, the mother-figure, which mediates it, and, on the other hand, the paradoxical fascinating object which turns lethal. The subject finally receives her/his own message:

'We are old friends. More than that. We are like twins. You said so yourself.... You wake up every morning of your life and you know perfectly well that there is nothing in the world to trouble you. You go through your ordinary little day and at night you sleep your untroubled ordinary little sleep, filled with peaceful stupid dreams. And I brought you nightmares. Or did I? Or was it just a silly, unexpert lie? You live in a dream, you're a sleepwalker, blind! How do you know what the world is like? Do you know that the world is a foul sty? Do you know if you ripped the fronts off houses you'd find swine? The world is a hell!'

The confession scene takes place in a bar, a place like hell with its heavy smoke and the atmosphere of vice. She cannot betray her uncle, her hands are bound by her mother; that would be her end. The mother who has endowed the object with its wonderful secret is now the figure who prevents its disclosure. There is a paradox in her position: on the one hand, she is the one who takes care of home and family, the protectress of domesticity (in contrast to the incompetent father); on the other hand, what emerges as the irruption of an alien body, the disruption and destruction of homely security, is precisely the object of Mother's desire. When Charlie wants to be saved from the domestic boredom, the uncle appears as the saviour in so far as he is the object of Mother's worship, the hero of a family romance (as Freud would call it).

When Charlie discovers the 'secret and wonderful' object the duality vanishes, the imaginary universe is torn to pieces, the fronts of the houses are ripped off. She finds the uncanniness at the point where she most intimately recognizes herself. It does not occur as an outside catastrophe; the catastrophe is that it emerges in a point closest to the subject, as her own message, the answer of her narcissistic image. She experiences in the most immediate sense that the object of desire is lethal.

The confession sequence in the bar, the structural kernel of the plot, has no double – young Charlie has never set foot in that place before, and never will again. We have seen that the condition of the doubling is the exclusion/inclusion of a third, and that goes also for the duplication of the scenes: the double scenes are roughly centred around this pivotal one which has no double and serves as their hinge.

Charlie's discovery of her own implication in her uncle's world prevents any maintenance of her own purity or a meta-position. The fascinating object is her fate: she has loved that 'more in him than himself', and it doesn't simply vanish with his death. 'She is doomed to love her uncle Charlie till the end of her life', Hitchcock once commented – this ending is far from the standard Hollywood happy ending.

So the position of the third in the duality is occupied both by the fascinating and lethal object (which is also the object of exchange and circulation) and the mother's desire, Mother as the bearer of the law. It is the convergence and coincidence of the two that provides perhaps the best clue to the fundamental Hitchcockian fantasy, and *Shadow of a Doubt* reveals it in perhaps the most striking way.

Strangers on a Train presents a similar case of doubling, albeit on a smaller scale and formally not so pure. In the opening shots, we get the symmetrical presentation of two pairs of shoes that we follow from a taxi to a carriage; the shot of rails, parallel and inevitably intersecting in the distance, just as the shoes will inevitably bump into each other, thus linking another pair, Guy and Bruno, fatally bound together. The couple again serves as the axis of duplication: there are two towns, Washington and Metcalf, linked by train, the place of the exchange and the contingent; two ladies in Guy's life – Miriam, his ex-wife in Metcalf, and Anna, the senator's daughter in Washington, opposed as vulgarity versus glamour; two young men accompanying Miriam; two detectives shadowing Guy; two scenes at the funfair with two guardians and two little boys; and, on the verge of the film, two Patricias H. – Patricia Hitchcock, Hitchcock's daughter in her most extensive part (she made 'cameo appearances' in *Stage Fright* and *Psycho*), and Patricia Highsmith (the film was based on her first novel, endowing her with sudden – and wholly justified – fame). Finally, Hitchcock himself, in his cameo appear-

ance in a key moment of the film, is doubled with a double bass, the instrument later played by the 'wrong man' Manny Balestrero.

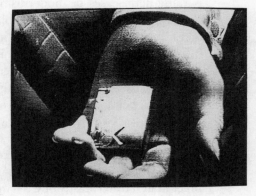

Here too, this duality, this device of formal symmetry, is finally just the background for the circulation of an object. In *Strangers on a Train*, the privileged object is the lighter which again summarizes the whole tension, serves as a pledge, holds the couple together and disrupts it at the same time. If *Strangers on a Train* were a story in *Decameron*, it could bear the title 'The story about Guy from Washington who lost his lighter and, after long and disagreeable complications, finally got it back'.

The opening shots have established two symmetrical partners, and the plot turns around an object circulating between the two. This situation looks remarkably like tennis, and indeed Guy is a professional tennis player – in contrast to the book, where he is an architect (in the book, the object left on the train is nothing less than the book of Plato's *Dialogues*; but the book is altogether different in its structure and implications). The alteration is perhaps not entirely fortuitous; it corresponds to a necessity.

One can think of another famous tennis game, in Antonioni's *Blow-up*. There is a group of people playing tennis without a ball; David Hemmings, in the end, enters into their game by fetching the nonexistent ball. He accepts the game in which the place of the object is empty, just as the social game could go on without a body. There was the illusion that the object could be detected by a blow-up, that the blow-up would seize or capture it, but all one could see were the vanishing contours of an elusive object which, the next morning, was no longer there.

The supposition that the place of the object is empty, that the social as well as aesthetic game is organized around a central void, was one of the essential suppositions of modernism. In modernism, Godot never comes; and both *Blow-up* and Godot were taken as paradigmatic cases of modernism by Slavoj Žižek.[7] In Hitchcock, however, the presence of the object is essential – the object that takes hold of the gaze is situated in a special place at the core of the intersubjective relationships: it instigates and triggers off these relationships, it provides their necessary support, and at the same time it blocks them, it embodies their inner impossibility, it prevents them from being specular, it provokes their break-up.

How does Guy get involved with Bruno? The question is an instance of one of the basic Hitchcockian problems: how does an accidental encounter cause fatal consequences? This is another key to Hitchcock's universe: an apparent order of the ordinary life is precipitated into catastrophe by an accidental encounter.

Raymond Chandler, who wrote the script, had only ten minutes of the film at his disposal to get an honest and law-abiding citizen entangled in a murder. It seemed like an impossible task, yet the result is quite convincing. There are two moments on which this opening depends: the first one concerns the way the subject is related to the Other of social conventions (in the last instance, to the Other of signifier); the second one implies the relationship to the object.

We can approach the first moment in a roundabout way. There is a hilarious incident at the beginning where we see Bruno with a necktie that bears his name. He introduces himself by referring to the name on his tie – the tie which was, significantly, a present from his mother and which he wears only for his mother's sake, to give her pleasure. One can detect the connection with *Shadow of a Doubt*, where Mother was the agency of naming – Bruno's mother is exactly halfway between Mrs Newton (Charlie's mother) and Mrs Bates. (If one wanted to do some wild psychoanalysis, one could point to the fact that there is also an image of a lobster on the same tie – lobster the castration animal? Anyway, it doesn't seem to be a good omen to be presented with such a tie by one's mother.) There is something hilarious in the way Bruno is, quite literally, the bearer of his name – the name is like a label, included in the image. But there is the same tendency in Bruno's treatment of language, his position in discourse, in the way he treats words as labels for things – which is essentially the psychotic handling of language. We can see this in two pieces of dialogue:

> *Bruno*: Surely we speak the same language?
> *Guy*: We do....
>
> *Bruno*: Do you think my theories are OK?
> *Guy*: I think all your theories are OK.

Guy answers with a form of politeness, with a civility, a tactfulness – that is, with a yes which is a no. The very form of politeness implies a capacity to read the implications, to read between the lines, not to take words at their face value, as labels for things. The form of politeness demands a form of subjectivation – that is, in its minimal form, a complication, a mediation of reference. The place of subjectivity entails a circularity in the reference; it runs between the lines; it cannot be pinned down to a signifier. But Bruno has a psychotic incapacity to read between the lines; he takes words for their immediate referents. Bruno and Guy say: 'we speak the same language' and 'your theories are OK'. Furthermore, on an even more minimal level, politeness implies reciprocity, an exchange of rejoinders, a formal co-operation. The very fact that Guy carries on with the form of conversation, that he answers politely, is taken by Bruno as a kind of guarantee of exchange, on the same level as the exchange of murders. Guy says no, but in the polite form of carrying on the conversational reciprocity, and the very form of co-operation is seen as an engagement: a word for a word, a murder for a murder.

This scene has its counterpart later, when Guy takes the train at the time of the murder. Again, there is an accidental encounter on the train, and Guy gets involved in a conversation with a drunken professor of mathematics who approaches him with some inchoate theories and incoherent mumbling. When asked 'Do you understand what I mean?' Guy answers again: 'Yes, sure'. His attitude is exactly the same – he keeps up the form of politeness and reciprocity, only this time the professor, drunk as he is, is capable of taking a yes for a no. He is baffled that Guy should understand his confused effusions, so he stops talking immediately, he gets the message. There is a correspondence between the two encounters; Guy's identical attitude produces two opposed reactions. The first time the form of politeness is taken literally, and will be all too well remembered; the second time its message is understood, but will be entirely forgotten. The professor will not be able to remember the conversation and will thus leave Guy without an alibi. In both cases, the consequences will be fatal.

Later in the film there are two more accidental encounters on the train. Guy takes the train four times during the film, and on each occasion there is an accidental encounter, the train being the place of the contingency and the exchange. In the third instance Guy witnesses two passengers, two other strangers on a train, bumping their legs accidentally into each other, but nothing follows – only a polite 'Excuse me', 'Sorry'. In that universe, accidents can be without consequences only if they happen to others.

The fourth one occurs in the concluding scene, when Guy is again approached by a stranger: 'Excuse me, are you Guy Haines?' – the same opening Bruno used. But this time, Guy very rudely turns away and leaves the compartment; he gives up the form of politeness and reciprocity; he has learned by now that the form itself contains deceptive pitfalls. So the first accidental encounter has three further repercussions in the film, like three variations, reflections, developments on the same theme. The red thread of the whole is a phenomenology of chance encounters.

The second moment that entails Guy's involvement with Bruno is centred on the object.

Accidental encounters, as already pointed out, are essential for Hitchcock's universe. It is a universe governed by a 'malign spirit' which makes a chance event plunge a normal citizen into a nightmare, and it is the chance accident that reveals the structure into which the subject is implicated. The chance encounter basically takes the form of a joint between an element and an empty place, a void that was awaiting the subject like a trap. *North by Northwest* is the most obvious example: the name George Kaplan, a nonexistent agent, an empty signifier, is the pitfall into which Roger O. Thornhill tumbles; he fills the empty space. In *Strangers on a Train*, the empty space is the place in the contract in which Guy gets caught as a partner. The contract itself seems ordinary enough: do for me what I will do for you – crisscross, the reciprocity at the base of social life. It is here that the object comes into play: the empty place becomes occupied by an object, the lighter.

Guy takes the lighter from his pocket to light Bruno's cigarette. The lighter is marked 'A to G' (Ann to Guy), it was a present from his fiancée, and this dedication sparks off the conversation about Guy's marital troubles, leading to Bruno's fatal proposition. At the end of the conversation, Guy forgets the lighter as he leaves the train, and Bruno keeps it – as a pledge, a gage, a handsel, a signature on the contract. This is the second moment: there would be no contract without the object, this little piece of materiality, this 'little-bit-of-the-Real'. Later on, Guy tries in vain to protest his innocence, to dismiss Bruno and deny any link with him – the lighter is there as his object equivalent, his *tenant lieu*, his material representative, his stand-in, holding his place against his will. So when Guy won't keep his side of the contract, Bruno can use it to plant it as evidence and to implicate Guy. Bruno holds to it all the time, he cherishes it, he won't use it to light cigarettes, he won't let it out of his hands, except once when it accidentally falls into a gutter.

The object as the object of a slip – being accidentally forgotten – calls for another slip: Bruno, too, is part of an unconscious contract – a murder for a murder, a slip for a slip. Bruno, too, depends on the object: it makes sense for his action, it provides his certainty, his sense of purpose. It is what he clings to till the end, as to his life, pressing it in his hand as he dies. Only when Guy can get it back from the hand of the dead Bruno – only then – is the contract broken.

Let us now draw some general conclusions. Hitchcock himself was very much aware of the problem of the object. In his famous remarks in the conversation with Truffaut, he pointed out the central function of a certain kind of object in his films, the one he has called the McGuffin – an 'irrelevant' object, a 'nothing at all' around which the action turns. Hitchcock tells the joke that gave the name to the object, which is actually a 'strangers-on-a-train' joke. It also has a Yugoslav version, an alternative ending:

> 'What is the package on the rack?'
> 'It's a McGuffin.'
> 'What is it for?'
> 'To kill the lions on the Highlands.'
> 'But there are no lions on the Highlands.'
> *Punchline A*: 'Actually, this is not a McGuffin either.'
> *Punchline B*: 'You see, it works.'

One has to read the two versions together: the object is a nothing, it is actually not a McGuffin, but it works.

We almost never learn the content of the McGuffin – the microfilms in *North by Northwest*, the plans for aeroplane machines in *The Thirty-Nine Steps* (the plans that we never even see), the encoded melody in *The Lady Vanishes* (the immaterial object that has to be entrusted to the voice and to the memory); my favourite example is from *Foreign Correspondent* – a secret clause in a defence treaty, a clause so secret that it had to be memorized by those present; it couldn't even be put on paper, a sublime ideal signifier beyond writing (of course, one never learns what the clause was); and so on.

The McGuffins signify only that they signify, they signify the signification as such; the actual content is entirely insignificant. They are both at the core of the action and completely irrelevant; the highest degree of meaning – what everybody is after – coincides with an absence of meaning. The object itself is a vanishing point, an empty space; it does not need to be shown or to be present at all – as in *Blow-up* – an evocation by words is enough. Its materiality is inessential; it suffices that we are merely told of its existence.

There is a second type of object, however, that follows a different kind of logic. It is a fascinating, captivating, bewitching, spell-binding object which necessarily possesses a kind of materiality and a certain lethal quality. The two examples I have tried to single out in some detail are the ring in *Shadow of a Doubt* and the lighter in *Strangers on a Train*. One can find them in many other Hitchcock films.

There is the key in *Notorious* – the key that Ingrid Bergman steals from her husband to give to her lover and by returning it reveals herself as a spy; in a beautiful tracking shot at the reception, the camera, after a complicated movement, seeks out the key in Bergman's hand, all the glamour of the reception gradually fading away, becoming the background for the object within a single shot. There is the key in *Dial M for Murder*, the key given by the husband to his wife's murderer, by which 'the man who knew too much' gets apprehended by his surplus knowledge (but it remains unexploited in a Hitchcockian way, the whole film being rather un-Hitch-cockian). There is the necklace in *Vertigo*, the necklace that the false Madeleine was wearing and which persists as the only object in the second half, worn by Judy Barton, that completely different woman who is nevertheless the same – the object is the core of her identity, her 'material equivalent', the little-bit-of-Real. Other variations are possible: in *The Man Who Knew Too Much*, the boy becomes the object of exchange between two couples – passing, as it were, from one side of the mirror to the other.[8] In *North by Northwest*, the empty space (the name George Kaplan) becomes accidentally occupied by Cary Grant: he himself, so to speak, takes the part of the lighter and becomes the object of exchange between two Intelligence Services.

So a distinction can be drawn between two kinds of Hitchcockian object: one is a vanishing point, immaterial in itself, which instigates the infinite metonymy; the second one has the massive non-transparent presence; it is endowed with sublime and lethal materiality; it is the evocation of what Lacan (following Freud and Heidegger) called *das Ding*. One could propose the following Lacanian distinction: the first one is the object of desire, a vanishing semblance pushing the desire in an infinite metonymy; the second one is the object of the drive, the presence incorporating a blockade around which all the relations circulate. The logic of the second object is the 'superstructure' of the logic of the first, its supplement and counterpart, as in Lacan's famous 'graph of desire'.[9]

Notes

1. *Cahiers du cinéma* 39, October 1954, pp. 48–9.
2. Donald Spoto, *The Dark Side of Genius*, Boston, MA: Little, Brown 1983, p. 263.
3. See Raymond Durgnat, *The Strange Case of Alfred Hitchcock*, London: Faber & Faber 1974, pp. 33–4.
4. Durgnat (ibid., pp. 187–8) even suggests some possible improvements of the script to obviate those deficiencies.
5. See Michel Chion's chapter on *The Lady Vanishes* in this book, pp. 137–42.
6. See Jacques Lacan, *The Four Fundamental Concepts of Psycho-Analysis*, Harmondsworth: Penguin 1979, p. 263; also Jacques Lacan, *Le Séminaire, livre VIII: Le transfert*, Paris: Editions du Seuil 1991, pp. 163–213.
7. Slavoj Žižek, *Looking Awry: An Introduction to Jacques Lacan through Popular Culture*, Cambridge, MA: MIT Press 1991, pp. 143–5.
8. See Pascal Bonitzer's chapter on *The Man Who Knew Too Much* in this book, pp. 178–84.
9. See Jacques Lacan, 'The Subversion of the Subject and the Dialectic of Desire in the Freudian Unconscious', in *Ecrits: A Selection*, London: Tavistock 1977, pp. 303–24.

Spatial Systems in *North by Northwest*

FREDRIC JAMESON

Themes and meanings can be detected in *North by Northwest*: some of them form-intrinsic, some of them form-extrinsic, but all essentially trivial, since they substitute other codes and languages for the filmic one, at the same time as they seek to justify and rationalize, by way of portentous significance, an experience marked as excitement, diversion, genre-adventure. Form-extrinsic: you look outside the text at other fragments of this director's *œuvre* and, driven by a synoptic passion, stereoptically combine the auction sequence here with other public and ceremonial situations in which the protagonist, as in a nakedness or examination nightmare, must perform (Cary Grant, here seated in the public and heckling the auctioneer, is the inverse of Robert Donat standing on the podium in *The Thirty Nine Steps* and improvising a stump speech).

This kind of operation is based on the decision to take recurrent formulaic gags not as filler but as deeper symptom and repetition: it is of a piece with an older literary stylistic or image-frequency criticism and, like them, depends on the *auteur* hypothesis – that is, the phenomenological positing of some central subject or consciousness embodying itself in a distinctive 'world' and 'style'. Predictably, this kind of rewriting (which constructs a new transtextual object) leads on to the false problem of subjectivity unless it raises the (historical) question of its own conditions of possibility: in the present context, the fact of a semi-autonomy of episodes which allows us to extract something like the auction sequence in the first place and to juxtapose it with other equally semi-autonomous episodes. But this line of inquiry leads us, not towards Hitchcock's genius or his libido, but rather towards the history of form itself.

Form-intrinsic meanings, however, tend to be deduced by hypothesizing or constructing a relationship between two situations in the work, most often its beginning and its ending: thus, the film is somehow 'about' the way in which Cary Grant, an advertising executive with two divorces and a mother, comes to the possibility of a 'fulfilling relationship' in marriage. The main body of the film can then be seen as a quest or a test, trial by fire, struggle with the adversary, the experience of betrayal, action not with images but within images, and so on. It is something that works better with *The Birds*, where the attacking forces have been libidinalized from the outset (in the pet store) and can always, in one way or another, be read as spilling out of Tippi Hedren's psyche. There, however, the message is as ominous as it is overt (the 'taming of the shrew'), whereas here it is merely pop-psychological ('maturity').

These two temptations – the stylistic and the structural – are in fact dialectically related projections of the two poles of the dilemma of modernist form: the content of the episodes and the organizing device or overall pretext of their formal totality – fancy versus imagination again, or the molecular versus the molar. The modernist work seeks to retain this tension and to live within it, to feed off it, to resist the impoverishment of the most obvious solutions: either to relax the work into the absolute heterogeneity of the text, with its swarm of local, random fragments, or to turn the work into the 'idea' of itself and affirm its 'concept' so stridently that what results is either 'pure' or 'empty', depending on one's mood and sympathies. But it is harder for the analyst than for the *auteur* to respect this tension, since any interpretation that seeks to lay simultaneous stress on the logic of episodization and the 'concept' of the whole (the overall movement through these episodes) will, in spite of itself, lean towards totalization and oversuggest some ultimate formal unity which is much more feebly at work in our actual experience of the film – which is to say, of the film's concrete episodes.

To call for a *mediation* between these two levels is only apparently to appeal to an antiquated piece of conceptual machinery; in fact, it involves a modification and an enrichment of the very concept of mediation which cannot be further explored here in an abstract methodological way. The notion that space itself might provide such a mediation is far from being as empty and as general a suggestion as it might at first seem. All films, no doubt, register and record space; but we have tended largely to recontain and to make that banality manageable by inserting the specificity of the visual, by rewriting space as *seen* space, by translating the larger category imperceptibly back into this or that notion of the image.

In contemporary image culture, there are evidently good and objective reasons why this temptation should be so strong: anyone who has leafed through Hitchcock stills, however, in the attempt to illustrate – or at least to peg for memory's sake – this or that signifi- cant moment in his films (including this one), learns, with a certain salutary astonishment, that the isolated frame in Hitchcock conveys very little of what we then rapidly come to identify as the crucial matter: namely, movement itself. In spite of the fetishization of the visual and the voyeuristic in Hitchcock (or perhaps because of it), these films rarely work towards the supreme moment of the produc- tion of the modernist image as such, the dissociation of the moment of vision from the narrative which becomes its pretext, as in the Dance of Death in *The Seventh Seal,* or the dramatic caricature of the whole process of image-production in the unexpected Last Supper of *Viridiana.*

The publicity stills for *North by Northwest,* however, which face this same theoretical dilemma for rather more practical purposes, 'solve' it mostly by offering Cary Grant in arrested motion, most notably in the stylized or contorted fall at the moment of his mock assassin- ation. But this image-possibility probably has more to do with Grant's acting style than with Hitchcock's aesthetic: one hesitates, indeed, to describe Grant's acting as Brechtian, yet it involves a shorthand use of the body to sketch in gestures which are never the fully realized 'expressive' thing itself, but merely designate this last – as, paradigmatically, when the hands in the pockets in the field sequence half-withdraw, to convey the anticipatory feeling that the vehicle now arriving may be the one he's waiting for. Neither face nor body here acts out the concrete experience of impatient waiting ('on tenterhooks'), but they certainly quote that experience and rehearse its idea. Yet such abstract, well-nigh Eisensteinian concepts

49

– which, one after the other, make up the tangible character called 'Roger Thornhill' or 'played' by Cary Grant – are essentially one endless stream of *reactions* to a situation they do not control, which one can in turn describe as various movements through space.

It may also be useful to specify the conception of space to be deployed here as a dialectical and historical one, which has more affinities with Henri Lefebvre's philosophy of space and spatialization than with Kant's abstract and immutable category. We are given, in *North by Northwest*, a whole series or sequence of concrete spaces which are not too rapidly to be reduced to mere *places*. The places are named, of course (as so often in Hitchcock: Phoenix, Arizona; or Quebec City; or San Francisco – several times); but place and place name alike are only the starting points, the raw material, from which a rather different realization of concrete space is produced which is no longer scene or backdrop for an action or for actors, but includes those in some new, qualitative way. The vocation of these new space-signs is often so imperious as to master the individual episodes and to transform each into the occasion for a qualitatively distinct production: indeed, the very special interest of *North by Northwest* in this respect is that, as in *The Thirty-Nine Steps*, it goes further in this direction than most other Hitchcock films, identifying each new episodic unit with the development of a radically different type of concrete space itself, so that we may have the feeling of a virtual anthology of a whole range of distinct spatial configurations, pinned side by side in some photograph album.

Such new scenotopes, however, inevitably begin to enter into comparative and dialectical relations with each other, as some unconscious 'persistence of the image' reads fresh spatial co-ordinates and qualities in terms of what the previous ones were not. Nor is it a matter of variable features against an unchanging substratum: the process of unconscious and differential spatial experience is dialectical very precisely in the way in which each 'type' of space vehiculates its own inner logic and laws and 'produces its own concept'. Yet in this heterogeneous series of spaces, where we learn the logic and meaning, the world-ness, of each *against* the others, it follows that some deeper 'system' of these spaces is at work that might, at a pinch, be crudely and abstractly articulated. Such a synchronic system of the languages of the various types of space is, however, only a way of representing graphically what also governs the narrative logic and movement of the episodes in time.

This is, indeed, finally how we will read the overall formal and narrative movement of *North by Northwest* (with all the reservations indicated above): as a transformation of one kind of space, through intermediary combinations and catalytic operations, into another. This story – of the adventures of space, if you like – will not turn out to be terribly different in its form from the psychological or char-acter-development story already caricatured, in which the Grant figure evolves towards love and marriage. But it offers a better, non-subjective way of telling that story (doing away with consciousness, 'character', and the anthropomorphic), and thus may not really be 'the same' any longer in the important senses.

As for the way in which the specific spaces may be characterized, the auction sequence offers some first clue for exploration in the striking construction of public formality it systematically tests and probes with a series of calculated transgressions (Grant's aberrant bids). The withdrawal of the villains from this scene of public scandal was already given a more abstract spatial expression in the drunken-driving sequence: when Grant's car finally comes to a halt within policed legality, the assassins' vehicle, which has been following him at a prudent distance, executes a slow and meaningful U-turn: renunciation, finality, withdrawal – this filmed trajectory of an inanimate object is more expressive than most human gestures; it is indeed itself a gesture of a heightened but constructed type. The withdrawal from the auction, then (Leonard and Valerian observing in discomfiture, Mason guiding Eva-Marie Saint away), is retro-actively unified by the earlier 'signifier'; but it will also be used and transformed later on in its turn – most notably in the ultimate with-drawal, the walk to the plane with its divisions within unity, each member of the group attending in a different direction (hesitation, caution, urgency), with the wind ruffling their hair (a detail to which I will return later). But here, for the first and last time, withdrawal is head-on, *into* the camera and towards us, and not the prudent and inconspicuous retreat from the auction room.

These effects, however, are not the most interesting ones: at best they play upon the logical possibility that public decorum or order may have not one, but two opposites (or that the antisocial can come

51

in two distinct and unrelated forms): the antisocial individual and the criminal organization; it is a lesson worked out paradigmatically in Fritz Lang's *M*, but only tactically relevant in Hitchcock, whose public villains (the Professor in *The Thirty-Nine Steps*) are also always sinners and private criminals.

The key to the auction scene seems to me rather to lie in the psychological disintegration of the auctioneer, who proves literally unable to handle antisocial conduct and provocation of the Grant type: it is a beautiful comic detail, to be included in the anthology of Hitchcock's other (minor) public figures, such as the venomous coroner in *Vertigo*; and what it underscores is the overwhelming predominance of public space in this film, from the Seagram Building to Mount Rushmore, passing through police stations (but is that *public* space exactly?) and railway stations and the lobbies of great hotels, as well as this auction room. Where people live 'privately' is here always problematic, even to the secluded private house of the final episode: perhaps, indeed, the strictly private is as limited and as evanescent as that collapsing upper berth in the Pullman, which can always be folded away without a trace. The berth is, however, not a statement, or a symbol, or a proposition; but, rather, a problem.

The opposition between private and public is, first of all, an ideology, like all such binary oppositions, but in a way that has genuine social and historical content, if one rehearses its exclusion of work (which is neither public nor private, or else both), its affinities with bourgeois or representative political systems, and its rather obvious mobilization of gender. Interesting and dramatic reversals can be achieved within such an ideology (most notably Hannah Arendt's notion that 'public' life today is in fact 'private'), but one cannot think within it, and one certainly cannot 'solve' the false problems it generates (such as, in the present context, the true or authentic nature of the 'private' in a public society). Hitchcock's film can scarcely be said to subvert or to 'estrange' this ideological opposition, within which it works and from which it draws its effects; what it can be seen to do is to attempt to 'produce' or 'construct' a concept of the private which need never be tested, since – ideal marriage – it lies beyond the closure of the film and thus beyond representation.

The various spaces of *North by Northwest* are therefore all ad-
mixtures of public and private in such a way that the public dimension predominates and the private one can never be separated out as
an independent element or contemplated with the naked eye. This
means, however, that there are no purely public spaces either –
none is genuinely anonymous or impersonal, since they are all in
this film, without exception, the scenes of distinctive personal
drama: not even elevators or bathrooms are exempt. Yet the logical
possibility of pure forms of each pole is certainly registered in this
film, as though *pour mémoire*, and in a simultaneous bit of filler which
is at one and the same time the obligatory explanation for the plot
and its most embarrassing low point (what is *necessary* in art, as
Valéry said, always being what is worse or bad).

What must be dealt with are two distinct problems, both urgently
relevant for the continuation of the intrigue: (1) Why, now that
'Cary Grant' knows that he is not really a fugitive from justice and
the police are not really after him, must all this continue? Why can't
everyone simply go home? (2) How are we to account for the
'sincerity' of Eve-Marie Saint's love for 'Cary Grant' in the light of
her earlier love affair with 'James Mason'? She does not have the
excuse of Ingrid Bergman in *Notorious*, where the second love was
simulated, virtually under the direction of the first lover (here the
time sequence is reversed); meanwhile, if the affair with James
Mason was 'insincere', then she is really 'a tramp' (to use the
ideological category of the period and the language of this film).
How can this seeming promiscuity be reconciled with her function
as the ideal love image?

Both these problems are summarily liquidated in the same scene,
one of the most wondrous settings in the film (to which we will
return) – that of the pine grove, whose strongly aesthetic surcharge
and bonus perhaps serves as a cover, as compensation and distrac-
tion, for the flimsiness of the constructional excuses in question. The
answer to the first question, given by 'the Professor', is simply: 'War
is hell, Mr Thornhill, even a Cold one'. The struggle is worth it, a
priori, and it must go on (along with the microfilm in the statue –
'let's just say, government secrets': this is what Hitchcock famously
called the McGuffin, the unexamined pretext).

Leo G. Carroll brings this off with more aplomb than Eve-Marie

Saint, whose embarrassment is palpable and understandable when she is obliged to field the following replies:

> *Thornhill*: Has life been like that? ... How come?
> *Eve*: Men like you.
> *Thornhill*: What's the matter with men like me?
> *Eve*: They don't believe in marriage.
> *Thornhill*: I've been married twice.
> *Eve*: See what I mean?

What is interesting in both these obligatory 'explanations' is not their banal ideological content (Cold War liberalism, marriage as the supreme vocation for a woman), but rather their relationship to the opposition between private and public, of which they offer virtually absolute and antithetical expressions. The Professor's position is that of the primacy of the public, in the face of which no private claims (love, for example) can be taken into consideration; while Eve's endorsement of ideal marriage is traditionally the affirmation of the existence of a private sphere as a privileged and unique space and an absolute value. But that 'space' cannot be represented, it must be taken on faith, as existing somewhere off screen (and beyond the ending of the film). Nor does the Professor's public space exist anywhere here (not even in the meeting in the FBI office, where humane and charitable objections are raised to his cynical – but 'heroic' – *Realpolitik*: a representation of such space is certainly conceivable, but not in this genre or in this particular film, nor even in Hitchcock in general, who has no interest in the political dynamics such a representational space would imply).

We therefore come to the conclusion that these two abstract conceptual affirmations mark the places of the ideological opposition between public and private, which will be explored concretely through the mixed spaces of the actual filmic episodes. The semiotic rectangle has the merit not only of positioning the various logical combinations dialectically (the complex term is a concrete experience; the lateral possibilities are abstract ideologies) but also of raising the question of some apparently indispensable but missing term, which would stand as the synthesis or combination of the two negative terms, and lay in place something that is neither private nor public (both 'not-private' and 'not-public'). Whatever this term is, we may also expect it to combine features of the other two – that is, to offer something like a concrete represent-ation, which is also (as with the ideologies) an absence or a non-space (or the simple affirmation of a space elsewhere or really existing – only not on screen).

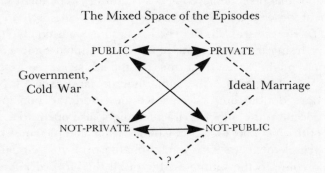

The Mixed Space of the Episodes

'Determination is negation', Hegel famously affirmed; and one is therefore tempted to search for that specific form of not-being, that specific boundary line or definition, that allows the visual experi-ence, the episode-spaces of this film, to exist in their plenitude and their own specificity. That genuine Other of the images and their pleasure is unlikely to be 'merely' the real world outside the cinema, while its position as a distinct fourth category makes it clear that it is relatively distinct from the phoney absolute categories of public life and private life (absolute movement and absolute stasis, in filmic terms). Yet surely some such Other space does exist within this film, in a unique and extraordinary fashion to which conventional notions of closure can scarcely do justice.

For the finale, the chase on the monument, is surely not merely one more type of space in a varied series but itself concludes the series with a flourish that demands analysis and explanation. Indeed, the entire spatial sequence system of the film – beginning with Mies's newly erected Seagram Building, and moving (with an excursus to Long Island and then a return to the United Nations building) to Chicago (with an excursus to an open field somewhere north of Urbana-Champaign), and thence to North Dakota and the conclusion – this sequence of spaces generates a sense of complete-ness (or a 'totality-effect') which can scarcely be explained by its content alone. Comparable formal problems (and 'solutions') can be found in Raymond Chandler's equally episodic (and spatial) detec-tive stories, where the successful mapping of the Los Angeles region – in other words, our sense that, in spite of necessary selectivity, 'totalization' has been achieved – is structurally dependent on the inclusion of some ultimate boundary or verge of Being itself (in *Fare-well, My Lovely*, the sea).[1] In the Hitchcock film, the stereotypical or imaginary frame is clearly some phantasmic United States, about which one might argue that the open-field sequence sets the Midwest in place, while the mountainous landscape of North Dakota does double duty for the Rockies (and the non-specific popular accent of the minor characters might also open up a space for the South). Yet here too, as in Chandler, the completeness of the enumerated elements (of such a map-phantasm) is not enough: we must also come to the ultimate edge of all this, in order for it to recohere retroactively as a satisfyingly exhaustive itinerary.

The final sequence provides exactly that in so far as it offers the spatial image of a jumping-off place at the end of the world. The evident structural analogies with the end of *Saboteur* – the villain hanging and falling from the torch of the Statue of Liberty – were evidently posited on a reverse-field movement from Los Angeles to New York and the very gateway of the nation; but Mount Rush-more and the Canadian border are not exactly that, nor would this locality seem the most obvious or convenient port of exit to the Soviet Union. But no one is going to the Soviet Union here; they are leaving the world itself, as when, in medieval times, navigators approached the edge of the map. The twinkling rows of landing lights direct our attention off into the void; meanwhile, this spatial structure is powerfully reinforced by the peculiar cantilevering of the house itself, which also juts out into empty space (and various spatial arrangements in the scenes themselves – Cary Grant looking down on the vast central living-room, for example – echo and mimic this phantasmic relationship to the edge and the void).

What is here set in place on the level of the Imaginary is then, in the next and final sequence, kinaesthetically redramatized as a material *analogon* on the level of the body itself:[2] the faces of the statues standing as a sheer wall and an abrupt end, below which a different forested landscape spreads: these are so many material manifestations and variations, not on the formal matter of mere closure (ending, completeness, and so forth) so much as on the concept of the 'verge' – the dramatic place in which something comes to an absolute end, beyond it lying the unknown or what does not compute within the system. This, then, is the sense in which it seems appropriate to inscribe this complex and unique space of the 'edge of the world' into the empty fourth slot of our combination scheme, as that impossible representation of absolute non-space, the Other of space, which is required for 'space' itself, concrete space, to constitute itself as a meaningful language.

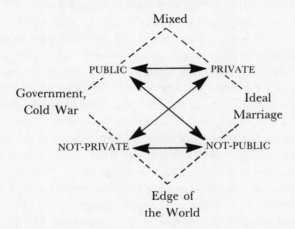

None of this even makes a beginning on the matter of the specific spatial episodes themselves, nor on the kind of reading or perception they imply, require, enforce and programme. The argument being made here, in other words, presupposes that spatial experience in this film has been uniquely constructed as a language (something that may be paradigmatic of the essence of film itself in some more general aesthetic and philosophical way, but does not necessarily hold for individual films in general, nor even necessarily for other films by Hitchcock himself). Something must therefore be done in order to train us in this language; we must be rapidly programmed to its use, in the process of unlearning habits of 'viewing' developed in other occasions and for other kinds of films.

Perhaps the process of *un*learning undesirable viewing habits indeed offers the most convenient way into the specificity of those now to be described. What is to be avoided, one may suppose, is on the one hand the Bazinian aesthetic, and on the other the aesthetic of the glossy image – filmic realism and filmic postmodernism respectively, whose mutual exclusion opens up a place for the properly filmic modernism in terms of which 'Hitchcock' is, in our general context, the marker and one characteristic realization. Everything that in Hitchcock is redolent of trick shots or gimmicks is in fact endowed with the deeper function of excluding the Bazinian 'deep shot' or deep space, even when it would seem to draw precisely on the capacities of deep focus to juxtapose a foreground detail and a background action in some 'meaningful' way.

The deep shot, however, is an invitation to stasis and to contemplation: nature as an overfurnished and traditional room around which you can slowly gaze, lingering on its objects: the ephemerality of the single shot, the relentless forward movement of the narrative camera, only exacerbates this longing for contemplation in the form of loss and the sting of time itself. That this longing marks Bazinian realism, or the deep shot, with a necessary and constructive incompletion is evident from the immediate impoverishment, the evaporation of being, suffered by such framed space when the image is artificially detained and frozen like a photograph.

The constitutive relationship between this aesthetic and black-and-white film stock is harder to argue, except *a contrario*, in its immediate exclusion by colour (whose full equivalent for this visual plenitude is no longer realism, but the nostalgia image). *North by Northwest*, then, obviously forestalls 'realism' in this special sense, a priori by virtue of its colour, but more substantively by way of its specific narrativization, which systematically distracts the eye from ontological inspection. (My argument here, therefore, differs from the positions of both Cavell and Heath, who affirm a deeper affinity and consonance between narrativization as such and black-and-white film or realistic representation respectively.[3])

That Hitchcock's space, even in colour, also excludes the peculiar libidinal investments of the postmodern or nostalgia image has also been 'empirically' argued above. Here too a certain type of narrativization is rigorously inconsistent with the aesthetics of the image, which solicits sensory overload of a kind that tolerates only the crudest and most stereotypical attention to plot (hence the perfunctory nature of most nostalgia-film narratives). Another type of structural difference can, however, be identified in the relationship of the two aesthetics to content, and in particular to the historical markings of such content. I will argue elsewhere that nostalgia film necessarily includes a (constitutive) reference, if not to the actual historical 1920s, then at least to our stereotypes of that period; what can equally well be argued is that in that sense Hitchcock's images are *never* historical (the overtly historical films testifying to the absence of historicity by the very traditionality of their costume-drama format). Historicity – the urgent sense of the year, the date, the decade, the cut of the hair or the dress, the model cars, the ideological and current-event preoccupations of a time in a particular place – is never active in Hitchcock, not even in the pretexts of the 'Balkan' or Nazi films, much less in the feeble Cold War efforts. The hallucinatory San Francisco of *Vertigo* is undateable, out of time; its very foregrounding of the mesmerization by the image and of voyeurism in some sense subverting and precluding the *practice* of nostalgia film and image culture.

When, however, we try to formulate Hitchcock's spatial programme in a more positive way, the concept of narrativization leads to misunderstandings and demands specification: not narrativization in general any longer, then, but Hitchcock's, and even Hitchcock's in this film! Yet it should be clear already that under the sign and regime of the modernist *episode*, where in any case larger narrative unities have been banished to the realm of the Idea, or to the concept of themselves, narrative logic can be expected to take on what – on some older conception of narrative – appear to be 'non-narrative' characteristics. Meanwhile, if the general concept of a tendency towards episodic semi-autonomy holds for all modernisms, the narrative logic whereby these Hitchcock films secure their semi-autonomization can probably not, at this stage, be expected to be generalizable even to other forms of modernist film, let alone the other arts.

In all these respects, the early drunken-driving sequence of *North by Northwest* takes on a significance not necessarily inferable from its status as a traditional Hitchcock 'number' (of which other versions are used in *Notorious*, and in *To Catch a Thief* and *Family Plot*) or as an optical gag or trick. Bellour's identification of the downward gaze from the precipice in this scene with analogous 'vertigo'-type perspectives in the flight from the UN and finally in the climactic Mount Rushmore sequence[4] already restores a certain thematic content to this otherwise formally conventional visual *tour de force* in which the audience sits behind the wheel of the careening limousine as the screen itself veers giddyingly into space, taking the entire cinema with it out of control. Now if this is grasped as sheer technique or 'effect', its logical opposite or structural antithesis could be expected to be the reverse of this – the aggressive movement of the screen towards the audience, space or spatial features emerging from the screen into the cinema, rather than the cinema plunging 'blindly' into the space of the screen.

This kind of effect is clearly what is associated with the various experiments in 3-D in the early 1950s – Hitchcock himself experimented with it in the unreleased stereoscopic version of *Dial M for Murder* (1954). But there was a certain formal logic in the spatial compensation of that filmed play (bound to a single interior) with a convulsive movement of the screen out into the audience (the fatal scissors would surely have provided the most dramatic exercise of the technique); nor were these lessons lost on Hitchcock, as we shall see in a moment; but spatial variation is more subtle in *North by Northwest*, and it is even arguable that the operative constraint in this film's structural system can be identified as a taboo on just such trick movements out of the screen. But this taboo, as we shall see shortly, does not foresee the complete elimination of the spatial system associated with 3-D technology, but rather its reorganization in a new way.

Under these circumstances, the 'structural opposite' of the drunken-driving sequence can more plausibly be identified elsewhere: if the logic of the car sequence is formulated as an attack, or an aggression, by the camera upon the space within the screen, then the inversion of this formula proposes one form or another of an aggression, directed upon the camera, by the space within the screen itself. That is certainly one way of describing the empty-field sequence and the assault of the cropdusting plane. Other significant features of this scene will be discussed in a moment: what is

important for us here is that the emptiness of the field constitutes a
veritable hypostasis of space itself – an attempt, as it were, to think
and to represent the latter's empty category. What would space look
like, in other words, if everything were removed? 'Everything' here,
however, is still the urban; and at the same time the representation
to be produced at this point is not yet the more consequent dialectical answer to the question – namely, Nothingness itself (which the
final sequence will ingeniously stage as the 'edge of the world' and
the ultimate boundary of Being).

What results is thus still necessarily invested with content in spite
of itself – a content which does not want to know or identify itself as
such, and therefore takes on the form of a degraded ideology of
nature: so empty space is conceived as an empty field, at the same
time as everything in this scene undermines its 'naturality' and
unmasks this seeming 'nature' as nature's opposite, as 'civilization'
and industry, as human praxis. What we actually see, therefore, is
not nature but industrial agriculture: this is the only moment of the
film in which concrete production is alluded to, the very vehicle of
the attack being itself a key instrument in the industrialization of the
agricultural process, and the high point of the scene constituting a
vivid experience of toxic pollution and asphyxiation (except that
since the political elements are removed, the viewer scarcely reads it
that way), while finally the collision with the oil truck can certainly
be read – if one is, for whatever reason, that way inclined – as an
allegory of the contradiction between industry and agriculture.

Before we see where this 'deconstruction' of apparently *natural*
space leads us, however, we must return to the matter of movement
in order to articulate the relationship between this kinetic moment
and the car sequence already mentioned: the plane strafes the
'Grant' figure from above but does not penetrate the camera (as is
the case with the final revolver-suicide sequence – in colour – of
Spellbound). It therefore seems best to co-ordinate these two kinds of
movement verbally, by opposing the movement of the vehicle-
camera *into* the screen not with its logical 3-D opposite, a movement
out of the screen, but rather with a movement *on to* the great sheet of
space with which the Grant figure is associated, and away from it
again. If we try, then, to correlate these two sets of variables which
are direction and movement itself (the negation of this second term

61

being, logically enough, something like *position*), we reach a preliminary scheme that looks like this:

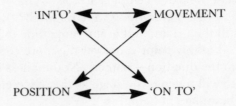

It remains to be seen whether the combinations implied by these features will yield a sufficiently exhaustive and articulated graph of the kinaesthetic 'system' of *North by Northwest*.

Two additional features of the empty-field sequence suggest directions that have not yet been explored. First, 'Grant's' relationship to the expected vehicle is initially embodied or manifested by an exploitation of the wide screen itself: the waiting figure searches the screen-space at one end, and is then obliged to follow the movement of the passing cars or trucks to the other in a caricature of a peculiar and very special kind of spectatorship. If we leave aside the retribution in store for this kind of voyeurism (and the way in which the 'correct' vehicle, as the essential machine-component of this scene, then serves as a grim representational equivalent for the camera itself: not seeing, finally, but being seen), a scene elsewhere in the film may occur to us which stands as a kind of rhyme or inversion to this one – the wondrous scene in the pine wood, in which the lovers are reunited after 'Grant's' fake assassination. The two appear on either side of the screen, separated by its entire width and by the wood of lodgepole pines it contains, so that until they slowly begin to approach each other and to diminish the distance between them, the spectators are obliged to turn their heads from side to side, in order to observe the character who happens to be speaking: it is we, therefore, who are now placed in 'Cary Grant's' position on the dusty road, as he follows the cars and trucks from one side of the screen to the other.

Similar Hitchcock tricks come to mind – the zoom shot of the maniac's face in *Strangers on a Train*, which, alone immobile in the swivelling heads of the fans in the bleachers, seems to leap out at us

(and its target); even the lovebirds in the opening drive to Bodega Bay (in *The Birds*) who, vertical within the twists and turns of the car, seem none the less to register its oscillations like a counter. But here the trick is projected into the audience, and requires us to complete it: nothing is visible on the screen, save the three-dimensional space of the deep shot of tree trunks aligned against each other – a remnant of Hitchcock's 3-D experiments used to open up inner space in a new way, which interrupts Bazinian depth just as effectively as it evokes the intangible 'supplement' or excess of a spatial dimension beyond the mere 'image'. Not only this excess, but the very trunks of the trees themselves seem to surcharge this scene with the sense of the 'aesthetic' as such, evoking the style of a distinctive Cézanne landscape in order to seal the identification of this version of 'nature' with Art itself.

This scene, then, completes the ideology of the empty field with a dialectical opposite in structural complicity with it: the notion of nature as agriculture, as the empty cornfield (which is in fact an industrial site), now redoubled by the equally conventional and stereotypical notion of nature as landscape and as painting or 'fine art'. The kinaesthetic structure of this scene also reverses the peculiarities of the aeroplane sequence, which involved movement on to and away from a surface of space: here we are given not narrative movement but, as it were, contemplative positioning of a static and 'aesthetic', lyric type; and at the same time a convergent movement of both lovers into the frame and into the three-dimensional magic space of the wood. (Meanwhile, within this lyrical stasis, Hitchcock's dialogue 'places', as we have already seen, his crudest ideological alibis, and gets his narrative presuppositions out of the way as unobtrusively as possible.)

But this is not the only feature of the empty-field sequence which 'rhymes' with scenes and spaces elsewhere in the film. We must also note the peculiar inscriptions here, which streak both versions of the empty surface of space – the expanse of the sky fully as much as the expanse of the empty land below. Both are furrowed with a set of parallel lines that is not without some distant affinity with the 'trauma' of *Spellbound*: the fateful ski tracks in the snow, reproduced by Gregory Peck's fork upon the white linen of the dining-table. The plane leaves its ephemeral traces on the sky fully as much as the empty fields retain the serrated grooves of tractor and plough.

But these are details which – otherwise mere realism of an obligatory, if artfully framed, kind – are endowed with heightened significance only retroactively, by a peculiar and obsessive – and otherwise incomprehensible – return of the same pattern in the final scene of the film. For what is most striking about the monument is not its only-too-familiar statuary, but rather the grain of its surface revealed by the uncustomary proximity of our perspective, and in particular the striations of the rock upon which the representational heads are embedded. Here, far more abstractly, we confront the same grid of parallel lines, systematically carved into the rock surface like a strange Mayan pattern. Again, what is confirmed by this pattern, and scored into the space of the scene, is the primacy of surface itself: the earth as a surface upon which the ant-like characters move and agitate, the sky as a surface from which intermittently a mobile and deadly technological mechanism dips; and here finally the upending of the surface into the vertical monument, prodigious *bas-relief* which has no inside and cannot be penetrated; upon which, as in some ultimate lunar landscape – neither country nor city – the human body, in its most vulnerable manifestation, must crawl, itself taking on something of the merely implicit or potential volume of the carved relief.

As in the reconquest of the painterly surface by modernism, this final avatar of space coincides tendentially with the screen itself, so that only the actors and characters remain, in some ultimate dissolution of context. Whence a new and heightened autonomy of physical detail: in particular the dreamlike floating of the figures as they approach the plane (in a scene that has already been mentioned) and the slight breeze on the mountaintop that plays almost imperceptibly in their hair: this will finally crystallize in the ultimate vision of Leonard standing above the lovers in some other hallucinatory space distantly reminiscent of the baroque and of Tintoretto's swarming altitudes. It is as though 'Leonard's' body had already been destroyed, everything that is heavily mechanical about it (his peculiar gait and shoes) condensed in the awkward fall, in which the human body seems for an instant an inert collection of material parts, like the collapse of a puppet. Now, however, high up, the wind plays in his hair for one last moment, as though this ultimate production of a strange new abstract space released a range of heterogeneous visual impulses hitherto contained by the 'realism' of the narrative.[5] It is from the retrospective production of this ultimate form of space that our earlier kinaesthetic moments fall into place and can now be systematically read:

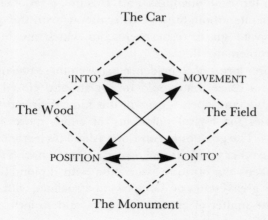

The spatial and kinaesthetic programming of the spectator by the film, therefore, moves towards the 'production' of that ultimate 'non-space' of the monument itself, an annulment of movement (and of narrative), which is, however, secured within the film as its final episode, or its final combination: it will be noted that this final episode therefore 'unifies' the film's various segments, but not after the fashion of some overall immanent meaning.

The preceding analyses, however, remain purely formal in so far as they fail to address the content of such spatial production, and in particular the dialectic of public and private which the formal description shows to be at work within the concrete episodes, without articulating its logic or its possible significance. To do so means returning to the concrete episodes in order to determine the relationship of private and public within each, rather than (as in our first graph) their overall conditions of possibility in the first place; in order, however, for this ideological and conceptual opposition to become a problem – an antinomy, a contradiction, a systemic gap, such that various logical combinations can be generated and, along with them, qualitatively distinct types of space as well.

I believe that such a gap can be identified or formulated in the (unconscious) attempt to co-ordinate one stereotypical opposition with another, which seems closely related to it but does not coincide at all points: the first such opposition is clearly that of private and public, to which we have referred here at various points. It would seem productive to formulate the second, related, but competing opposition in terms of 'openness' and 'closure', a set of characteristics which are often thought to be coterminous with the qualities of public or private space, respectively, but which are in this film concretely problematized.

For the purer forms of coincidence between these two oppositions or systems – a space that would be private and closed, one that would be public and open – exist in this film; their very existence, however, raises the logical possibility of other, more anomalous combinations. The great estate on Long Island is clearly private and closed: on the other hand, its real owner's affiliation with the United Nations awakens the obvious association with diplomatic housing generally, the great estates on Long Island associated with big power embassies, the matter of extraterritoriality, and so forth. That this association can also be argued by way of Hitchcock's own *œuvre*, any number of situations in his other films suggest – most notably, perhaps, the last sequence of the second version of *The Man Who Knew Too Much*. There, as here, the categorial *malaise*, the conceptual dysfunction, betrays itself in our nagging feeling that what is institutional, as in the diplomatic representation of a foreign state, can no longer really be thought to be private any longer, even though it is certainly closed (and also, as here, assimilated to the private dwelling: but are such mansions of the very rich themselves exactly *private* dwellings any longer ...?).

The unstable nature of this combination or 'pure' term – which threatens to break down into a range of other possible (more 'mixed') combinations – is also observable in that term (or type of space) which is its logical inversion: namely, an entity that would be both public and open all at once. This combination is, like its opposite number, by no means as obvious or self-evident as it might at first seem: the Seagram Building is public, for example, but is it really open? (Going a little further, the FBI is a public institution, but scarcely open at all in that sense.) How, then, to stage this second type of 'pure' space in as unambiguous a way as possible? What is 'open' here in all senses is certainly the empty cornfield which has figured prominently in our previous discussion; and that it is also 'public' in several senses seems plausible as well – you can see into it, for example; there are no fences; the highway is itself traditionally a public space *par excellence*. None the less it is not public in the sense in which the Capitol Building can be so designated, for example; at which point this 'strong form' begins itself to be undermined, and to deteriorate in as troubling a fashion as did the great estate. Farm land, and in particular agribusiness, is certainly not public, but private property: and the vision or space of the empty field rapidly unmasks itself – not as the demonstration of a space which is open and public simultaneously, but rather as the confused attempt to image such a space, which may in fact be unimaginable.

The problem suggests that one of the underlying semiotic and ideological difficulties with the very opposition of public and private lies in the inconsistency between the very conception of a public space or public sphere and the regime of private property, and in particular of the commodification of land, in a virtually universalized stage: thus, you may well think of the cornfield as open, but when you begin to speculate about its putative 'public' character, not only does that characterization seem open to question, but it begins to seem problematical whether *any* North American space could ever be rigorously so described.

At any rate, the combinations are now developed as follows:

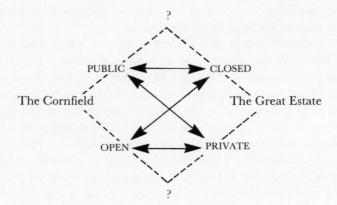

This diagram has a somewhat different function from the previous ones, in so far as it opens up lines and directions of disintegration or conceptual, semic integration, and proposes speculative categories we would not normally think to explore – as for example in the so-called 'neutral' term here, the combination of the negatives of the principal opposition: a term which would be neither 'closed' nor 'public', and therefore *might* be both 'open' and 'private'. This empty slot or merely logical possibility, therefore, formalizes the ideological dilemma, the speculative worry, that emerged from the previous discussion: how a space could be conceived (and then 'visualized' – that is, concretely and filmically experienced) which was open and private all at once.

But of course such a space is present in *North by Northwest* and is even in some sense 'central' to it, despite the representational dilemmas it raises for a *mise-en-scène*. Here, after all, 'private' remains stubbornly associated with dwelling and the 'domestic' – that is to say, it contains an inner tension or oscillation between images of the 'family' and more physical conceptions of privacy associated with closed bedrooms and bathrooms. That the (ideological) conception of the purely private to be produced turns on the vision of ideal marriage has already been demonstrated, but this kind of space is not available *within* the film or its world. A semiotic pun will therefore occur in which, for that 'strong' and 'positive' form of privacy, an easier representational one – the space of bedrooms and bathrooms – will be substituted. The problem at hand, therefore – the concrete term or 'space' to be generated – lies in the way in which such 'privacy' can be imagined, not as *public* (this was the drift of our unconscious speculation about the great diplomatic estates) but rather as *open* – that is, as a space through which anyone can wander at will.

The 'movable feast', the 'vanishing toyshop': clearly enough, this 'ideal form', which never coincides with any empirical physical reality but moves endlessly, invisibly, restlessly, from one locale to another without altering its fundamental 'spiritual' reality, can only be 'Mr Kaplan's' hotel room, as it is inexorably and dialectically teleported (with no one in it) from Atlanta to Manhattan, thence to Chicago, and finally to Cedar Rapids.

It is difficult to imagine a 'representation' better suited to capture the paradoxes of the so-called neutral term (*neither* public *nor* closed) than this evanescent yet 'objectively real' entity, which, although not empirically observable (the various physical hotel rooms – of which we see only one – are depersonalized and anonymous), organizes perceptions and frames the data of the empirically visible. The mobile Kaplan room is therefore a 'form' in the most rigorous sense of the word, so that Hitchcock's ingenuity lies in giving representation to what is somehow, by definition, beyond it. The various psychological or psychoanalytic interpretations to which this narrative situation is largely open – doubles, for example: the nonexistent Other which 'Mr Thornhill' must become – constitute something like a 'surplus of signifier', a space of exegetical excess and play, which certifies the 'depth' of the modernist product without being substantively (or in their content) essential to it: what is essential is the formal structure that enables such interpretive multiplicity, of which the empty hotel room is the precondition.

How, finally, might the structural inversion of this term be imagined – in other words, the complex term or 'Utopian' synthesis of the two poles of the positive contradiction itself, a form of space which would be *both* public *and* closed all at once? Everything in our preceding analyses conspires to propose the monument itself as the realization or manifestation of this peculiar final combination: a public space *par excellence* which is, however, uniquely closed by virtue of its sculptural existence as sheer representation (and representation best seen from over a great distance at that). Unlike the earlier public monuments in the film – the Seagram Building, the United Nations, even the dome of the Capitol viewed from the offices of the FBI – this one cannot be penetrated or explored within: indeed, the 'rhyme' with *Saboteur* – which also conjugates 'monumentality' with the nightmare of heights and falling – underscores the specificity of the structural inflection in this film, since the earlier thriller staged an elaborate sequence *within* the Statue of Liberty itself. Yet, as we have also seen, *North by Northwest* not only posits this spatial characteristic of the monument, it exploits it in ways that greatly transcend the staging of the plot itself and the ingenious working out of the final chase sequence. If the monument is the mere pretext for that sequence, the chase itself can now be seen as a 'mere pretext' for the production of this strange new space of unnatural exteriority, on which the bodies of the actors/characters crawl, and by virtue of which they take on something of the volume and sculptural relief of the monumental heads themselves.

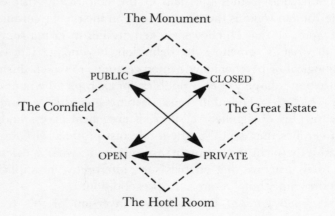

What this final permutation of our scheme also achieves is the decisive replacement of the episode of the monument in a positive position. In the two earlier schemas, we read this sequence in an essentially negative or privative way, as what set a boundary or limit to the world itself – or, in a somewhat different fashion, what constituted something like the zero degree of the film's system of movement. Reckoned into the present articulation, however, these seemingly negative or neutral functions can be grasped as that towards which the film moves, as what it ultimately sets out to 'produce', as the ultimate semic climax and 'solution' to a whole series of articulated but provisional combinational possibilities.

The monument sequence and its space, however, cannot be said to be the 'solution' to the contradiction that informs the film (and which we have formulated as the conceptual incoherence or inconsistency between the ideological opposition of public and private and that between the equally stereotypical terms of open and closed): that contradiction – which springs from ideology and false consciousness in the broadest sense – cannot be 'solved' but only done away with and transcended towards some more adequate mapping of social space. Representation, however, emerges in the empty place that conceptual resolution is unable to secure: 'seeing a solution' then replaces thinking one, and suggests that the latter is unnecessary and superfluous. At the same time, however, the successful, achieved representation – in so far as it does not succeed on the ideological level – has the capacity of projecting its own failure and undermining its own representational claims: something implicit in the oneiric nature of the final sequence that hollows out the reality claims of the image from within in a kind of 'internal haemorrhage of being', as Sartre once described what he calls *derealization*.

Notes

1. See my forthcoming 'Synoptic Chandler' in Mike Davis and Joan Copjec, *A Noir Reader*, Verso: London 1993.
2. But see Raymond Bellour's interesting discussion of 'ancestors' in this film in 'Le Blocage symbolique', *Communications* 23 (1975), pp. 235–350.

3. Stanley Cavell, *A World Viewed*, New York: Viking 1971; Stephen Heath, *Questions of Cinema*, Bloomington: Indiana University Press 1981.

4. See Bellour on downward shots.

5. Wind is often, in occult films, the signifier for another space: witness what happens to James Woods's hair at climactic moments of *Videodrome*. It is also a favourite image of Benjamin, and not only in the famous *Angelus Novus* evocation of the 'storm blowing from out of paradise'.

4

A Perfect Place to Die:

Theatre in Hitchcock's Films

ALENKA ZUPANČIČ

In Hitchcock films, one of the most frequent and interesting references is theatre. There are two films which are constructed around the relationship between film and theatre: *Murder!* (1930) and *Stage Fright* (1950). Furthermore, there is a whole series of films based on stage plays: *The Secret Agent, Rope, I Confess, Dial M for Murder* – counting only the most famous. A number of films follow where the key sequence (usually the denouement) takes place on a *stage* in a broader meaning of the word: besides *Murder!* and *Stage Fright*, there are *The Thirty-Nine Steps* (Mr Memory, who answers from the stage all the audience's questions, including the question of the leading character: 'What are the thirty-nine steps?', paying for this with his life), *I Confess* (Keller, the murderer, runs from the courthouse to the Hotel Château Frontenac, right on the stage of a concert hall, where he meets his end and where, fatally injured, he 'confesses' for the last time to Father Logan), *The Man Who Knew Too Much* (the memorable shot in the concert hall when we are waiting the crash of the cymbals – a sign to the killer), *Young and Innocent* (an even more famous tracking shot which ends on the stage on the twitching eyes of the drummer who is also the murderer) and, last but not least, the title of the film *North by Northwest* is taken from Shakespeare's *Hamlet*.

The Curtain between Theatre and Film

We can begin at the end, at the closing scene of *Murder!*,[1] which can be seen as a sort of definition of the fundamental relationship between theatre and film. The camera slowly tracks back and suddenly the frame of a stage appears within its field, then the curtain falls and the film ends. If we leave aside for a moment the consequences this ending has for our understanding of the plot, and limit ourselves only to the 'formal' level, we could say that it is the end not just of this film, but of the film as a concept. Film in today's sense of the word is born or constituted precisely as a step over a specific threshold – the stage threshold or the perimeter of the stage. The camera cuts into the tissue of some already-existing fiction – this is the elementary move which enables and produces the close-up, the cinematic time, the parallel montage, and so on – in short, the totality of the diegetic content, of the narrative line, which originates from a heterogeneous multitude of partial shots/views.

For Hitchcock himself, the birth of a 'pure film' is the moment when Griffith's camera overstepped the barrier of the stage and thus discovered a new subject of the gaze – the film subject: 'The most significant of these [techniques proper to film], you know, occurred when D.W. Griffith took the camera away from the proscenium arch, where his predecessors used to place it, and moved it as close as possible to the actors.'[2] The important point, in this context, is the following: when the camera detaches itself from the proscenium arch as the place of theatrical perspective on the action, we can speak about the moment in which, *within the film itself*, the stage perspective (which has initially dominated the cinematic perspective) is transformed into a cinematic perspective. The emergence of the specific cinematic view does not coincide simply with the invention of cinema. The decisive break between film and theatre occurred within film itself, when filmmakers 'changed the paradigm' by ceasing to think in terms of theatre and beginning to think in terms of film; more precisely, when the camera stopped being a mere mediator, the recorder of a specific theatrical vision, and became an 'organ' with which the filmmaker thinks – a creator of its own vision. The final shot in *Murder!* most explicitly reminds us precisely of this. But this reminder has still far from exhausted the role of this shot in the film.

In classical theatre, the curtain (besides the obvious fact that it is the 'signifier of theatre') is the bearer of the function of theatre time and the creator of the specific feature of theatre time. When the curtain falls between two acts, it has a double role. On the one hand, it promises that we won't miss anything in the interval should we leave the hall. It is a sign that theatre time does not coincide with real time – with 'our time'. The lowered curtain 'freezes' and 'petrifies' the figures of the story and halts their time. It is only the presence of the gaze which makes the images (the figures on stage) come to life, and it seems that these images stand still the moment the curtain cuts into the field of vision. However, this veiling is not only the *suspension* of theatre time but also its condensation. Dramas are usually constructed so that the cut between two acts implies a certain period of time. The following act, measured with the time of the story, usually commences a day, a month, a year ... *later*. In classical theatre the curtain is, so to speak, the 'transcendental condition' of fiction.

In a film shot, the curtain has a different function. When Hitchcock's camera stops on the curtain at the end of the film and the sign *The End* follows, this by no means implies that the film ends with the ending of the stage story, and that both realities or fictions coincide. Such an interpretation would neglect the fact that while the curtain is not *part* of the stage story (but, rather, its 'transcendental condition'), it is very much part of the film story. The end of the film story is actually this fallen curtain – a shot which gives the film's answer to the question of the relationship between Diana and Sir John. *It is precisely the curtain which literally balances or 'regulates' their relationship*: Sir John can confront Diana only through the medium of the stage play, and their relationship 'progresses' only while the 'curtain is raised'. Sir John can approach Diana only by translating her story into a stage play, in 'The Inner History of the Baring Case'. An intimacy not mediated by the gaze is unbearable for him. This paradox of the relationship between Diana and Sir John is best represented in the shot of Sir John visiting Diana in prison. In the foreground there is a large, imposing wooden table – the real image of a stage. Diana and Sir John are seated at either end, so it seems

75

they would have to shout to hear each other. There is also an 'audience' present in the form of a warder – an arrangement, therefore, which hinders any possibility of intimacy and imposes a relationship over a great distance. On the other hand, this setting is precisely what enables Sir John to confront Diana. Not only is it an obstruction to intimacy, it is the fundamental condition for both characters to achieve some kind of 'communication', a relationship and a dialogue. When, towards the end of the film, Sir John comes to prison to fetch Diana, who is now absolved of guilt, she weeps on his shoulder in the car, and instead of telling her about his love – for which this would be a perfect opportunity – he says: 'Now my dear, you must save those tears. They'll be very, very useful – in my new play.' In the (love) story about Sir John and Diana, we won't miss anything – until the curtain is down. This, I think, is the message and the function of the last shot in *Murder!*, the shot where we see nothing but the fallen curtain.

Hitchcock has offered one more paradigm for reading the relationship between Diana and Sir John: in the scene of Sir John's inner monologue, which takes place in his bathroom immediately after the trial. In this scene, Sir John stands in front of the mirror absorbed in his thoughts, which we hear as a voice-over and which concern Diana and her conviction. He is listening to the prelude to

Tristan and Isolde.[3] In the legend about Tristan and Isolde there are at least three moments that can assist us in conceiving the relationship between Diana and Sir John:

1. 'Mechanically produced love' – Tristan and Isolde unintentionally drink the love-potion which makes them fall in love.

2. From Tristan's point of view Isolde is, of course, an 'inaccessible woman', a woman from 'another world' (betrothed to King Mark).

3. He can unite with her only through her *'semblante'* or 'double' – another Isolde, Isolde of the White Hands, whom he marries in order to 'flee from love'.

The same paradigm regulates the relationship between Diana and Sir John. Their love is the consequence of a specific stage layout: we have already stated that Sir John falls in love with Diana the moment he begins to 'translate' her story into a stage play – he didn't even notice her before, he didn't see anything special in her, and even sent her away when she came to him looking for a job. One could say that he did not notice her until she became a star. As Bennett, Sir John's secretary, puts it: 'You know, you have met the lady before. A year ago that was. She wanted to become a star. I suppose you can say in a sense that she has, star in the Baring murder case ...' Furthermore, Diana is 'inaccessible', closed to this world, sentenced to death. And thirdly, Sir John can confront and unite with Diana only through her *semblante* or double – the Diana from 'The Inner History of the Baring Case'.

Let us return to the curtain which, in its unique way, demarcates throughout the relationship between film and theatre. The curtain (or fade-out as its stand-in) is the basic means for a theatrical 'construction' of the story, as already pointed out, and it gives the theatrical narrative its basic framework. On the other hand, it is the editing that gives the basic framework to the film. At this point, both fictions differ from each other considerably. However, in one of his films Hitchcock focused just on this moment and succeeded in reducing the difference between theatre and film to just a thin line inscribed in its very title: *Rope.*

Rope is based on a stage play and, as is well known, it is unique in its narrative and technical aspects.[4] Hitchcock explains why he decided to shoot practically the whole film in one shot as follows:

'The stage drama was played out in the actual time of a story; the action is continuous from the moment the curtain goes up until it comes down again. I asked myself whether it was technically possible to film it in the same way. The only way to achieve that, I found, would be to handle the shooting in the same continuous action, with no break in the telling of the story that begins at seven-thirty and ends at nine-fifteen. And I got this crazy idea to do it in a single continuous action.'[5]

And Hitchcock succeeded – not only in preserving the basic dramatic disposition in the film, but at the same time in preserving film as film – and a fine one at that. He actually succeeded in maintaining the balance on a thin rope which separates both worlds of fiction. Not without problems, however:

'To maintain that continuous action, with no dissolves and no time lapses, there were other technical snags to overcome, among them, how to reload the camera at the end of each reel without interrupting the scene. We handled that by having a figure pass in front of the camera, blacking out the action very briefly while we changed from one camera to the other. In that way we'd end on a close-up of someone's jacket, and at the beginning of the next reel, we'd open with the same close-up of the same character.'[6]

What is that paradoxical piece of cloth that covers our field of vision, that 'close-up of someone's jacket', other than an inscription of the function of the curtain which is absent in classical montage? And what is this inscription of the stage signifier *par excellence* other than the capacity of the film medium used to its full extent and brought to its edge – the camera's capacity not only to pass beyond the edge of the stage and approach the actors, but even more: to approach them *too much* – to generate, in this inner circle, the effect of the theatre again?

The Stage

We have already stated in the introduction that in a series of Hitchcock's films the key scene is enacted on stage. Or, to define the 'key scene' more precisely – the stage is a place of truth and a place of death. *Murder!*, *The Thirty-Nine Steps*, *Stage Fright* and *I Confess* are four instances in which these functions of the stage are most striking.

In the final scene of *Murder!*, we encounter a 'cruel' intrusion of the Real in (stage) fiction. Fane appears on a trapeze, and at the end of the performance *he stages his own death*. For his last act on the trapeze he chooses suicide, actual suicide, writing 'in blood' the last chapter of 'The Inner History of the Baring Case', Sir John's stage play – thus making the reality of theatre coincide with that of film.

In *The Thirty-Nine Steps*, the stage's primary function is entertainment. Mr Memory, the 'subject supposed to know', answers all the questions from the audience that tries to find a gap in his knowledge. But regardless of his 'real', actual abilities, irrespective of the fact that he indeed has a 'photographic memory', Mr Memory, while standing on the stage, nevertheless *acts*; he plays the role of *sujet supposé savoir*. And it is precisely this professional *milieu* which at some point transforms knowledge into truth and costs him his life. If someone in the street were to ask him, 'What are the thirty-nine steps?', he could simply say that he does not know. However, the moment this question is addressed not to his off-stage person but to his *stage appearance*, to his *role on the stage*, he cannot do so. Hannay, the protagonist of the film, gambles on this very split – on the fact that Mr Memory 'abuses' or duplicates his stage role and his function off stage, in some other reality. This is the fundamental mechanism of 'the mousetrap', the trap of a play-within-a-play. The culprit (or in this case his auxiliary) is forced to play the role and to pronounce the words that incriminate him, the words which are a repetition and a 'materialization' of something concealed or repressed. One could say that his death is precisely the consequence of the intrusion of some 'foreign reality'. It is, therefore, the price claimed by the stage for breaking 'the rules of the game'.

This moment is even more strongly emphasized in *Stage Fright*, where a similar intrusion of the real into fiction causes, so to say, 'the subjectivation of the stage': the stage becomes the 'executioner'.

Jonathan (the actual murderer, as we learn towards the end) attempts to frame Charlotte (who is in love with him). Together with his girlfriend Eve, whom he has convinced that Charlotte is guilty, he connects Charlotte's wardrobe in the theatre with the stage, trying to ensnare her in a trap (and actually succeeds, because Charlotte protects him). Their conversation over the public-address system reverberates on stage, overheard by Jonathan and the police inspector. (This is a case of a 'fake' mousetrap whose function is to frame.) When Jonathan subsequently confesses the murder to Eve and attempts to strangle her, she is rescued by the police. The iron stage curtain falls on Jonathan and kills him – as if the stage 'knew' what was going on, and not only 'knew', but was able to inflict punishment as well.

In all these three examples, we are faced with the intrusion of some 'alien reality' in a specific fictional disposition. This intrusion is directly linked with *death*. Of course this 'alien reality' that intrudes on the stage is the very reality of the film itself in which this stage framework appears. Hence the relationship between film and theatre could be defined in the following terms: *Every time cinematic and theatre realities coincide*, every time cinematic and theatre narratives overlap, *there is a corpse*. (When Fane chooses the theatre for his film exit, when Mr Memory enacts his film role on stage, when Jonathan abuses the stage for his cinematic survival.) But this corpse, this death, is as much a punishment for erasing some fundamental difference between both 'fictions' as it is the price for the re-establishment of this difference. Only the corpse convinces us that the stage fiction is over (that the actor will not appear in the next performance) and that only 'cinematic fiction' is still on. The stage or theatre corpse can rise from the dead only in the next *film*.

Let us now consider *I Confess*. This film is particularly interesting because the appearance of the stage in it is somewhat surprising, as it is in no way connected to the plot itself. In all the above films, it was related to the storyline in one way or another. But here, at least at first sight, there is nothing in the story that would lead up to the theatre or the stage. In the final scene, Keller, the murderer, simply runs (as if by chance) on to the stage of the Hotel's concert hall – and it seems that he could run anywhere else. However, as we shall attempt to show, this 'stage surprise' is well founded, if not a 'logical necessity'.

In the first place, Hitchcock achieved the maximum dramatic effect with such a scene of denouement. Not because the stage, by definition, evokes the context of drama. The reason is here explicitly connected to the logic of the film and is played out as the device of the absolute contrast the audience was forced to bear throughout the film, and its burden is taken from them only right at the end, in this stage scene. It is the contrast between a *confessional* as the place of extreme, radical intimacy and secrecy, which will not and must never be revealed, and a *stage* as the public setting *par excellence*, where everything that is said is intended for the audience.[7] Throughout the film we are put in the paradoxical position of *a public without a stage*, a public who knows what has to take place on stage and what must be brought to light, and demands this performance but does not get it. We are put in the position – surprisingly identical to the situation of the main character – where some knowledge is entrusted to us, but we have nowhere to place it, and we cannot locate it in the symbolic – right until the end, when we literally get a stage and a stage denouement. This function of the stage is present in the background throughout the entire film as the setting of some impossible knowledge, and is evoked through its radical contrast: the confessional.

In all the above films, the stage is also the setting through which 'the truth' is inscribed in cinematic reality. It is not that we learn the truth on stage; we already know it before these stage scenes take place. The point is that on the stage, the truth *is inscribed in the symbolic universe of the film*. This role of the stage is also connected with the moment of death. In none of those cases was Hitchcock satisfied with the arrest of the murderer as the conclusion of the film. In all four examples the culprit has to die, and to die in a literally 'theatrical' way. One could attempt to find the reason in the condensation of three dramatic events into one scene:

1. confronting the suspect with the '*representatives of the law*' who are always among the audience (an analogy to arrest);

2. *the trial* – the proof of guilt (the culprit gives himself away in front of the audience as in front of the 'jury') and the verdict;

3. *execution of the sentence.*

Because of this condensation, the stage in all these films appears as 'the Other Scene' – as the place of the Other. It is the silent place through which the subjective truth emerges, the place that bears witness to the subjective guilt, and with its very 'muteness' demands punishment.

A Play-within-a-Play

'There were also several references to *Hamlet* because we had a play-within-a-play. The presumptive murderer was asked to read the manuscript of a play, and since the script described the killing, this was a way of tricking him. They watched the man while he was reading out loud to see whether he would show some sign of guilt, just like the king in *Hamlet*. The whole film was about the theatre.' (Hitchcock's comment on *Murder!*[8])

The play scene, the play-within-a-play, is certainly one of the most interesting moments produced by narration – not only 'practically', but also 'theoretically'. Jacques Lacan, in interpreting the play scene in *Hamlet*, developed the thesis that the truth has the structure of fiction. Gilles Deleuze resorted to this thesis in putting forward the concept of the image-crystal; he applied this concept precisely to Hitchcock's *Murder!*. What is so interesting and fascinating about the structure of a play-within-a-play?

First of all, it can tell us a lot about the nature of reality and the nature of fiction, within the framework of a story. The device of a 'play-within-a-play' can be conceived, in a general form, simply as 'fiction-within-fiction'. From this point one can argue that *fiction-within-fiction is the moment where fiction is faced with its own exterior at its own interior.* For fiction to be structured in the classical sense (after all, we are discussing two classics: Shakespeare and Hitchcock), it is essential that something is excluded from it. This something is, as a rule, a crime which, on the grounds of its exclusion (we do not see it in the film, we see only its tracks), acquires the status of 'the original crime', the crime *par excellence* which belongs to the Real in terms of Lacan's paradigm. Fiction is then established through the disjunction regarding the Real, sustaining itself through something *that it cannot show* – with the essential postscript: *that it can show only by duplicating itself* in the form of a *mousetrap* in which 'some sign of guilt' is captured, as Hitchcock put it. This is the fundamental mechanism of 'fiction-within-fiction'.

Here one has to underline the distinction between this kind of fiction and the *whodunit* genre. It is known that Hitchcock did not like whodunits where, in his own words, we coldly and without emotion await the end to learn who committed the murder. The whole interest is concentrated in the ending. Nevertheless, he made two films on the basis of scripts belonging to the whodunit genre – precisely *Murder!* and *Stage Fright.* In response to Truffaut's question why, despite his aversion towards this genre, he decided to make these two films, Hitchcock, in both cases, unambiguously answered: 'The aspect that intrigued me is that it was a story about the theatre'. If we consider *Murder!*, we could say that it is precisely this theatrical aspect – and, more to the point, the play scene as the crux of the film – that enabled Hitchcock to devise something completely different out of a whodunit.

It appears at first glance that in whodunits, too, it is essential that we do not and must not see the crime. On closer inspection, this is not entirely true. What has to be disguised is only the criminal him- or herself (we get, say, a shot of the crime scene with a masked murderer). Let us stay, however, with the whodunits that begin with a corpse and do not show the crime itself: the detective's task is therefore to *deduce* the truth, to gather clues, facts and evidence, and to use them to establish the identity of the murderer by means of reconstructing the crime. The murderer is buried under the weight of evidence. This is the moment when the film simply shows what has previously been omitted: the precise and 'realistic' account of the crime (usually accompanied by the detective's commentary). There is no 'duplication of fiction' here, only a simple displacement and a time-shift. Structurally, the whole suspense is built on the fact that the initial scene is 'cut out' and 'attached' to the end of the film.

That distinguishes the whodunit genre from the genre *Murder!* belongs to, which can be labelled a *'play-scene genre'*. If the climax of the whodunit is the moment when the murderer's identity is revealed, when the Name is announced, the set-up in the 'play-scene genre' is quite different. The knowledge about the murderer's identity precedes the play scene, and the dramatic quality of this knowledge is not essential to that scene – which, however, represents the peak or climax of events. The fascinating point is not the revelation of the murderer's identity, the reconstruction of the crime and the deduction of the truth, but the manner in which the truth is displayed – or is gazing at us, if we can put it that way, in the glint of the murderer's eye. We witness the situation in which the truth *surprises* the only person who knows it from the very beginning – the murderer.

On the one hand, it is the distinction between 'digging up' the truth and making the truth reveal itself on the surface that is at stake. On the other hand, we are dealing with the difference between the truth of facts and the 'subjective truth', the truth of 'desire and guilt'. In other words, the answer we, the audience watching the play scene, get is not the answer to the question 'Did you kill person X?', but the answer to a much more fundamental question, which has no direct relation to the first one: 'Are you guilty?' (Neither in *Hamlet* nor in *Murder!* do we see the murderer stand up and announce: 'Yes, I am the murderer.' All we see is 'some sign of guilt'.) It concerns a dimension which does not revolve around mental exercises, 'the little grey cells', and has nothing to do with the narcissistic satisfaction that we ourselves, maybe long before the end, have made the right deduction. We are moving in a universe of 'desire and guilt'. The mousetrap captures not only the murderer's guilt, but also our desire – and this is what makes it so fascinating.

One essential question still remains. If we go back from the broader framework of fiction-within-fiction to the device of 'a play-within-a-play', the following problem appears: what justifies Hitchcock saying 'we have a play-within-a-play', when in fact we are dealing with a 'play-within-a-film'? What distinguishes a 'play-within-a-play' is also its formal side – namely, that it doubles the *form* of the narration itself, that it represents the 'crystallization' of the image on the level of the form itself. How does the play scene in *Murder!* differ from other theatrical contexts in the film which could be described as 'a play-within-a-film'?

Under the pretext of an audition, Sir John asks Fane to play the murder scene in front of witnesses. The scene which Fane has to play begins with the murderer entering the room on a cue from one of the girls: 'Friends? I can tell you things about your friends that you don't know'; it ends with the murderer raising his weapon upon hearing how this girl says to the other, 'You fool! Don't you know that he's a half –'.[9] Before Fane begins, the camera frames a kind of 'stage' in the room in which the scene is to take place. After giving Fane basic directions, Sir John moves to the audience and directs him from there. During this time the camera goes through many different movements and defines the setting, situation and circumstances 'from within'. When the climax is reached, when Fane should raise the murder weapon and complete what is missing in the script, he stops, and in the next shot we see that he opens his mouth in a silent scream. Now the key point of Hitchcock's direction appears: the cut which moves us 'out', so that we get a view from above, 'from the ceiling', on to the stage.

The scene is divided into black and white areas. Fane and Sir John stand motionless opposite each other with scripts in their hands, one

in the light, the other in the dark. A cut follows, and a close-up on the script – a hand turns a page and a blank page appears. It is precisely this camera jump, when we are transposed out of the events, displaced in a bird's-eye view, and then thrown back again, that is of key significance. By way of this method, the effect of two fields is produced, one within the other, 'a film-within-a-film', 'a play-within-a-play'. The structure of Hitchcock's mousetrap can thus be illustrated as follows:

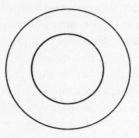

– which is nothing else but Bergson's plan, seen from above, with the aid of which Deleuze[10] illustrates the phenomenon of the crystal-image:

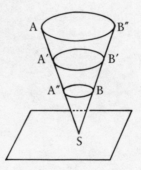

The crystal in question is a time crystal defined by Deleuze as the present that coincides with its proper past – precisely the basic structural moment of the mousetrap. We have a certain time, the time of the crime excluded from events and from cinematic reality, yet hovering continually in the background as a kind of threat. And we have the present, the actual moment of the play scene itself, in the 'crystal' of which the excluded time − that is, Deleuze's 'virtual' time − finally finds its place in this reality. Hitchcock could not point out more directly this coincidence of two different registers of time: we actually know that the murder happened at 1.30. The play scene begins so that we are shown the time on someone's watch, and it is exactly 1.30. The circle of virtual and actual time is therefore closed. It is possible to see in this the echo of Hamlet's famous words:

> The time is out of joint; − Oh, cursed spite,
> That ever I was born to set it right!

The function of the mousetrap is that it captures this derailed time and allocates a place for it in cinematic (or drama) reality − that it allocates the *proper present* to the time which did not have a future and was 'frozen' at the moment of the crime.

One can put it another way: in the 'play-scene genre' we deal not with the reconstruction of the crime, but with *Vorstellungs-Repräsentanz* of the crime. The structure of the play scene is precisely the structure of what psychoanalysis conceptualized as *Vorstellungs-Repräsentanz*: we are dealing with the representation of something which is originally (and structurally) missing; with something that can appear only as *duplicated* and appears already the first time as its own *repetition*: *its only original is this very repetition*.[11] The original crime which propels the whole *Murder!* (or the whole *Hamlet*) can be materialized and presented only in the form of *Vorstellungs-Repräsentanz*; it is structurally inaccessible in any other way. This is the only way the lack of the original presentation itself, or the impossibility of its adequate representation by a signifier, can be inscribed into reality.

When, seventeen years later, Laurence Olivier undertook his film production of *Hamlet*, he encountered the same problem of structural duplication in shooting the play scene − the problem of how to make a 'play-within-a-play' from a 'play-within-a-film'. Olivier succeeded as well, and because his solution in many ways recalls Hitchcock's, it is worthwhile to examine it in more detail.

So how is the mousetrap shot in his film? In the basic set-up, the actors perform the play; the king, the queen and a host of courtiers are the audience of this play, while Hamlet and Horatio (whom

Hamlet previously acquainted with his suspicion and with the words of the Ghost) watch the king. In some sense we have two stages or two centres of events – the crossing point of both is, of course, the king: the actual murderer.

Olivier shot the mousetrap in such a way that the king loses control over himself in the very first circle of the mousetrap (we know that the mousetrap-play is first performed as a pantomime and afterwards repeated with text). It is sufficient for the king to see the scene enacted *silently*. The camera movement during the time of the play scene is illustrated in the accompanying scheme.

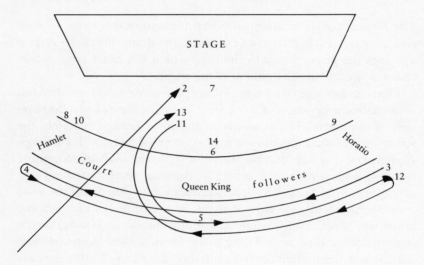

The camera – except in the middle (6–10), where it constructs, with the series of six cuts, a cross and so defines 'vectors' of the gazes (the king looks at the stage, Hamlet and Horatio alternately watch the king) – moves as if it were fixed on a pendulum. With such a movement, it outlines and defines the focus or the 'gravity centre' of the action. In the first part, until the scene of the poisoning (5), this centre is on the stage, and the camera travels, oscillating behind the backs of all the spectators (3–5). Then, after the series of exchanged gazes (6–10), the focus shifts to the king in the audience (the poisoner) and he becomes the centre of the last two swings of the camera (11–13).[12] The layout is gradually reversed: from the turning point of six cuts the audience's attention begins to follow the persistent gazes of Hamlet and Horatio, until at the end everyone is staring at the king. The circle of surprised, frightened and curious gazes is closing around the king, and it makes him respond with the famous outburst 'Give me some light!', followed by general panic and confusion.

While one play is performed on the stage – the 'mousetrap' to capture the king's gaze – the other trap is set in front of the stage, a trap no less 'fictitious' but no less efficient. The king is entangled up to his ears in the net, in the 'cobweb' of gazes. In Olivier's interpretation of the mousetrap, the light demanded by the frightened king undoubtedly shows how 'aware' he is of the quandary he got into on the level of the scopic field.

What, then, does Olivier do concerning the 'structural duplication'? First of all we must bear in mind that the trap for the king is set in the scopic field and not at the verbal level, as it is in the drama. This already provides a partial answer to the question of the 'structural duplication' of the mousetrap in the film. Taking a step further, we can say that the dramatic effect of what we otherwise view as cinematic reality culminates in the series of six cuts/gazes. We know that the cut or editing is the instance where we are least aware of the presence of the camera. At the same time this dramatic, explicitly cinematic sequence is framed by almost too obvious wanderings, swings of the camera behind the protagonists' backs. (This moment, when we are suddenly well aware of the presence of the camera as a mediator of our gaze, is equivalent to the effect Hitchcock achieved with a jerky movement of the camera to the bird's-eye view and then back again.) First the camera encircles and outlines the field of vision (3–5), while the cross made by the camera within this field (6–11) represents a real intrusion of the camera into the forbidden place: into its own field of vision. By this means, Olivier came as close as possible to the structure of the film-within-a-film: the 'first' film would be the one we are watching through the perspective of the swinging camera. Once this circle is defined, the series of cuts takes place and knits the drama of gazes – that is to say, another 'mousetrap' within this scene of the mousetrap outlined before. The next moment the camera is again, 'as if nothing has happened', thrown in the track of swings behind the backs of the audience (11–13), as if it wanted to convey: what you saw before, I might as well not have shown you.

Olivier's method could be seen as an inversion, but retaining the basic paradigm of Hitchcock's procedure. In both cases we have the structure of a cone: in Hitchcock's case it is placed horizontally, in Olivier's vertically. And in both we come across the exchange of 'internal' and 'external' view: in *Murder!* the sequence is inside–outside–inside, while in *Hamlet* it is outside–inside–outside. This inversion may be due to the fact that in *Murder!* the murderer stands *inside*, in the play itself; while in *Hamlet* he is *outside*, in the audience.

What conclusion could be drawn from this? Are we to say that Olivier was Hitchcock's disciple? Or would we do better to conclude with the thesis that they were both masters of some basic insight into the paradigm of the relationship between film and theatre?

Suicide as the Structure of the Act

In the previous section we were building our interpretation on the way Hitchcock shot the play scene in *Murder!* We particularly stressed the moment when the camera 'jumps' all of a sudden to the 'bird's-eye view'. In the next scene this dizzy height will be given a new retroactive meaning: it will appear to be the virtual point of the murderer's death. It is exactly the height chosen by Fane as the place to commit suicide.

Fane's suicide is the moment in *Murder!* that rather dilutes and diminishes Sir John's final triumph. It is, in the strict sense of the word, the sublime moment of the film, the image that makes all other images to fade in comparison. Moreover, it is the moment of Fane's 'moral victory' over Sir John. One can illuminate this with a digression into the theory of an (ethical) act, the theory developed by Kant that could be related to some concepts of Lacanian psycho-analysis.

The first key point of Kant's theory of pure ethical act lies in the distinction between the act that is done only *in accordance with* duty and the one that is done exclusively *from duty*. Only the latter is ethical in the strict sense. One may act in accordance with duty because of various personal interests: one wants to avoid inconvenience, one wants others to have a good opinion of oneself, one expects a benefit, and so forth. For Kant, any such action is pathological, and although it is done *in accordance with* duty, it is never an ethical act. The ethical act is only the one done exclusively *from duty*.

First of all, this means that the act in the strict sense has no exterior: its foundation must always be an *auto-, self*-foundation. An act could not occur on the basis of reasons that are external to it (our 'inner' impulses and motives also belong to such reasons). It can arise only from itself as identical with the moral law, otherwise it is 'non-pure', 'pathological', not an act in the proper sense of the word. On the other hand, an act has no exterior in the sense that all its effects, consequences – everything that comes *after* – must be abstracted and put in brackets. In an act there is no after. This is what Kant repeats tirelessly: an act is beyond all criteria of usefulness, efficiency and suchlike; it is – to use Kant's own metaphor – a jewel that glitters by itself and bears all its value in itself. What counts is only an act without a purpose outside itself, confining the purpose to itself, being the only purpose of its own realization – being, so to say, '*a purposeless act*'. If we act to achieve this or that, it is not an act.[13] Ultimately, an act is *essentially a by-product of itself*. It represents something absolutely firm, albeit groundless. It is the point of absolute firmness and certainty that floats in emptiness: it is '*in itself*'.

Another essential moment of the act is its being explicitly placed 'beyond the pleasure principle', beyond the care for subject's welfare [*Wohl*]. In the structure of the act there is no place for any pleasure or satisfaction. As Lacan points out in his seminar on *The Ethic of Psychoanalysis*, Kant goes as far as allowing only one emotional correlate to moral law: *pain*.[14]

Furthermore, the act is beyond any compensation (I sacrifice something here in order to gain something elsewhere); it is beyond any exchange, calculation, beyond any model or logic of equivalence. If the act is a sacrifice, it could only be a 'pure' one; there is nothing equivalent to it, nothing that could compensate it.

However, if we formulate the criteria of the moral act in such a way, a problem occurs that we never know for sure whether they are really satisfied or not. We can never state with certainty that every 'pathological object' is excluded from our act. Kant translates this problem into the problem of the structure of the act itself by exposing it on the level of language. What we have in mind is the passage in *Metaphysical Foundations of Morals*, where Kant discusses various kinds of imperative. One of the most important distinctions here is the difference between the hypothetical and the categorical imperative. The form of the hypothetical imperative is this: 'If you want to obtain X, you have to do Y'. Here the act is only the means to obtain a certain goal or purpose. The categorical imperative, in contrast, imposes the necessity of the act, the necessity that belongs strictly to the act-in-itself, regardless of any purpose. Let us consider the command 'You must keep your promises!'; its problematic character and its ambiguity (as well as the ambiguity of our acting in accordance with it) are due to the fact that the supplement can be hidden or implied in it: '... otherwise you will lose your reputation'. With this supplement, the categorical imperative immediately turns into – or, better, turns out to be – the hypothetical imperative in disguise. All the imperatives that seem categorical might be just *disguised hypothetical* imperatives. Or, as Kant puts it, 'Rather is it to be feared that all those apparent categorical imperatives may actually be hypothetical.'[15]

To put it briefly: the problem with (moral) acts is the fact that they are bound up with language, inscribed in the symbolic network – or, in Kant's terms, of the fact that they are not 'in itself' [*an sich*]. This is the very reason for their ambiguity, which they share with words, with signifiers. The ambiguity that is at stake here is not something one could 'get rid of'; it arises from the fact that the speech of a subject is always (more or less disguised) discourse of the Other, and that the subject – to paraphrase a well-known formulation – does not act but 'is acted'. In other words, the problem is that the subject of the act is the subject of the unconscious, which is why the status of the act is that of a *failed, miscarried act*, not of a fulfilled one. In this perspective a successful act would be something that would overstep the threshold of the symbolic and therefore enable the subject to detach itself from the ambiguity of words. It would be possible only as a 'borderline' entity in the literal sense of the word.

Kant insists on the process of infinite 'purifying', infinite approaching this limit of the act (and even introduces the postulate of immortality of the soul to 'support' it). Nevertheless, there is one act that conforms completely with the structure of the act required by Kant: *suicide* – the act of suicide as described and defined by Jacques-Alain Miller in 'Jacques Lacan: Notes to His Concept of *passage à l'acte*'.[16] Miller states that Lacan made a model of the act from the act of suicide; every real act is a 'suicide of the subject'. The subject may be born again in this act, but only as a new subject. The act is an act only if afterwards the subject is no longer the same as before. It is always structured as a symbolic suicide; it is a gesture by means of which symbolic ties are torn up. What are the key, distinctive features of the suicide as the model of the act? What are the characteristics of this act *par excellence*?

It is always *auto*. On the level of foundation, it is the act of self-authorization. It is radically beyond the pleasure principle, and it rests on what Freud designated 'the death-drive' and Lacan later conceptualized as *jouissance*. In it, the subject evades the ambiguity of words, oversteps the threshold of the symbolic. It is a borderline act. (Miller gives the example of Caesar's crossing of the Rubicon.) It is the only *successful* act, and it is something completely different from 'doing' or 'action'. It incorporates some radical *no!* to the universe which surrounds it and involves an irreducible moment of risk. It is indifferent to its exterior and its future, and as such it is external to the sense, to meaning. Act is in its kernel without any *after* (since, as stated above, after the act the subject is no longer the same as before), and it is, says Miller, *in itself*.

The structure of the act demanded by Kant actually corresponds to the structure of suicide – except in one sole aspect: suicide does not seem to survive the criterion of universality, it cannot become a universal law (according to the requirement of the categorical imperative: Act only on that maxim through which you can at the same time will that it should become a universal law). It is true that this impossibility seems self-evident, but the beauty of Kant's theory lies in the fact that it is none the less possible to prove that we are able to do this as well. Kant's elaboration of the concept of pure, radical evil arises precisely from such a gesture, where we *explicitly* put something particular in the place of the law, and particularity itself acts as the form of the supreme legislation. This evil is not a matter of weakness, lacking, transgression or temporary 'pathological' impulses; it is the Evil as an 'ethical attitude'. The finest example of this may be found in *The Metaphysics of Morals*, where Kant analyses the difference between the murder of a monarch and his formal execution, and defines the latter as 'an act of suicide by the state'.[17] Murder is a crime, of course, a crime to be punished by the law. The murder of a sovereign – the supreme legislator – is also a crime: the 'supreme', 'borderline' crime, but still a crime. It is a borderline crime in the sense that it probably will not be punished, since it is committed against the very person who could punish it. And it is committed with this very intention: from fear of eventually being punished afterwards. It may happen that the competence of the new sovereign would radically change with a new, 'revolutionary' legislation, but it is most unlikely that the new authorities would legalize killing as such. This is why the murder of a sovereign could be thought of, without any problems, in terms of the category of crime.

The formal execution of a sovereign, however, is quite a different matter. Its unbearableness is due to the fact that it is something absolutely scandalous and yet not a crime in the proper sense of the word – it is accomplished in the name of, and has the form of, the law. The formal execution of a monarch is thus in a way the realization of the Sadeian idea of radical crime. In contrast to death, which he sees as an inherent moment of life-cycle, of permanent transformation involving dissolution and rebirth, Sade develops the idea of a radical crime which would destroy, stop, the life-cycle and the process of transformation itself.[18] It is precisely the same logic that could be identified in Kant's reading of the execution of a monarch as a radical crime, the crime beyond all crimes: other forms of changing rulers and systems are all part of a 'normal' society cycle, whereas the (formal) execution of monarch throws the society out of joint; it throws it into the point of no return. What is it about this act that is so unbearable for Kant?

As mentioned above, Kant defines this act as a *suicide* of the state, and suicide turns out to be the unique point, in the territory of Kantian philosophy, in which the act of pure, radical evil and the pure moral act paradoxically coincide. Kant's conditions which an act has to fulfil in order to count as the moral one all lead to one fundamental disposition: the pure, immaculate moral act would be the one that succeeded in emerging and remaining in the register of *the Real* (in Lacanian terms). An act is moral only if all our efforts to explain or symbolize it fail – that is to say, if we cannot find any reasons for it, any motives or purposes the subject wanted to achieve by it, or any interests that made the subject do it. To put it briefly: if the subject acted motivated by anything but the act itself (if, therefore, he/she did not act 'purposelessly', 'non-functionally'), he/she accomplished not the moral act but an ordinary action.

It is precisely in this dimension of the Real that the act of radical, 'uncompromising' evil, evil as 'ethical attitude' (the evil that is not due to weakness or temporary pathological impulses), meets the pure moral act, since the ethic here is strictly beyond good and evil. The reason why Kant is so terrified by the formal execution of a monarch lies in the possibility that one could commit 'a crime of such formal and completely futile malice'[19] – it is because of this feature that the formal execution of a monarch is 'a pure idea representing ultimate evil'.[20] In other words, if the people want to get rid of their monarch in an outburst of rage and fear for their own future existence, why not kill him? – it is a crime, and as such it could be explained and comprehended. But why – and this is the question that irritates Kant – why take the trouble to perform a formal execution, which is nothing but the act of pure malice, a useless 'waste'? It complies with the form solely for the sake of form – *which is exactly the definition of the pure moral act.*

The origin of Kant's horror and fascination with a crime of this sort could be discerned in the fact that whenever he comes across it (which is by no means rare) he is compelled to describe it in the same words as the pure moral act – all he can add to this description is the 'perversity' of this act. Kant was able to maintain the ideal of the Good only at the price of abandoning the possibility of the pure moral, ethical act: the only unambiguous examples of this act he can find are examples of radical evil, with their agents in the role of 'the guardians of the being of crime as such' – words used by Lacan to demonstrate the position of Antigone and her act. Although suicide in this perspective appears to be the act of radical evil, it nevertheless preserves the dignity and structure of the act *par excellence*, since the kernel of this structure – in Miller's words – is precisely a *delict*.

Between the Act and the 'Hysterical Theatre'

In view of the argument developed above, what can we say about the denouement of *Murder!*? What are the consequences for the positions of Sir John and Fane?

Sir John is a 'real man'; he incarnates the sum of the identificatory features that are considered 'the manifestation of masculinity': he is strong, successful, handsome, unbendable.... Fane is the exact opposite: unhappily in love, unsuccessful, of 'impure' race and uncertain gender. He is not only half-caste but also 'half-gender'; his entire appearance is wrapped in sexual ambiguity and transvestism (on the stage he often performs dressed as a woman). At the beginning of the film somebody describes him as 'a hundred per cent he-woman'. As for his sexual identification, he is closer to the feminine side. Sir John and Fane are thus the opposites of one another; more precisely, each represents everything the other is not. This fundamental layout of complementary opposition should itself suffice to recall another disposition that is at stake here: *the disposition of the double* and the antagonism connected with it. In *Murder!* this dimension could be discerned on several levels.

First of all, in the scene following the trial scene. Sir John stands in his bathroom, absorbed in thoughts, sipping his wine; he puts down his glass and looks at himself in the mirror. This shot in which we see his silent mirror-image and the glass in front of him is accompanied by the voice-over question 'Who drank the brandy?' (At the scene of the crime an empty brandy glass was found, so that Sir John's glass in this scene directly evokes the murderer.) We are confronted here with the function of the mirror-image, with the murderer as Sir John's double. The same could be said of the mousetrap scene discussed above, where Fane and Sir John stand facing each other, both with scripts in their hands, one in the light, the other in the dark, just like the body and its shadow. What makes them doubles is also their rivalry over Diana. And, last but not least, the dimension of the double is the only way to explain Sir John's *hatred* towards Fane. Not only is he trying to find the murderer, he seems to hate him (especially towards the end of the film). He is hitting below the belt – the allusion to Fane's being half-caste in the scene Fane has to play – and his reaction to Fane's death is absolutely cold. He hates him, because somehow he is too close to him. Fane reminds him of some uncanny dimension of his own desire, of the mortal feature of the Thing around which his desire circulates.

As for that desire, Sir John's position is quite a paradoxical one; it is perfectly described by William Rothman: 'Sipping the wine, perhaps he imagines himself possessing the object of his desire. On the other hand, his gesture, enacted in front of a mirror, seems so theatrical that we might take him to be absorbed not by his desire, but by the *role* of a man possessed by desire.'[21] And this is not the only instance where this aspect of his desire could be discerned. It is even more striking in Sir John's monologue that follows his conversation with Bennett, during which it comes out that he has met Diana before. When Bennett leaves, Sir John assumes a perfectly 'Hamletian' pose: leaning against the wall, his eyes fixed upon the ceiling, he begins to think aloud about Diana and their relationship. The setting is so theatrical that it borders on comedy.

And then there is also the fact of his translating the whole story of resolving the crime into the theatre play that provides the frame within which he can enact his relationship with Diana, *enact his desire*. One could say that Sir John *never ceases* to play 'the role of a man possessed by desire'. Two lines of interpretation are possible on this point. Sir John's enacting desire could be conceived as his way of concealing some radical impossibility, some incapacity to desire – he is ashamed of this 'impotence' and therefore pretends to be 'possessed by desire'. However, is it not more plausible to interpret it the other way round: the impotence that Sir John is ashamed of is *the impotence due to the presence of desire itself?* By *enacting his desire*, he is concealing not the lack but the overwhelming presence of desire; he is concealing desire itself. The enactment of desire is his strategy of keeping it on a distance, of 'organizing' it adequately. It is the strategy by means of which he seeks to control it and become the *master* of desire instead of its subject. His anxiety and fear of his desire, of the real of this desire and of the fact that Diana actually possessed him during the trial, become the driving force of his enacting desire. It is the technique with the help of which he keeps events under control and prevents them from slipping out of his hands. To put it briefly: *the enactment of desire equals perfectly the escape*

97

from desire; it is a manoeuvre to avoid confrontation with the real of desire, with the Thing, *das Ding*.

Sir John incessantly enacts some sort of 'hysterical theatre', where he can play the role of a master (the role of a man who holds all the strings and dominates the game), and in this role he compromises his desire. In this sense, Fane appears to him as the ideal figure to justify his compromising his desire: Fane embodies the threat of what will happen if Sir John does not control his desire. He personifies the undesirable, disturbing shadow of Sir John's own desire, the shadow Sir John is trying to escape from and to leave behind the scene: the lethal, mortal dimension of desire. The problem, however, is that this shadow 'emancipates' itself and appears in front of him – where else but on stage, in the guise of the suicide in which the triumph of pure desire, the desire of death, embodies itself? If, throughout the entire film, Fane is a mere shadow of Sir John, at the end he will radically subvert this situation by his act of 'pure autonomy': now Sir John emerges as nothing but Fane's pale shadow.

What exactly is introduced by Fane's act, what does he accomplish? He chooses the path of absolute *persistence*, of a persistence that is – at least in the perspective of the reality principle – utterly senseless. However, it is precisely the fact that it is senseless, *hors-sens*, that bestows on his act the ethical dimension. Fane persists even where desire hesitates, on the edge of the ultimate limit which separates desire from its focus, whence one can henceforth speak only of a 'pure desire', of the desire of death as such. *He persists in his desire even when this desire no longer has any ground*, when he can no longer expect anything in return for his persistence; this is what makes it ethical. So it is Fane who, unlike Sir John, all the way along embodies the paradoxical position 'in-between', the position of symbolic 'indetermination' and ambiguity which, at the end, is capable of the act *stricto sensu*.

It is essential to any proper moral act that it involves a break which 'rearranges' the previous symbolic code, restructures the very symbolic universe within which it emerges. In order to exemplify this characteristic of the act, let us approach another film in which suicide plays a crucial role: Peter Weir's *Dead Poets' Society*. The action takes place in a classic Victorian school; its regular life is disturbed by the arrival of Keating, a new teacher of literature. In his very first lesson he surprises the students by proposing the imperative '*Carpe diem!*', 'Seize the day!'

Keating resorts to peculiar pedagogic approaches and justifies them by the fact that he teaches poetry, not a 'positive science'. His appearance provokes four different responses among the students. Some go on living as previously and are as well prepared to satisfy 'the caprices' of their new teacher (if necessary they step on the table, write a poem, or march in the backyard). Others are immediately willing to substitute new authority for old: they are enthusiastic about doing everything they suppose Keating would appreciate; the main protagonists of this attitude are Dalton and Neil. Neil finds out that Keating, who studied in the same school, was a member of the 'Dead Poets' Society', and the boys decide to form their own 'Dead Poets' Society'; they meet at night in a cave near the school and read poetry. The third type of response to Keating's procedures is the one represented by Todd Anderson: he is reserved about Keating, he doesn't want to change, to 'open himself up', and is the only one who refuses to write a poem for homework (and probably the only one who has a chance to become a poet); his attitude changes only in the second part of the film. The fourth type of response is the one of the leading character, Neil. It is true that he belongs to the group of the enthusiasts; nevertheless, he is not willing to replace the paternal Law with a new one so easily – and here, things get complicated.

Neil most desperately wants to become an actor, yet his father strongly opposes it. So he fabricates his father's permission to take a part in the school performance of *A Midsummer Night's Dream*. His father finds out about it and, a day before the opening night, he once again forbids him to perform. In his despair Neil turns to Keating, who advises him to tell his father what he has told him: that acting is simply the only thing he wants to do in his life. When Neil comes back from a meeting with his father, he claims that, on hearing his plea, his father has allowed him to perform on the opening night. Neil acts brilliantly, but before he can enjoy his success, his father puts him in the car and drives him home. The result of a most awkward family discussion is that he is forbidden to act as long as his parents are 'supporting him': he should go to

Harvard and study medicine for the next ten years.

In the night following this discussion, Neil commits suicide. In order to avoid scandal, the school authorities are desperate to find someone on whom to pin the blame for his death, so Keating is accused. Members of the 'Dead Poets' Society' are forced to sign a statement saying he was seducing them. The film ends with the scene of Keating leaving the class; the school principal (the chief 'exorcist') is giving the lesson instead of him. Todd Anderson shouts to Keating that they were forced to sign the statement and then, in spite of the headmaster's threats, he steps on the table, saying 'Captain, my captain!'. One after the other, the boys are stepping on their tables, and the headmaster is yelping powerlessly. Keating thanks them and leaves.

Let us first consider the consequences of Keating's arrival on the intersubjective level. If – as indicated in several scenes – the relationship between students and teachers in this school is based principally on fear and discipline, Keating 'complicates' this relationship considerably by arousing in the students a different kind of 'transference', namely love. This liaison could be discerned most clearly in the relationship Dalton–Keating; two scenes are of crucial importance here. The first one is the backyard scene when Keating orders his students to march and to find 'their own walk'; Dalton refuses to do so. Here we witness defiance, one of the most fundamental forms of love. The message is clear – a demand for a look and attention, an appeal to Keating: 'Look at me, look at what I am doing!' Keating, of course, gets the message. The second scene is the scandal Dalton provokes at the school assembly, mockingly imitating a phone call and shouting to the headmaster that God wants to speak to him – a gesture that questions the headmaster's authority and makes it look ridiculous, a gesture that poses the question 'What authorizes you?', 'What supreme knowledge do you possess?'. The true aim of this provocation becomes manifest soon afterwards when Dalton (after being punished) chats with his friends and is definitely the star of the evening; Keating enters and tells him that he did a very stupid thing, yet Dalton looks at him with great surprise and says, 'I thought *you*'d like that!'. In short, it turns out that his act was meant for Keating to see – that is, it was again a demand for a look. The second feature that becomes manifest in this scene is the fact that

Dalton was able to nullify one authority only by relying on another, on Keating. Keating's demand 'Think with your own head!' has therefore failed: everybody who took it seriously *started to think with Keating's head or act for his gaze* – a lesson to Keating that is worth its price. Regardless of what pedagogic ideas and approaches one endeavours to introduce, the fundamental disposition *student (subject)–teacher (subject supposed to know)* is irreducible.

Once the transference is established, *Carpe diem!* loses its inno-cence, too. It loses its form of advice and begins to function as an imperative – more precisely: as the imperative of the superego, since what it communicates is ultimately an injunction to *jouissance.* It is true that the verb *carpo* signifies enjoyment in a broad sense of the word, from consuming fruit to expressions like 'enjoy your youth', yet the moment it attains the status of an imperative of the superego, this command loses its innocence. Enjoy! – the impossibility of this command with which the boys are confronted arises from the fact that it puts us in a cleft stick. We can never be certain that we have been enjoying ourselves enough, that we have profited by all the opportunities offered to us, that we have really 'seized the day'. We are constantly worried about missing something – in short, the situ-ation here is strictly homologous to the deadlock of the Kantian subject who worries all the time whether he/she has really accom-plished a moral act or not, since he/she can never be certain that he/she has really eliminated all pathological impulses. This bears witness to the fact that it is precisely the dimension of *jouissance* which makes the moral act so difficult to realize: Keating is a Kantian, saying to his students 'Do your duty!', 'Do your Thing!' – do the Thing that is really *yours* and not the school's, your parents', or anybody else's. Do the act because it is the only thing that will make your life worth living. Most students fail at this; Neil does not.

Neil's situation can be described as follows: he has his Thing – acting – but Father forbids it. Two alternatives are possible here, either of which is worse, if we may put it that way. The first would occur if the paternal Law were to win, if Neil were to submit to the will of his parents. This would be the path of a lifelong antagonism: the Other (Father) would be considered by Neil as the one who is constantly preventing him from realizing himself fully, realizing his Thing. With the second possibility – that is, if he were to choose acting and to refuse to obey the will of his parents – he would lose the Thing itself. Why? According to the elementary 'dialectic of desire', it is the paternal Law – that is, the interdiction itself – that makes a thing the Thing. So Neil, if he were to become an actor, would sooner or later realize that *this is not It*. Neil decides not to take a choice in this alternative and commits suicide: he realizes that he can carry out his Thing only at the price of his life.

This suicidal act is a clear and unambiguous answer to the pressure of the symbolic universe that surrounds him: *the answer of the Real*. The school apparatus activates itself immediately and tries to *symbolize* this act; they are looking desperately for 'external causes', trying to deprive this suicide of the dignity of the act, to reduce it to an ordinary action: Neil was seduced, and, as mentioned above, Keating is chosen to play the role of scapegoat. The first to realize the falsehood of this scapegoating is Todd, Neil's roommate, who persistently repeats that acting was Neil's Thing and that Keating had nothing to do with it – the boy who was the last to join the 'Dead Poets' Society' is the first to step on the table in the final scene of the film when Keating has to leave the school. In this perspective, the final scene (students stepping on their tables, saying 'Captain, my captain!') could be read as the gesture by means of which the dignity of the act, its non-symbolizable status, is returned to Neil's suicide.

This gesture is in itself inherently 'theatrical', an act of public defiance, intended for a look – in contrast to Neil's suicide, which was a lone act. Yet the distinction of Fane's suicide in *Murder!* consists precisely in its being committed in a theatre, in front of a large public – does this make it any less 'pure'? Just the opposite! Hitchcock could have shot the suicide scene in a standard way, say, with Fane finishing his performance, going to the wardrobe and hanging himself there. Yet by placing the suicide on the stage, he succeeds perfectly in staging *the act's failed encounter with the gaze*. That is to say, when Fane finishes his performance on the trapeze, his gaze changes into the gaze of a blind man: staring in front of him but seeing nothing, he tries to reach the rope and misses it two or three times; when he finally gets hold of it, the whole disposition is repeated. When Fane lets the rope slip slowly through his hands, he appears hardly to attend to it, giving no sign that he is aware of the audience – this effect would surely escape our attention if his suicide were committed in private. *It is only when it takes place in public that we become fully aware of the fact that it aims past the public,* that it is not designed for its gaze. In spite of the large audience, Fane is alone at this moment: this absolute seclusion reminds us of the true dimension of his act.

Notes

1. The film begins when the body of the murdered actress Edna Duce is found. All the circumstances point towards Diana Baring, an actress in the same troupe: the murder happened in Diana's flat – the actresses were rivals who detested each other. Diana is found on the scene of the crime in a sort of trance. The trial follows; Diana's only defence is that she does not recall anything, so she is sentenced to death. Among the jurors is Sir John, a famous playwright who is convinced of Diana's innocence and decides to discover the real murderer on his own. He intends to use his art for this purpose – in his own words: 'Life permits a beautiful and unfortunate girl to go to the gallows. Unless art, for once, can bring its technics to bear.' He is writing the drama 'The Inner History of the Baring Case' (as we learn only towards the end of the film) – a 'true story' about a murder case. His intention, or even fantasy, turns out to be that he will appear together with Diana Baring on stage performing this very play.

After some detective work (a cigarette case is found which Diana recognizes) it turns out that the murderer is Handell Fane – a quite unfortunate character – an actor 'condemned' mostly to giving circus and entertainment performances (with a considerable degree of transvestism). He is unhappily in love with Diana – to whom, at the key moment, Edna wanted to reveal something shameful about him. Sir John decides to capture Fane in a theatrical trap *par excellence*, a 'mousetrap' – a play-within-a-play. Under the pretext of an audition he makes him act (in front of witnesses) an unfinished scene of the play he is writing, calculating that Fane will 'fill the gaps', or betray himself in some way. Yet in spite of his excitement, Fane nevertheless succeeds in getting through the act and does not make any fatal mistakes.

A scene follows where Fane performs a spectacular trapeze act in a circus. In the audience are Sir John and Markham, a theatre manager who is helping Sir John with his detective work. After Fane finishes his performance (still high above the stage) he ties a noose in the rope and commits suicide. He also leaves a letter in which he tells Sir John that he decided to participate in his play after all (to fill 'the empty gaps') and continues in the style of dramatic stage direction: 'Both women are standing, beholding each other in a deadly silence. Both are absorbed in the tension of the moment, so that they do not hear the murderer creeping through the door.... He walks home, a murderer, a murderer on impulse who silenced the mouth of the woman who knew his secret and began to reveal it to the woman he dared to love. Here is the melodrama for you, Sir John.' (What makes Fane's death even more melodramatic is the fact that Diana knew 'his secret' all the time.)

The letter is sufficient to acquit Diana. The closing scene of the film seems at first

103

like an emphatic 'happy ending'. Sir John and Diana enter the flat and he kisses her. The camera tracks backwards slowly until the frame appears – the frame of the stage. Then the curtain falls and the film ends. What really happened in the relationship between Diana and Sir John we never learn. We know only that Sir John succeeded in staging his 'fantasy' – as we have obviously seen the last scene of 'The Inner History of The Baring Case'.

2. François Truffaut, *Hitchcock*, London: Panther 1969, p. 65.

3. Hitchcock emphasizes it, since the radio announcer tells us what we are about to hear.

4. 'In *Rope* each shot runs to ten minutes, that is, the entire film roll in the camera magazine, and is referred to as a ten-minute take. In the history of cinema this is the only instance in which a full-length film has been shot with no interruption for the different camera set-ups' (Truffaut, p. 259).

5. Ibid.

6. Ibid., p. 261.

7. For the way this opposition of 'public' and 'private' spaces works in Hitchcock's films, see Jameson's chapter on space in this book (pp. 47–72).

8. Truffaut, p. 83.

9. Half-caste, a term applied directly to Fane. In the second part of the film Sir John visits Diana in prison and reproaches her for protecting the murderer because she is in love with him. She claims in her defence that this is impossible. When Sir John 'irritates' her further, saying, 'I see no reason why it should be impossible', Diana finally erupts: 'Why, the man's half-caste!'

10. Gilles Deleuze, *Cinema 2: The Time-Image*, London: The Athlone Press 1989, p. 294.

11. See Chapter 17 of Jacques Lacan, *The Four Fundamental Concepts of Psycho-Analysis*, Harmondsworth: Penguin 1979.

12. Such a movement of the camera follows exactly the principles of Galilean physics, as it is seen in the following scheme:

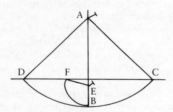

In point A there is a nail from which the pendulum hangs. If the pendulum starts swinging from point C, it will travel through point B and come back to the starting point on the other side – i.e. to point D. If we add another gravity point by positioning another nail in point E, the pendulum will swing to point B normally, but then curve towards point F. See Galileo Galilei, *Two New Sciences*, transl. S. Drake, Madison: University of Wisconsin Press 1974, pp. 162–4.

13. 'An act done from duty derives its moral worth, *not from the purpose* which is to be attained by it, but from the maxim by which it is determined. Therefore the act does not depend on the realization of its objective, but merely on the *principle* of volition by which the act has taken place, without regard to any object of desire. It is

A PERFECT PLACE TO DIE

clear from what precedes that the purposes which we may have in view for our acts, or their effects as regarded as ends and impulsions of the will, cannot give to actions any unconditional or moral worth' (*Metaphysical Foundations of Morals*, in *Immanuel Kant's Moral and Political Writings*, ed. Carl J. Friedrich, New York: Random House 1949, p. 147).

14. See Chapter 4 of Jacques Lacan, *Le Séminaire, livre VII; L'éthique de la psychanalyse*, Paris: Editions du Seuil 1986.

15. Ibid., p. 168.

16. Jacques-Alain Miller, 'Jacques Lacan: Bemerkungen über sein Konzept des *passage à l'acte*', *Wo es war VII–VIII*, Vienna: Hora Verlag 1990.

17. *Kant's Political Writings*, ed. Hans Reiss, Cambridge: Cambridge University Press 1970, p. 146.

18. For a more detailed elaboration of this 'Sadeian project' and its relationship to Lacan's concept of the 'between-two-deaths', see Slavoj Žižek, *The Sublime Object of Ideology*, London: Verso 1989, pp. 134 ff.

19. *Kant's Political Writings*, p. 146.

20. Ibid.

21. William Rothman, *The Murderous Gaze*, Cambridge, MA: Harvard University Press 1982, p. 62.

5

Punctum Caecum, or,

Of Insight and Blindness

STOJAN PELKO

Out of sight, out of mind.
(Advertising slogan for Moschino spectacles)

Out of sight, not out of mind.
(Slogan for TV clip in support of a kidnapped journalist in Beirut)

I

At the juncture of the eye and the mind many a philosophical head has been breaking, and some cinema skulls must have cracked. Surely, one of the most famous skulls is on the photograph titled '46, Burnham Street' in *Shadow of a Doubt*. It belonged to little Charlie, who slipped on the ice and fell off his bicycle under the wheels of a tram. 'He fractured his skull and he was laid up so long.... He didn't do much reading after that, let me tell you. It [the photograph] was taken the very day he had his accident. And then, a few days later, when the pictures came later, when the pictures came home, how Mama cried! She wondered if he'd ever look the same, if

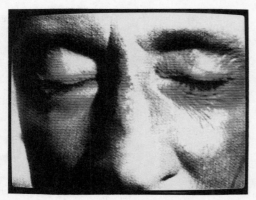

he'd ever be the same,' summarizes sister Emma. Uncle Charlie knew nothing about this photograph: it was out of his sight and at the same time out of his (morbid) mind. But once he faced that torpid evidence of the traumatic day, his whole body became torpid and his sight was replaced with goggling blindness. *Out of sight, but not out of mind!*

Raymond Bellour derived from this case some far-reaching conclusions about the role of a static photographic image in the dynamic stream of cinematic moving pictures:

> By creating distance and another time, the photograph allows me to think in the cinema. It allows me to think the film as well as the very fact of being in the cinema. In short, the presence of the photograph allows me to cathect more freely what I see. It helps me (a little) to close my eyes, though they keep on being open.[1]

It is no coincidence that Bellour titled his text 'Le Spectateur pensif' (The Thinking Spectator). After all, it is precisely this elusive juncture of pondering eyes and dimmed mind around which Alfred Hitchcock builds his cinematic universe. Because of that, by necessity, he himself appears at a similarly elusive juncture – at the juncture of classic and modern cinema. The shortest definition of Hitchcock by Gilles Deleuze is this:

> He is, perhaps at the juncture of the two cinemas, the classic that he perfects and the modern that he prepares.[2]

Hitchcock wins this thankless role of milestone and linkage at the same time, of the pure relation between one and the other, precisely as he 'introduces the mental image into the cinema. That is, *he makes relation itself the object of an image*, which is not merely added to the perception, action and affection images, but frames and transforms them.'[3] That is why Deleuze can emphatically claim that with Hitchcock a new kind of 'figures', the *figures of thoughts*, appear in film history, and place their 'inventor' side by side with English philosophy: 'Hitchcock produces a cinema of relation, just as English philosophy produced a philosophy of relation.'[4]

So what has happened to our starting point, the relation between the eye and the mind? What happens when our eyes are closed, yet kept open?

II

You must remember Hitchcock's story about a scriptwriter who had his best ideas at night, but could not remember anything in the morning. So he put paper and pencil on his night table. After one of his turbulent nights there was a note: *Boy meets girl.*

I mention this story because this is precisely the disposition at the outset of the text that is going to serve as a kind of legend in our examination of Hitchcock's images – of *Mémoires d'aveugle. L'auto-portrait et autre ruines* by Jacques Derrida. A 'legend', since the text explains images (the author's selection of pictures on the subject of blindness from the archives of the Louvre), but also because it keeps on falling back on the very legends that have fundamentally deter-mined the (blind) imagery of Western civilization – from Homer to Borges.

It all began one restless night (6 July 1989) with a pencil and a notebook by the bed. In the morning, the author managed to read the following traces of an interrupted dream:

> ... duel de ces aveugles aux prises l'un avec l'autre, l'un des veillards se détournant pour s'en prendre à moi, pour prendre à partie le pauvre passant que je suis, il me harcèle, me fait chanter, puis je tombe avec lui par terre, il me ressaisit avec une telle agilité que je finis par soupçonner de voir au moins d'un œil entrouvert et fixe, comme un cyclope (un être borgne ou louche, je ne sais plus), il me retient toujours en jouant d'une prise après l'autre et finit par user l'arme devant laquelle je suis sans défense, une menace contre mes fils ...[5]

Although the author explicitly adds that it was his dream and nobody else's business – 'il ne regarde personne' – we nevertheless dare to follow the traces of his dream, for besides the surprisingly similar outset, it contains a condensation of literally everything that is to be discussed in relation to Hitchcock: the real and the false blind, the annoying and the passing-by, the one-eyed and the cross-eyed, fathers and sons ...

III

We begin with a dream ('Last night I dreamt I went to Manderley again' – *Rebecca*), so that from the light and lights ('Keep your lights burning, America!' – *Foreign Correspondent*) through short-sightedness (*Suspicion*) we could achieve blindness (*Saboteur*) and finally fall into the shadow of a new nightmarish dream ('And I brought you nightmares.... You live in a dream, you're a sleepwalker, blind!' – *Shadow of a Doubt*).

In contrast to the ordinary topical classification of Hitchcock's films, we are therefore rather more interested in the five consecutive films that roughly mark his passage from Europe to America at the time of the Second World War. Again, there is the elusive break between two periods, analogous to Deleuze's 'break' between movement-image and time-image. And of course, it is no coincidence that Deleuze's classification of cinematic images, in piling up evidence for the break, should finally resort to an altogether external, historical argument – to the Second World War as the most radical break between the 'old' and the 'new'!

The key innovation of time-image is that it became a cinema of the seeing, *un cinéma de voyant*, says Deleuze. Though situated on the edge of the old movement-image, Hitchcock succeeded in staging precisely this essential innovation of time-image. Contrary to the usual statements, he is not revolutionary in *involving the spectator with on-screen characters*, but mainly in *making the very character a spectator*![6] As the basic action of the character is reduced to watching and is thus literally embodied in a unique object – gaze – so a wide range of opportunities appears to subvert this basic attitude: the character may see too much or too little, may be near-sighted or cross-eyed, may be blinded or hypnotized, and, finally, blindness may be staged in the literal sense – in tearing out the eye! In this text, we shall be interested in these *figures of blindness*, as, perhaps, through the radical absence of the object, they reveal most of the theme of sight that directly touches the *figures of thoughts*.

IV

So let us begin with *Rebecca*, as blindness is at the outset of its biblical reference. Of course, it was Rebekah's husband Isaac who was blind, thus making possible the paradigmatic scene of the choice between two sons, the first-born Esau and the second-born Jacob. The notorious fact is that the real 'director' of the whole scene was Rebekah – more precisely, she provided the cast and the costumes (she was the one who 'took goodly raiments of her eldest son Esau, which were with her in the house, and put them upon Jacob her younger son. And she put the skins of the kids of the goats upon his hands, and upon the smooth of his neck.'[7])! However, the classic interpretation, which reduces Rebekah's act to a mere deception, is a trifle too weak. It overlooks, first, the fact that Rebekah in fact merely follows the Lord's advice about how 'the elder shall serve the younger',[8] and second, the fact that the paradigmatic scene of the blind man's choice is repeated in the next generation of grandchildren when Jacob, instead of blessing his first-born Manasseh, blesses the second-born Ephraim!

At least two conclusions may be derived from this more sagacious interpretation: on the one hand, *it shows deception to be the necessary means for the accomplishment of fate* (what else does Hitchcock's Rebecca do but arrange a deception – stage her own death – where she is anyway being led by the inevitable – fatal illness?); on the other hand, the key dimension of the whole game is inscribed precisely through *repetition* (in Hitchcock, its 'agent' is, of course, Mrs Danvers – who, by the way, replicates Rebekah's biblical gesture: she distributes the roles and provides the costumes!).

It seems to us that the precise formal analogue to this duality in content can indeed be found in a certain fundamental duality of the shot. With Hitchcock, Deleuze offers what may be its most beautiful illustration: in every shot, *two sides of a movement* can be discerned – the moving of the distinct parts of a multitude which changes their mutual positions; and the moving that crosses the whole and delineates its change. If the intersubjective relation that undermines the mutual positions of protagonists is precisely the *necessary deception*, then *repetition* changes the status of the whole itself by way of inscribing its inevitability through duration.[9] Both are best summed up in a conceptual pair used by Deleuze as the title of his doctoral dissertation: *Différence et répétition* (Difference and Repetition).

Moreover, this double necessity (ordered *in advance* and confirmed *retroactively*) calls into question the status of the very subject of choice: what if a (wrong) decision is not the *consequence* of blindness, but rather blindness is the *condition* of a (right) decision? Or as Derrida puts it – a little differently: what if it is not the choice (and the sacrifice which inevitably follows it) that blinds, what if it is, rather, blindness itself which is the condition of choice and sacrifice? – blindness in which the subject is no longer seeing, because he actually sees 'too far and too well'?[10] The blind man thus, at the very first confrontation, turns out to be seeing, to be the *voyant* with whom we have set out into the darkness of the modern cinema in the first place. True, we are still far from the voyeur in *Rear Window*, yet the link between them is by no means negligible. By seeing less, they both see more! *Out of sight, not out of mind!*

v

The same structure as the one registered in the case of the biblical blindness (deception is necessary if the mission is to be accomplished) may be found again in the case of the only really blind Hitchcock character of this period, Philip Martin in *Saboteur*. We might even make a little joke by saying that here we are not very far from the Bible – more precisely, from the Old Testament: instead of Cain we have both Ken and Kane (the first, guiltless, dies in a set fire; the other, just as guiltless, is charged with setting the fire – so again, it is *sacrifice* and *choice*); and instead of Sodom we are led to Soda City! After all, at the very beginning, blindness and overlooking are indicated by the name on the envelope that makes Barry Kane follow the traces of crime: Charles *Tobin*! Was not Tobias the biblical son who restored his father Tobit's sight?[11] Philip Martin is therefore anticipated in Tobit's name – anticipation being, as Derrida has it, first of all a matter of *hands*. As distinct from haste, or precipitation (*prae-caput*, head-on), anticipation primarily concerns touch, grasp (*capere*, to hold; *ante*, in advance).[12] And the blind old man is actually in a situation where he must – like Isaac – choose between what is

111

said by hands and what is said by voice. We know that Isaac was misled by dressed-up hands and thus he dismissed the voice ('The voice is Jacob's voice, but the hands are the hands of Esau'). Naturally, Philip Martin does not repeat this mistake: even though the handcuffs on Barry Kane's hands indicate his guilt, he listens to his voice and recognizes innocence in it.

(Kane's) deception once again proves to be the only way to the fulfilment of the mission (to disclose a network of sabotage), and the blind man to be the most penetrating seer. But what about repetition? If we are to answer this question, we have to introduce into the game the third sight, that of Martin's niece Patricia.[13] Patricia thinks with her head, and in her haste she sees guilt in Kane. That is precisely why there must be the other structural consequence: *repetition*! Not until the scene in the circus caravan – a kind of spectacular repetition of the original choice between guilt and innocence – is she definitely convinced. It is almost redundant to state that this decision of hers is once again conditioned by blindness – it is the blind love called transference that emerges between the characters on their common path.

Hitchcock, as the director of relations, knew very well, of course, that a couple never sets out on account of love, and that it is only the path itself that engenders love. That, after all, is the stake of *Mr and Mrs Smith*. It was on the basis of this film that Deleuze introduced the key term of his interpretation of Hitchcock – the thirdness [*la tierceité*].

VI

That is to say, the double movement of the shot (change in the mutual position of the parts of multitude – change in the status of the whole) is properly interesting as long as there is, between the two sides of an action, some sustained interaction; as long as a *relation* is entwined between them. This 'thirdness' may, of course, be expressed in different ways. What is 'primary' on the cinematic level is no longer character (in this case we would have a whodunnit, scorned by Hitchcock) nor action, but the very multitude of relations that represent both action and character. On the metacinematic level, however, the bipolar relation between director and film is enriched with the third party, the spectator. We have already mentioned how the interpreters have recognized Hitchcock's first great innovation in the inclusion of the *spectator*; thus they have only repeated, for the history of the cinema, the gesture carried out for art history by Michael Fried, who discerned in the mid-eighteenth century 'a major shift' in the process of the absorption of the spectator. It is no coincidence that this revolution took place precisely in relation to the paintings the topics of which are closely related to blindness (Greuze's 'The Deceived Blind Man', Fragonard's 'Blind Mice'). Derrida's recapitulation of this revolution in art history is the exact replica of the characterization of Hitchcock summarized by Deleuze after Truffaut and Douchet:

> [Derrida:] 'The Deceived Blind Man' attracts and implies the spectator. The latter becomes indispensable to the dramatic narrative. The spectator's place of a visible witness is marked in the very disposition of representation. We might say that in it, the third is included.[14]

> [Deleuze:] In the history of the cinema Hitchcock appears as one who no longer conceives of the constitution of cinema as a function of two terms – the director and the film to be made – but as a function of three: the director, the film and the public who must come into the cinema, or whose reactions must form an integrating part of the film (this is the explicit sense of suspense, since the spectator is the first to 'know' the relations).[15]

It should be clear, now, why we used the term 'the third sight' apropos of the introduction of Patricia in *Saboteur*. If we continue to speculate about the possible parallel between the blind seer Martin and the director himself, and confide the film action to its main character, Barry Kane, what is left in the triad director–film–spectator is the place of the third party, occupied by nobody but Patricia! But with an essential enrichment: the spectator becomes one of the characters – or, more exactly, *the character becomes a spectator*! Thus we come to the second, far more innovative Hitchcock move which we mentioned at the outset: *the character is reduced to a gaze*; he is literally embodied in it. Hence his inevitable entrapment into the dialectics of sight, the cleavage between the almighty surveillance and the impotent punishment. Indeed, Patricia *sees* the handcuffs on Kane's hands – but that is precisely why she *overlooks* their truth and errs about his guilt.

Saboteur was the film in whose context Slavoj Žižek has pointed out the similarity between the problems of sight in Hitchcock and the specific dialectic of the simultaneous omnipotence and radical impotence of gaze as developed by Poe in 'The Purloined Letter'.[16] In both instances we have three parties: the *agent*, the *adversary*, and the *innocent third party*. Of course, the scene of charity ball in Mrs Van Sutton's palace is paradigmatic in this respect, but it seems to be conveniently applicable also to the interpretation of the meeting of our three protagonists: Kane, the blind old man, and Patricia. Entangled in this scene, we find practically all the threads we have tried to lay so far. We could untangle them only through understanding Patricia as the agent of the 'thirdness' that not only embodies the relation, but is literally substantiated by it.

Yet we must understand this embodiment in a very specific sense. In order to explain it, we must return once again to the scene in which Tobias restores his blind father's sight. Art history roughly distinguishes two ways of staging this scene, the distinctive feature being the presence or the absence of angel Raphael. He is the one who *leads the hand* of Tobias and thus in fact *restores sight*. But as soon as we ask about the actual significance of the restoration of sight, things become unexpectedly complicated. For what is the first 'object' offered to the cured eyes? Is it the son who restored sight, or the angel who in fact made it happen? True, it is Raphael who gives sight, but he himself is a pure *vision*! After all, this nature of a pure simulacrum, substantiated only by what he himself produced – sight – is explicit in his own words:

'Thank God now and for ever. As for me, when I came to you it was not out of any favour on my part, but because it was God's will. . . . Even though you watched me eat and drink, I did not really do so; what you were seeing was a vision.'[17]

Before he leaves this world of bodies and flesh, Raphael commissions the astonished witnesses carefully to 'write down all these things that have happened to you'. The vision is then necessarily followed by the act of writing, *graphein*, which retroactively substantiates the vision itself.

Instead of wondering about the sex of angels we shall, rather, try to justify the equation between this kind of *vision* that always offers itself to a precisely defined addressee and demands an inscription, and the *embodiment* we attributed to Patricia. Patricia is inscribed into that long chain of Hitchcock's female characters who persistently oscillate between presence and absence, whose paradigm, of course, is the eponymous heroine of *The Lady Vanishes*. Each and every one of them owes her status of simulacrum to the very cinematographic disposition that is capable, with a single stroke, of replacing presence with absence, and thus performing quotidian biblical visions. That is why that disposition is to be attributed the role of the demiurge of the 'thirdness'. Deleuze points out first of all that people in a film can act, feel and experience, but can never testify to the relations that determine them. This fundamental role is always reserved for the *movement of the camera* and the *movement of people* towards it. It may be *delegated* to another machine (the Hitchcockian analogue to camera *par excellence* is, of course, train); it may be literally *staged* (false film reporters at the launching of a ship in *Saboteur* are thus merely the other side of a very real movement of people on screen – more precisely, in front of the screen of a cinema), and, in the final consequence, it can even replace editing altogether (as proved by *Rope*). But the point is always that the content is literally *narrated* by a completely formal agency, such as the camera movement.

VII

In terms of narrative mode, the character of Patricia is of further interest. It makes trouble for the traditional theory of film identification, which in principle distinguishes a primary identification (identification with a disposition) from a secondary one (identification with a character): we have just tried to prove that Patricia embodies the cinematographic disposition and herself at *one and the same time*. How indeed are we to understand this concurrence of object with subject?

The same question emerges at the end of the survey of narrative modes in the second part of Deleuze's study of cinema, *The Time-Image*.[18] After evoking the dilemma of real and imaginary by questioning *description*, and the pair of true and false by questioning narrative, he is left with the *tale* [*le récit*]. And this is where he introduces into the game the fundamental philosophical pair of subject and object, yet both still within the cinematic disposition. That is why he first describes the usual division ('objective' as seen by a camera; 'subjective' as seen by a person in the film), but complicates it in the very next move: the camera must be seeing the seeing person, too! Thus we arrive very quickly at the person who sees and is seen at the same time. The other side of the person is the camera that offers to sight the person seen as well as what the person sees. The initial duality has thus multiplied within each of the two elements; in the course of this multiplication, however, the division itself has won independence and autonomy. The stake of the filmic narrative can thus be conceived as a persistent effort at merging this initial cleavage between 'subjective' and 'objective' images, an effort that is much more difficult if one of the parties is missing or if, in the final consequence, the roles of the parties are reversed (subjective camera; person–object).

That is why we dare to say that, in contrast to the traditional distinction between primary and secondary identification, Deleuze is interested precisely in the *identity of the two identifications*, and presume to recognize in the character of Patricia, in *Saboteur*, one of the few successful accomplishments of this identity. Inasmuch as Patricia is the carrier of the above-mentioned 'third sight' as well as being embodied in it, inasmuch as she is simultaneously both subject and object, she is in a way also simultaneously spectator and agent. Is it really by chance, then, that the film spectator finds in her the chief support of identification upon his or her calvary between true and false indices, between hands and voices?

If we were to judge by another, similar female character – the short-sighted Lina Mackinlaw from *Suspicion* – then it may seem that the spectator must inevitably be led into error by the heroine, only subsequently to see the truth. Moreover, in such a procedure the truth itself turns out to be fully arbitrary, based on a mere chance – which, after all, is testified to wittily enough by the episode of Hitchcock's 'purloined letter'.[19] From the radically different ending only the master's *cameo appearance* is left in the film: he throws a letter into a country letterbox. The term *punctum caecum*, the blind spot, thus takes on an additional meaning, since this time it is literally the concurrence of the director's *structural blindness* to what goes on in front of the camera with some *surplus-knowledge* that only he himself has at his disposal.[20]

Blindness as the condition of choice, error as the only way to the truth — are they not merely different forms of asserting the fundamental relation between chance and necessity that is so concisely encapsulated in the Nietzschean *cast of dice*, with its double structure:

> Once cast, the dice are the confirmation of chance; yet the combination they form as they fall is the confirmation of necessity. Necessity is asserted by chance just as being is asserted by becoming, just as one is asserted by plenty.[21]

The die, then, is cast. But what is also cast is the body — in *Shadow of a Doubt*! This fall of the body, *la chute du corps*, is duplicated, too: first, little Charlie fell under a tram, and in the end, adult Charlie falls under a train. Chance or necessity? The character of niece Charlie helps us to exit from what seems to be the non-reflectable identity of identification. For Deleuze sharpens the dilemma between subjective and objective images into a motion, a *becoming*:

> What cinema must grasp is not the identity of a character, whether real or fictional, through his objective and subjective aspects. It is the becoming of the real character when he himself starts to 'make fictions', when he enters 'the flagrant offense of making up legends'.[22]

Is not this *flagrant délit de légender* the most suitable label for the actions of all Hitchcockian female characters mentioned so far? What else, after all, is Patricia Martin doing in *Saboteur*, Lina MacLaidlaw in *Suspicion*, and Charlie Newton in *Shadow of a Doubt*, if not 'fictionizing' about guilt and innocence, love and hate, life and death.... Our own position in relation to them is of course difficult enough, for they lead us through the story of the film (this is very clear in *Suspicion*, where our sight is led by the short-sightedness of the heroine), while at the same time we can never get rid of the discomfort of having caught them 'legendizing'. But if today the term 'legend' generally means a *textual appendix to image* (e.g. the legend under a photograph), then their action of 'legendizing' is exactly the opposite – it is the *imaginary appendix to a text*; or, more precisely, it is the picturing of an already-existing text. With the last-mentioned female character, niece Charlie, this piling of *text* that plants shadowy images of suspicion is more than obvious: the telegram, the talk on the radio, the initials on the ring, the newspaper article, and last but not least the title of the melody which, pictured, bursts in among the first letters of the film (i.e. during the opening credits) – *Merry Widow*! Uncle Charlie tries to defend himself from such a strategy of 'legendizing' with a succession of defence mechanisms: from the *interdiction of taking pictures* (he does not allow himself to be photographed), through the smearing and *erasure of text* (the knocked-down glass at the mention of the melody title; the hidden newspaper article), to the attempt at *annihilating the very subject of legendizing*. With the latter we are interested not so much in the attempts at physical murder itself (after all, all of them fail) as in the words by means of which the uncle tries to shake his niece's basic attitude:

> 'You go through your ordinary little day and at night you sleep your untroubled ordinary little sleep, filled with peaceful stupid dreams. And I brought you nightmares. Or did I? Or was it just a silly, unexpert lie? You live in a dream, you're a sleepwalker, blind! How do you know what the world is like?'

Precisely because she is 'blind', the heroine can make the right choice – and the murderer's body *falls*, just as in *Saboteur*! The original sin, in the beginning was the Word, the fall of the body as the condition of merging the sexes ... – all these are the cornerstones of Hitchcock's cinematographic work, which, although the Catholic tradition may be recognized in it, can truly be conceptualized only if it is stretched on the relations substantiated by the cinematic disposition of the persistent exchange of presence and absence, word and image, writing and vision.

To conclude: we have to confront a specific figure of blindness that personifies all the entwinements mentioned so far: between hands and head, eyes and spirit, word and vision. It is *hypnosis*, of course. Raymond Bellour, certainly the most penetrating among contemporary film theorists to work on the parallelism between the cinematographic disposition and the hypnotic, conceived the very situation of the spectator in the cinema as the simultaneous super-position of the two phases of hypnosis: the *process of induction* that makes the subject sleep (and roughly corresponds to Freud's 'regression'); and the *hypnotic state itself* in which the hypnotized, through the hypnotist, makes the link to the outside world (Freud's 'idealization'). In short, the film spectator experiences regression in the form of idealization.[23]

The hypnotic situation, encapsulated in its fundamentals by the cinematographic disposition, is then precisely that juncture of blind-ness and surplus-value, eye and spirit, for which we are searching throughout this chapter; it is the particular *blanc sur blanc* ('Your mind is blank', says the hypnotist to his victim in the first version of *The Man Who Knew Too Much*); it is that *punctum caecum* which is the condition of sight. And if, in our chapter, we have been interested primarily in female characters, then this is certainly not without relation to the close link between hypnosis and *sexual difference* mentioned by Bellour:

> Mostly, the chosen subjects of a critical dream are women: it is through them that the hypnotist sees the best. In a lengthy footnote to the text 'Précis pour servir à l'histoire du magnétisme animal', Mesmer describes the case of Marie-Thérèse Paradis, which is literally the accomplishment of the pre-vision of photographic and cinematographic disposition through the body and the eyes of a woman.[24]

So, in the end, we have returned to angels – more precisely, to visions and Paradise! If there is a common denominator to all Hitchcock's flirtings with camera, it is to be sought in the realization that the hypnotic cinematographic disposition is female, and all its agents are women – *Women who know too much!*

Notes

1. Raymond Bellour, 'Le Spectateur pensif', in *L'Entre-Images*, Paris: La Différence 1990, p. 77.

2. Gilles Deleuze, Preface to the English edition of *Cinema 1: The Movement-Image*, London: The Athlone Press 1986, p. x.

3. Ibid., p. 203.

4. Ibid., p. x.

5. Jacques Derrida, *Mémoires d'aveugle. L'autoportrait et autre ruines*, Paris: Editions de la Réunion des musées nationaux 1990. [... duel of two blind men, one of whom turns to attack me, the poor passer-by, he molests me, forces me to sing, and then I fall down with him, he grabs me with such swiftness that I have serious doubts whether I do not see at least one eye half open and fixed like Cyclops' (that one-eyed or cross-eyed being, I cannot say), he keeps on holding me and moves me from one position to another, and finally uses the weapon I am defenceless against, a threat to my sons ...]

6. See Deleuze, *The Movement-Image*, p. 205: 'If one of Hitchcock's innovations was to implicate the spectator in the cinema, did not the characters themselves have to be capable – in a more or less obvious manner – of being assimilated to spectators?'

7. Genesis 27: 15–16.

8. Genesis 25: 23. For a closer scrutiny, see the comment in Derrida, *Mémoires d'aveugle*, p. 100.

9. See Deleuze, *The Movement-Image*, p. 22.

10. Derrida, *Mémoires d'aveugle*, p. 100.

11. The story about Tobit losing his sight actually reads as a condensation of *Antigone* and Hitchcock's *Birds*. In spite of interdiction, Tobit buried the dead. One night, when he fell asleep by a wall, with his eyes open, sparrows strewed him with their excrement and caused leucoma ('white spots') on his eyes. No doctor could help him, until eight years later his son Tobias restored his sight with fish gall. Divine and human laws, anal birds and torn-out eyes ...

12. Derrida, *Mémoires d'aveugle*, p. 12.

13. Patricia was also the name of Hitchcock's daughter. If we were to speculate about out-of-cinema details, perhaps we might, through blind father-seer, arrive at an understanding of Hitchcock's cameo appearances. Is not every appearance of a director – whose position is by definition behind the camera – on the other side of the barrier: i.e. in front of the camera, also the point of his blindness, the *punctum caecum* of our title? The voyeur becomes the *voyant*, and the self-portrait becomes the utmost form of blinding ...

14. Derrida, *Mémoires d'aveugle*, p. 97, n. 73. For a closer scrutiny, see Michael Fried, *Absorption and Theatricality: Painting and Beholder in the Age of Diderot*, Berkeley Los Angeles London 1980. For our purpose, the title of the French translation is more than significant: *La Place du spectateur: théorie et origines de la peinture moderne*.

15. Deleuze, *The Movement-Image*, p. 202. On references to the 'thirdness' in Truffaut and Douchet, see also footnote 7 on the same page.

16. See Slavoj Žižek, *Looking Awry: An Introduction to Jacques Lacan through Popular Culture*, Cambridge, MA: MIT Press 1991, pp. 71–3.

17. The Book of Tobit, 12: 17–19. Quoted from Derrida, *Mémoires d'aveugle*,

p. 35. In connection with the history of this book, see also footnote 24 on p. 33.

18. Gilles Deleuze, *Cinema 2: The Time-Image*, London: The Athlone Press 1989. See mainly Chapter 6, 'The Powers of the False'.

19. One knows that Hitchcock envisioned a very different ending: before her death, Lina writes a letter to her mother in which she warns the society about dangerous Johnnie; in the last scene, he throws that letter into the letterbox and thus, cheerfully whistling, seals his fate. Cf. François Truffaut, *Hitchcock*, London: Panther 1969, p. 164.

20. The same term, blind spot, was also used by Stephen Heath when he dealt with the other 'inexplicable' scene, the fight between Lina and Johnnie in the storm. 'Where is this plan seen from? With what gaze does it capture us?' asks Heath, and answers with the Lacanian notion of the object *a* that frames the field of reality inasmuch as it is absent from it. See Stephen Heath, 'Droit de regard', in Raymond Bellour, ed., *Le Cinéma américain* II, Paris: Flammarion 1980, pp. 87–93.

21. Gilles Deleuze, *Nietzsche et la philosophie*, Paris: PUF 1962, p. 29.

22. Deleuze, *The Time-Image*, p. 150.

23. (Conversation with) Raymond Bellour, 'La machine & hypnose', *Cinem-Action* 47, 1988, p. 69.

24. Ibid.

PART II

The Particular:

Films

1

Hitchcockian *Sinthoms*

SLAVOJ ŽIŽEK

The *auteur* theory of Hitchcock has taught us to pay attention to the continuum of motifs, visual and others, which persist from one film to another irrespective of the changed narrative context – 'the woman who knows too much'; 'the person who is suspended from another's hand'; 'the glass full of white drink', etc. The first motif – that of an intellectually superior, but sexually unattractive bespectacled woman who has insight into what remains hidden to others – runs through a series of Hitchcock's films from *Spellbound* to *Psycho*. In *Spellbound*, the unattractive 'woman who knows too much' is Ingrid Bergman herself, before she finds emotional release in the contact with Gregory Peck; in *Shadow of a Doubt*, it is the haughty young sister of the niece Charlie; in *Strangers on a Train*, it is Ruth Roman's sister, who quickly guesses that Bruno is a murderer (significantly, the role is played by Hitchcock's daughter Patricia, who portrays a homologous personality in *Psycho*); in *Vertigo*, it is Scottie's unsatisfied ex-fiancée Midge (Barbara Bel Geddes); in *The Wrong Man*, it is the bank teller who wrongly identifies Henry Fonda as the robber, etc.

As to the motif of 'the person who is suspended from another's hand', we encounter it for the first time in the final engagement on the Statue of Liberty's torch in *Saboteur*, and then in the three films from the late 1950s: in *To Catch a Thief*, the true robber is forced to confess when suspended from Cary Grant's hand on the roof's edge; at the very beginning of *Vertigo*, the cop who offers his hand to the suspended Scottie himself plunges into the abyss; in *North by Northwest*, Eve-Marie Saint is suspended from Cary Grant's hand, and the desperate clasp of their hands dissolves directly into the final scene in the sleeping-car with Cary Grant lifting her on to the upper berth. The famous glass of unnaturally white milk brought by Cary Grant to Joan Fontaine in *Suspicion* reemerges three years later in *Spellbound* (Dr Brulow, the psychoanalyst, passes it to John Ballantine – Gregory Peck – to put him to sleep) and then a year later in *Notorious* (Cary Grant offers it to Ingrid Bergman to sober her up after a boozy night).

How, then, are we to interpret such extended motifs? If we search in them for a common core of meaning (reading the hand which pulls the subject up as a token of deliverance, of spiritual salvation, for example), we *say too much*: we enter the domain of Jungian archetypes which is utterly incompatible with Hitchcock's universe; if, on the other hand, we reduce them to an empty signifier's hull filled out in each of the films by a specific content, we *don't say enough*: the force which makes them persist from one film to another eludes us. The right balance is attained when we conceive them as *sinthoms* in the Lacanian sense: as a signifier's constellation (formula) which fixes a certain core of enjoyment, like mannerisms in painting – characteristic details which persist and repeat themselves without implying a common meaning (this insistence offers, perhaps, a clue to what Freud meant by the 'compulsion to repeat').[1]

So, paradoxically, these repeated motifs, which serve as a support of the Hitchcockian interpretive delirium, designate the *limit of interpretation*: they are what resists interpretation, the inscription into the texture of a specific visual enjoyment.[2] Such a riveting of our attention to *sinthoms* enables us to establish links connecting Hitchcock's films which, on the level of their 'official' content, seem to have nothing whatsoever in common – let us just mention *The Trouble with Harry* and *Vertigo*: is it possible to imagine two more divergent films? Yet does not the story, in both cases, bear on the *difference between the two deaths, symbolic and real*: Harry, like Judy-Madeleine, *dies twice*?[3]

This tension between the 'official' content of the totality of the work and the surplus that comes forth in its details determines the typical Hitchcockian interpretive procedure which consists in a sudden 'leap', departure from the 'official' content ('although apparently a detective story, the film is actually a story about . . .'). The postmodernist pleasure in interpreting Hitchcock is procured precisely by such self-imposed trials: one invents the 'craziest' possible shift from the film's 'official' content (the actual core of the *Strangers on a Train* is the circulation of a cigarette lighter,[4] etc.), whereupon one is expected to stand the test by proposing perspicacious arguments on its behalf.

The first version of *The Man Who Knew Too Much* (1934) is perhaps the film which most directly calls for such a reading: a close look quickly reveals, behind the 'official' spy plot, a story about family, about how the intrusion of a charming foreigner (Louis Bernard) threatens its composure, about the price Mother has to pay for succumbing – albeit only in jest – to his charm. When, at a party in a Saint Moritz hotel, the mother dances off with the seductive stranger, the remaining part of the family (father and daughter) pin to the back of the stranger's dress-coat a thread from the woollen pullover on the table, so that the dancing couple gradually unravel the pullover, symbol of the family bond – the shot which, during this dance, kills the stranger is clearly a punishment for his intrusion into the closed family circle. (It is highly significant that this shot exerts a kind of deferred action identical to that usually encountered in cartoons: Louis Bernard first just casts a surprised look at his chest – that is to say, he falls down only after he becomes aware of the bullet in his chest, as if the detour through consciousness is necessary for the shot to become effective . . .) In the previous scene, a shooting match, the mother misses the clay pigeon, demonstrating thereby her agitation due to the impact of the seductive stranger; at the very end of the film, she successfully shoots down from the roof the murderer threatening her daughter, redeeming herself for her previous failure – her shot is now successful. One is thus tempted to say that the film is 'actually' the story of the two shots: of a mother who, a second time, rectifies her aberration and regains her capacity to shoot straight. (The rhythm of the entire film is regulated by a succession of shots: the shooting match at the beginning; the shot which kills Louis Bernard through the hotel window; the failed attempt on the foreign politician in the Albert Hall; the final shot which disposes of the threat to the daughter.)

Notes

1. On the notion of *sinthom*, see Chapter 2 of Slavoj Žižek, *The Sublime Object of Ideology*, London: Verso 1989.

2. Another case of it is, for example, the mysterious old villa in which Madeleine has rented a room in *Vertigo*: although it anticipates the mother's house from *Psycho*, it is totally wrong to look, in this resonance, for some common meaning – it suffices to conceive it as a 'Hitchcockian stain'.

3. See Slavoj Žižek, *Looking Awry: An Introduction to Jacques Lacan through Popular Culture*, Cambridge, MA: MIT Press 1991, pp. 26–7, and 83–7.

4. See Mladen Dolar's chapter on Hitchcock's objects in this book, pp. 31–46.

2

The Spectator Who Knew Too Much

MLADEN DOLAR

Sabotage produced a scandal and a general indignation at the time of its first release in 1936 (somewhat overshadowed by the practically simultaneous abdication of Edward VIII), and it seems that the scandal has not quite subsided yet. It still produces contradictory and sharply opposed judgements, ranging from praise as Hitchcock's best English film and one of the most radical in his career to deprecatory verdicts that it is crude and in bad taste, 'academic, cold and phony';[1] its 'cruelty is unmatched until *Psycho*, and, perhaps, even by *Psycho*'.[2] The latter judgement can find support in Hitchcock's own subsequent negative opinion about the film.

The first reason for indignation could be found in the disrespectful treatment of a literary classic, Joseph Conrad's *Secret Agent*, on which the film is based (the title was changed to *Sabotage* to avoid confusion with Hitchcock's previous film *The Secret Agent*, shot earlier the same year and based on two of Somerset Maugham's 'Ashenden' stories). This was the closest Hitchcock ever came to 'high' literature (later in his career, he considered Henry James's 'The Turn of the Screw' and even a new version of *Hamlet*, but – fortunately – nothing came of it). The general opinion was summarized by Borges:

> Conrad makes it possible for us to understand a man that causes the death of a child; Hitchcock, by his skill (and by the slant eyes of Sylvia Sidney), tries to make us emotional about it. The endeavour of the first

was intellectual, that of the second is, at best, sentimental. And that is not all: the film contains – oh! another tasteless horror – a love affair whose protagonists, equally virtuous and passionate, are the martyr-like Mrs. Verloc and the affectionate and handsome detective disguised as a greengrocer.[3]

Yet, paradoxically, the main reason for scandal was a scene where Hitchcock closely followed Conrad: the scene of the explosion with the death of an innocent child, around which the whole film is built. Hitchcock later regretted that scene; in his conversations with Truffaut and Bogdanovich, however, he gave two very different reasons for the outrage and fury provoked by it:

> I made a serious mistake in having the little boy carry the bomb. A character who unknowingly carries a bomb around as if it were an ordinary package is bound to work up great suspense in the audience. The boy was involved in a situation that got him too much sympathy from the audience, so that when the bomb exploded and he was killed, the public was resentful.[4]

The death of the boy broke all the traditional rules as to who, and under what conditions, can become a victim. Heroes don't die fortuitously; the victims must either have committed errors or sinned in some way, or they have some mark that prevents full identification with them, or they are marginal enough not to enjoy a great deal of sympathy, or they hinder the happy ending, and so on (to say nothing of negative characters). The murder of Janet Leigh in *Psycho* – practically the only murder of a star in Hitchcock's films – obeys those rules in an oblique way, since she has herself committed a crime: she stole the money, although the thing gets out of all proportion. A positive hero can die if his death is presented as a sacrifice on the victorious path of an 'idea': his death can always be 'economized', it brings a reward on a 'higher' level, it hasn't been in vain. Apart from this salutary effect, it has to be prepared beforehand by some kind of forewarning.

The boy's death in *Sabotage* has none of those features. He has all the sympathy on his side, without any side-effects; his death is unprepared and completely senseless; it doesn't bring an absolution. Moreover, it is accompanied by the death of a busload of innocent people. It appears as an irretrievable loss, a crack that cannot be patched up, not even by vengeance.

The second reason seems paradoxical:

> Oh, that was a big error. The bomb should never have gone off.... If you build an audience up to that point, the explosion becomes strangely anticlimactic. You work the audience up to such a degree that they need the relief.[5]

Why would the anticlimax be produced by an event that was entirely expected and served as the very basis of suspense? The expectation is then let down precisely because the expected happens and the audience feels cheated because it got precisely what it wanted. This happens in an even harsher form because of an additional Hitchcockian device, a delay before the catastrophe: the bomb was supposed to go off at 1.45, the moment has already passed and in the brief interval the public is almost relieved ('We knew all the time that it wouldn't happen'), awaiting some plausible explanation. After that brief moment which condenses the pulse of spectator's desire, the bomb explodes with double force; the expectations are doubly thwarted. Coming too late, the explosion nevertheless comes too early – it bursts on an unprepared spectator.

This delay can be matched with two other famous delays: the one in *Dial M for Murder*, when the phone call comes too late and the murderer is already preparing to leave (thus shifting the identification of the audience, which suddenly wants him to stay); and the other in *Psycho*, when the car containing Marion's body, while sinking into the moor, is stuck for a moment (again switching the desire of the audience to Norman's side, with the hope that it will sink). Those two delays play a role in the economy of suspense (and suspense is finally nothing but a form of economizing), whereas in *Sabotage*, the economy fails: the delay produces only frustration and anger; it cannot be economized or compensated.

The two reasons Hitchcock gave in support of his later regret finally boil down to breaking the rules of economy: the first one breaks the rule that every victim has to be compensated (and the one in *Sabotage* is not); the second one breaks the rule that suspense, too, has to be compensated. Every suspense has to be a suspense with absolution, but in *Sabotage*, the spectator feels cheated because s/he got what s/he wanted without an absolution. The problem of film fiction and its internal economy is posed in a particularly crude and radical way: the spectator wants both to believe and not to believe in film fiction; s/he acts on the assumption that s/he will be compensated for his/her belief. When the presupposition that founded the suspense is realized, it produces the effect of *menetekel* – it confronts the subject with a senseless destruction into which s/he finds him/herself thoroughly implicated with his/her desire. S/he has been caught in this disaster as in a trap, and the suspense retroactively turns into anxiety. The film fiction ceases to produce reality, it stumbles on its edge, it produces a trauma that tears asunder the balance of fictional universe.

Although all Hitchcockian films are centred around a traumatic event which involves a confrontation between the subject and his/her desire (in the purest form with that 'What do you want?' at the end of *Rear Window*), *Sabotage* remains perhaps the only one where the traumatic wound does not heal, it cannot be squeezed back into a fictional mould. The second murder only perpetuates it, it doesn't bring an absolution for Mrs Verloc. This unresolvedness leaves us with frustration, as it left Hitchcock, too.

Rohmer and Chabrol argue that *Sabotage* is an un-Hitchcockian film, that the crude mechanism of suspense is far from Hitchcock's finesse when he is at his best, and that *Sabotage* is mostly admired by people who otherwise do not like Hitchcock.[6] This judgement raises an interesting question and a legitimate problem: can a hero who unwittingly carries a bomb be counted as an instance of Hitchcockian suspense? More generally: is it enough, for the specifically Hitchcockian form of suspense, that the spectator knows more than the hero? This seems to be a very traditional form of producing suspense, amply used in literature.

The now classic paper by Pascal Bonitzer[7] has given the most concise argument about the specifically Hitchcockian suspense. He argues that with Griffith's introduction of montage, film lost its initial innocence. Up to then, it could be taken as a more or less 'neutral' presentation of objects and events, as a gaze that does not reflect on itself as a gaze. Hitchcock has radicalized this first revolution in such a way that the gaze itself has become the hinge and the main object of suspense. Bonitzer has shown that the function of the gaze had thus to be doubled; it had to be presented as a *blot*, a *fascinum* in the scopic field. The blot shatters an everyday idyllic life, a customary order; it emerges as a foreign body, a counter-natural element in a natural pattern. It estranges and perverts its orderly background, which suddenly becomes filled with uncanny possibilities. To achieve this Hitchcockian effect, the parallel montage is thus not enough (a knife approaches a body, then a rushing car – will it be on time?). It is based on a separated and therefore parallel presentation of two (or more) events, an interior and an exterior, and the suspense results from their concomitance. This device becomes Hitchcockian when the exterior threat is drawn into the interior, when the blot contaminates the whole. It is true, as Jean Narboni has argued,[8] that with Hitchcock the exterior of the field of vision is heterogeneous to its interior (in contrast to Renoir and many others, where the camera can move freely in a homogeneous and continuous space), but the heterogeneous exterior has to be inscribed in the interior, and that constitutes its internal tension.

Theoretically, one could speak of two clear-cut cases: parallel montage and the Hitchcockian function of the blot (Narboni calls it 'a sign which is not the sign of anything';[9] Deleuze[10] calls it *démarque*, etc.). Where, then, should one place the simple and very frequent case of the spectator knowing more than the hero? Bonitzer gives a basic example of how to achieve a 'Hitchcockian' suspense with a 'naive' shot *à la* Lumière. If we have a simple scene where a soldier tries to seduce a girl with a baby in a pram, all one has to do, he argues, is to append an additional knowledge (say, that the soldier is a murderer or that the girl wants to get rid of the baby). The same simple shot assumes a very different value; it becomes haunted by gloomy possibilities and anxieties.

However, this elementary case is not on the same level with his other examples taken from Hitchcock (the famous windmill in *Foreign Correspondent*, the murderer's cigar in *Rear Window*, etc.), since there is no counterpart of our additional knowledge in the field of vision itself; the gaze has no counterpart in the blot. No cinematic device has been necessary; the shot stayed as it was – we simply got the additional knowledge in another, separate shot. Yet the case is not reducible to a parallel montage: the two shots can be far apart, they do not need an alternation to produce the suspense (the parallel montage gets all its strength from alternation). The surplus-knowledge is itself enough to maintain the suspense for a long time. If there is no blot in the field of vision, then the blot is solely the surplus-knowledge as such – it is enough to disrupt the ordinary peace and to get hold of our vision from the inside, to structure the gaze. The blot is in the gaze, not in the visible.

The spectator's surplus-knowledge is thus the point of inter-section between the parallel montage and the function of the blot as the inner tension of the field. It is technically the result of two separate shots, where the first one is in no way represented in the second – except that the additional knowledge invades the whole, it inhabits the gaze and colours every detail. This could be called the zero degree of suspense: the neutral gaze loses its transparence, it becomes reflected as the gaze and thus the invisible blot on the same image.

The surplus-knowledge is first and foremost the knowledge about the gaze as the agent of the cinematic image. But that surplus-knowledge also produces lack of knowledge, it confronts the spec-tator with his/her ignorance: if the initial setting was well known and predictable, then the surplus-knowledge makes it opaque and uncertain, the outcome becomes entirely unpredictable, beyond the reach of knowledge – it becomes the place where the subject is torn between his/her surplus and lack of knowledge; the surplus turns into lack. The objects lose their functionality, they become secret signs that have lost their (usual) meaning and are therefore open to multiplicity of significations. So the function of the blot is finally nothing but the developed form and the reflected expression of the function of the gaze which is structured by the oscillation between the surplus and the lack. The blot is the counterpart of this gaze, concentrated in one point. In it, the zero degree achieves its positive expression.

The suspense in *Sabotage* is accomplished in a form that is still rudimentary and coarse. Hitchcock is still not the master of his own devices, and he plays with means that get out of hand. All Hitch-cock's films are built around a balance that is broken through a traumatic event, a murder, and is in the end established again. The standard Hollywood formula is always at least superficially satisfied, although the trauma usually casts long shadows on the 'normal' beginning and the 'normal' ending. It seems that in *Sabotage* the formula failed; the end could not do away with the trauma (even at the price of ambivalence, as in many other films). Hitchcock has gone over a certain edge, he seems himself like the boy unwittingly carrying the bomb. So Durgnat is perhaps right in claiming that the continuation of *Sabotage* is to be found in *Psycho*, which again reached over the edge, but this time at the height of the master's power, producing a trauma that neither Hitchcock himself nor film history could integrate.

Some further comment should be added on the famous scene of Verloc's 'murder'. Verloc is one of those negative Hitchcock characters with whom one cannot fully not identify (this is what makes some of his happy endings rather ambiguous). The knife lying on the table at dinner becomes a fascinating object – first for the spectator (this is the third meal in the film, and the motive has already been well prepared), then for Sylvia, and finally for Verloc himself, who follows Sylvia's gaze and gradually realizes its implications. Yet Verloc doesn't try to defend himself, he accepts his fate, so that the murder seems to be a half-hearted suicide. More precisely: Verloc's death is the result of two gestures, two movements that are suspended in the middle – a gesture being 'something that is done in order to be arrested and suspended'.[11] Sylvia's thrust with the knife is restrained, she cannot quite push it to the end, she can only produce a gesture, but the other half is accomplished by Verloc himself in a gesture of self-punishment, a suspended suicidal gesture. So the murder is actually the successful result of a coincidence of two failed gestures; neither the one nor the other could have accomplished it by him/herself. This is not enough to exempt Sylvia from guilt, and the ending leaves an uneasy feeling that the moral balance has not been achieved. The detective who is prepared to cover up Sylvia's crime takes his share of the guilt as well – similar to the outcome of *Blackmail*, and to some extent of *Shadow of a Doubt*, where the police heroes step on the other side, abandoning the straight course of law enforcement. If the police are, for Hitchcock, a worthy object of interest, the least they can do is to cover up crimes.

Notes

1. Eric Rohmer and Claude Chabrol, *Hitchcock*, Paris: Editions d'aujourd'hui 1976, p. 53.

2. Raymond Durgnat, *The Strange Case of Alfred Hitchcock*, London: Faber & Faber 1974, pp. 137–8.

3. Jorge Luis Borges, *Sur le cinéma*, Paris: Edgardo Cozarinsky 1979, p. 87.

4. François Truffaut, *Hitchcock*, London: Panther 1969, p. 118.

5. Quoted from Durgnat, p. 138.

6. Eric Rohmer and Claude Chabrol, pp. 52–5.

7. See Pascal Bonitzer's chapter on suspense in this book, pp. 15–30.

8. Jean Narboni, 'Visages d'Hitchcock', in *Cahiers du cinéma, hors-série 8: Alfred Hitchcock*, Paris 1980, p. 38.

9. Ibid., p. 33.

10. Gilles Deleuze, *Cinema 2: The Movement-Image*, London: The Athlone Press 1986, p. 203.

11. Jacques Lacan, *The Four Fundamental Concepts of Psycho-Analysis*, Harmondsworth: Penguin 1979, p. 116.

3

The Cipher of Destiny

MICHEL CHION

Nothing is more commonplace in a narrative, especially in cinema, than to establish a link between the destiny of a character and a tune.

For Rick and Ilsa, the lovers in *Casablanca*, 'As Time Goes By' is their song. It should be remembered that at first the song was banned from Rick's café, repressed, and that it was the woman who, in the guise of seductress and temptress, forced Sam, the easy-going black, to play it and to awaken all its charm: 'Play it for me, Sam'. Whereupon Rick, caught in the toils, himself says to Sam: 'Play it again'.

Likewise, in Genina's *Prix de beauté*, there is a love song through which the heroine, Lucienne, declares her fidelity to the love of her life, which he refuses to hear, since it is to the sound of the same music, and the same song, that he will kill her when, having herself become a film star, she watches herself singing it on the screen, immured in a recording like the singer in *The Castle of the Carpathians*.

The idea that a musical theme might be not merely something fatal but a coded message bringing death serves as a 'McGuffin' in two famous spy films of the 1930s, von Sternberg's *Dishonored* and Hitchcock's *The Lady Vanishes*.

In von Sternberg's film, the spy, played by Marlene Dietrich, is surprised in the act of noting down an encoded musical theme containing a secret message. Her enemy – a Russian colonel, played by Victor McLaglen – plays her the piece, which is oddly chromatic and 'modern' in style, and then observes: 'Each of these notes represents death for millions of men'. Hitchcock's film is a veritable narrative of initiation, which takes as its stake and signifier a snatch of music, the arbitrary nature of which is emphasized by the person responsible for devising it: 'I wonder why these counter-espionage people didn't simply send a message by carrier pigeon?'

Admittedly, *The Lady Vanishes* is also a sort of moral and political film, intended as a reproach to the democracies for their cowardly response to the mounting totalitarianism of the 1930s. Yet it is still more an adventure of initiation undergone by two young people, Gilbert and Iris, who are by and large selfish and irresponsible at the outset, but who meet each other, face up to various trials, and so grow to maturity.

Like other initiatory narratives (*The Magic Flute*, for example), *The Lady Vanishes* is punctuated by a series of vanishings and disappearances. Most of the story is set on a train, and the vanishings may be compared, on a metaphorical level, with the 'blackouts' or 'tunnels' which allow access to the second birth involved in all initiatory adventures.

The sequence begins, of course, with the disappearance of Miss Froy, the old lady, from the train. Furthermore, her disappearance occurs while Iris, who has sat down opposite her, is asleep. The second 'tunnel' concerns the vacillation around the name of Miss Froy, which she herself traced in the steam on one of the windows of the train and which, after her kidnapping, constitutes the sole evidence for her ever having existed, since when Iris starts looking for her, no one admits to remembering her. This name, written by the old lady when the train's entrance into a tunnel prevented her from making herself heard, will later be found again by the young woman, when she has lost all hope of proving that Miss Froy was indeed real. Yet no sooner has she seen it again than a blast of air caused by the train entering another tunnel erases the letters in the steam, which have served Iris as the sole evidence of the reality of what she has lived through. This flickering irruption of the real, torn away the instant it has appeared on a screen which of course, as a neutral support, reminds one of the cinematographic screen, is a sublime idea, and close in many respects to the example Truffaut liked to quote from *Under Capricorn* (where Ingrid Bergman sees herself in a window where the man who loves her has her look at herself); it too touches upon the essence of cinema.

Gilbert is with Iris in the buffet car when the fleeting reappearance of the lost name flashes before her eyes, and if he does not see it himself, it is because he is too taken up with contemplating her. He too will have to retrieve a name appearing in a flash behind a window – a name on a tea label (Harriman), which miraculously rises up before his eyes before being whirled away for ever. This was the favourite brand of tea of the old lady whose very existence Gilbert has until now been reluctant to acknowledge.

After the vacillation of the various names, Miss Froy's disappearance and Iris's falling asleep, the final vacillation concerns the coded melody, which Miss Froy, an English spy, had come to that particular corner of the Tyrol, where the action begins, to pick up and report to her Secret Service.

It is worth noting that Hitchcock, in order to strengthen the impact of the theme, avoids using accompanying music throughout the film. Music is employed only in a very general fashion, for the opening images, which depict the isolated, snowed-in mountain from which the protagonists of the story set out. On the other hand, several notations and gags warn of the part that music is to play in the film. Thus, one of the first interior shots of the mountain hotel is of a mechanical clock, from which emerges not a cuckoo but a little trumpeter, who sets up an interminable Lilliputian racket; later, the two English cricketers allude in their conversation to the excessive length of their country's national anthem.

A little later, Miss Froy makes her entrance and introduces herself to the two Englishmen as a governess and travelling music teacher. As she exchanges polite commonplaces with the two men, we hear, off frame, a tenor voice singing a sad folk song. Miss Froy, alleging her love of music, stands up and walks over to the window of her room so as to hear better.

This melody, which Miss Froy tries to learn by heart, is then overlaid and obscured by some other music, a screeching din of reed instruments and heavy dance steps coming from the top floor. This provides the cue for Gilbert, the young lead of the film, to make his entrance. We learn that he is studying musicology, and that he has come to the Tyrol to collect specimens of the local folk music. When one of the hotel staff comes to beg him, at the prompting of Iris in the room below, to make less noise, we see him playing a strident air on a kind of local clarinet, at the same time inviting the peasants to dance to it and noting down their steps.

An encounter between a young musicologist and a fake music teacher would be a pleasing prospect, but it is some time before Gilbert and Miss Froy actually meet. The old lady will have to be kidnapped and 'obliterated', then found again by Iris and Gilbert. For the time being, Gilbert has nothing whatsoever to do with the musical message around which the film turns, but is concerned with another, harsh, dislocated music which is itself, after its own fashion, a sort of coded message, since it is wedding music which, by creating the occasion for the first stormy encounter between Gilbert and Iris, already speaks to us of their ultimate betrothal.

Later, when silence has returned and the troubadour-spy takes up his sad and lovely chant once more, Miss Froy is able to hear the melody again and to note it in her head in its entirety. What she fails to hear, however, is the small strangled noise that issues from the throat of the singer when, after the final note has died away, a hand emerges from the shadows and kills him. Quietly, the old lady repeats the melody to herself in an undertone before going back to her own room.

We should note in passing how Hitchcock, having shown Miss Froy leaving her balcony, cuts rapidly to a dark background, and swiftly dissipates the impression the music has left by proceeding immediately to the beginning of the following scene (at the station, the next day, departure) and to *another music*, an unremarkable tune on the accordion. Like the din from Gilbert's room in the earlier episode, so too here the accordion serves to distract our attention from what we are not yet supposed to recognize as the heart and stake of the drama. At the same time, the delicate problem of *stopping the music* is raised.

The melody that is a message will reappear only when Miss Froy is safely installed in a train compartment with Iris, and hums it as she works. Indeed, it serves as a lullaby for Iris, who drops off to sleep as she listens to it. At the same time, it is to the sound of this air that Miss Froy will literally evaporate and dissolve into notes of music.

Miss Froy could, of course, have jotted down the melody on a scrap of paper the previous evening, and she would thereby have avoided having to be forever repeating it to herself, or running *the risk of forgetting*. Apart from the fact that this risk introduces an important element of suspense, however, I would argue that the strictly oral existence of the music participates in the symbolic rules of the game. Conversely, Gilbert's relationship with music is defined from the outset as written and scholarly. The first time we see him, he has a writing desk so that he can note down the dance steps. Moreover, in the train, he speaks to Iris of the 'very long book' that he is preparing on folk music, and indeed his attitude towards music seems to stem more from an instinct for compilation, inherited perhaps from his father, than from any deeper emotional involvement.

When, however, towards the end of the film, the fight is raging between the protagonists entrenched in the train and the fascists who are besieging it, it is to Gilbert that Miss Froy, before attempting to take flight, entrusts the message.[1] Here too, she does not give him the score, but simply hums through the tune a couple of times in the midst of the fusillade. In spite of his training as a collector of popular music, Gilbert likewise refrains from noting the tune down on paper, and therefore has to sing it obsessionally on the journey home.

Once Gilbert has arrived back in London, and is waiting in an antechamber in the Foreign Office to deliver his message, he has a memory lapse and exclaims: 'It's gone!', thus echoing the words which Iris herself had used when Miss Froy's name, which she had recognized on the window, had been obliterated. In his desperate attempt to recall the tune, he sings – predictably enough – Mendelssohn's 'Wedding March'. Gilbert and Iris are astonished when a piano in an adjoining room plays the forgotten theme in a solemn, stately fashion. The two young people are then shown into the room, where they recover, together with Miss Froy – who reaches out her arms to them and unites them in a single gesture – the lost, coded theme, which is their real Wedding March.

It is therefore after a final hole, a final tunnel, that Miss Froy's theme, which is really the theme of transmission, is able to resound in all its harmonized plenitude. To win Iris, Gilbert has had in fact not only to bring her another name (Harriman's tea) but also to run the risk of losing music (and of failing in his mission) by accepting a relationship with it which was no longer one of written, passive conservation but an oral, living thing. It is worth recalling that one man has already lost his life transmitting the message.

Finally, we should note that Hitchcock, consistent in this regard with his own intuition that a McGuffin is a mere nothing, takes good care not to give us the *translation of the musical message* – of what is, in fact, a cipher of destiny.

Notes

1. 'The Message? It's a tune. It contains a code, of course. I want you to memorize it.'

4

A Father Who Is Not Quite Dead

MLADEN DOLAR

We are watching a wife watching her husband: is he a murderer?
The basic pattern is extremely simple, yet it can encompass the
whole complexity of the drama of the gaze.

First of all, throughout the film our gaze is delegated to another
gaze: we watch somebody who is watching, we see only through
Lina's eyes and we see nothing outside her horizon. We do not
possess additional information to judge her 'objectivity'. But the
bearer of this gaze, being all the time in the centre of the story, does
not act as befits the heroine (at least during the last two-thirds of the
film, after her marriage against her father's will). Watching is her
principal activity: she is there, inert and passive, marking every
scene with her gaze full of worries, suspicions and fears. She is
watching, but she does not see.[1] 'They have eyes, yet they do not
see' – the biblical motto could stand at the head of almost every
Hitchcock film; but not seeing is the condition of the *mise-en-scène* of
the gaze.

Hitchcock's obsession with the gaze is omnipresent in his films,
but *Suspicion* presents it in a particularly poignant way. The same
pattern is later continued and radicalized in *Rear Window*, where
Jefferies (James Stewart), just like Lina, is doomed to inactivity,
quite literally immobile with his broken leg, reduced to a being of
the gaze, confronted with the enigmatic signs in the building
opposite his rear window. He, too, watches, but does not see: is it a
murder or just a series of coincidences? The same basic situation has

two different outcomes: in *Rear Window*, it turns out that the murder was real; in *Suspicion*, it turns out that the lethal signs were deceptive, they are retroactively transformed into a series of coincidences. The suspicion supporting the gaze (or the gaze supporting the suspicion) was justified in one case and unjustified in the other.

Rear Window is the Hitchcockian presentation of the Panopticon, his illustrative application of Bentham and Foucault. Stewart, in his armchair, is placed in the central watchtower where he is able to supervise the flats on the other side; the flats are situated like the cells in the Panopticon, constantly exposed to the controlling gaze. But what distinguishes Hitchcock from Bentham is the fact that the disposition works in reverse: in the Panopticon, the prisoners live in permanent fear of the ubiquitous gaze which they do not see, but which nothing escapes (and the disposition finally works equally well if there is nobody in the tower); whereas here, the inhabitants live their quiet ordinary lives (eating, sleeping, dancing, partying, making love and killing each other); Stewart, on the contrary, lives in constant fear in his watchtower – the fear that something will escape him. His problem is how to make his gaze ubiquitous (and the essential actually does escape him: he is asleep at the time of the murder). So the inhabitants are not the prisoners of the gaze of the Other, with its invisible omnipresence; it is rather the Supervisor who is the prisoner, the prisoner of his own gaze – a gaze that does not see.

Lina, too, is all the time confronted with opaque and ambiguous traces. She is silently awaiting the worst – a real contrast to her husband, who is bursting with activity, full of new ideas and projects. The Hitchcockian presentation of the gaze is based on the axiom that there is no good measure of the gaze: one sees either too much or not enough. Or rather: one sees too much and not enough at the same time. The drama of the gaze is triggered off when, by coincidence, the gaze catches something too much, something beyond the 'normal' field of vision; but this elusive surplus of visibility renders the whole vision non-transparent, ambiguous and threatening. Seeing too much entails blindness, the opacity of vision.

The traces arouse the suspicion, they remain enigmatic – that is, they demand new traces that would clarify them. The suspicions increase and decrease and we hope to find an unambiguous trace, a steadfast signifier which would stop the gliding and determine the sense. Yet this deferring movement, maintaining and nourishing the suspicion, cannot stop until the last scene. The ambiguity and indetermination of sense is the substance of the whole film. As spectators, however, we know from the outset that the ambiguity has to be dissolved and that in the end an unequivocal sense must emerge. Cary Grant is either a murderer or just a petty swindler – there is no third way out, and the suspense is an anticipated certainty of solution one way or the other.

It is well known that the final solution in the film is opposite to the one in the book, *Before the Fact* by Francis Iles. In the book, 'accessory before the fact' is Lina, who drinks the poisoned glass of milk of her own 'free will', out of her love for Johnnie, consciously accepting the fate of the victim. Hitchcock told Truffaut that he wanted to maintain the original ending, but with an additional twist: before drinking the milk, Lina would write a letter to her mother explaining Johnnie's guilt, and ask him to post it. In the last scene, we would see Johnnie happily throw the letter into the letterbox. Such an ending was prevented by Hollywood conventions – according to Hitchcock – which could not possibly tolerate Cary Grant as a murderer.[2] The only trace left in the film is Hitchcock's cameo appearance: we see him throwing a letter into a letterbox, thus assuming himself the part of the bearer of the lethal message.

The interpreters have either regretted the compromise which left us with a happy-ending cliché instead of a much more radical solution, or pretended that speculating about a different ending is just another of Hitchcock's gags, and that only the present outcome is consistent with the rest (this is also Truffaut's opinion[3] as well as Donald Spoto's[4]). Does one have to come down on one side or the other? Which ending is more appropriate? There is a third solution, however: some interpreters have remarked that the decision in one direction or the other is not really very important to the substance of the film (Raymond Durgnat: 'It seems that one way or the other there is no gain or loss as to the artistic depth'[5]). If we accept this view, we have to face the following paradox: that what one decides about the sense of the whole film is finally unimportant. Whether suspicion is grounded or not doesn't really change much, it has no major consequences for the substance of the film. From the point of view of its basic disposition, it is ultimately irrelevant whether Cary Grant was a murderer or just a small-time crook. Hitchcock knew very well that the *enjeu* of the plot is just an empty point, a McGuffin insignificant in itself; and so the final 'quilting point', although conferring sense, can be irrelevant for the effectiveness of the film. Yet a McGuffin can remain empty or entirely tautological, whereas the ending has to be filled up, it must resolve the matter in one of the two possibilities, even if it does not matter which. Whatever the solution, it always retroactively creates the illusion that precisely this ending was inevitable and the only logical one.

Since the ending cannot remain empty (as a McGuffin can), it also brings about a certain effect of disappointment. The suspicion is confirmed or rejected; the suspense turns into certainty. The disappointment is structural: it stems from the fact that *there is no final signifier which could match the gaze*, the bearer of the whole film – no signifier could resolve that suspended and anxious status of the subject, confronted with opaque traces and reduced to the gaze. The final signifier necessarily thwarts expectations. Fixing the sense dissolves the in-between status of the subject suspended between enigmatic traces. Sense as definitive, positive and irrevocable dissipates those intermediate, gliding and never fully existing entities: suspicion, gaze, suspense. The problem of the ending is that the alternative between the two solutions seemed to be exhaustive, yet what it did not cover was the evasive oscillation between the two; suspicion, as the substance of the film, was betrayed either way. The subject depended upon it: Lina existed, she had *being*, only in so far as the *sense* did not arise – that is, as long as the traces remained opaque. So if, in the end, there is no successful representation of that subject, is disappointment unavoidable? How could one conclude the film at all? Is every ending inadequate?

Let us confront the problem from another angle, through a famous literary example. The comparison with Henry James's 'The Turn of the Screw' has been suggested by Donald Spoto,[6] and the formal parallel seems to be evident: the young governess, the subject of suspicion, telling her story in the first person (let us leave aside James's complex narrative stratagems), is also constantly confronted with enigmatic traces, yet we are never certain, and we are never to learn, whether she is right or wrong: does she see phantoms and try to implicate the two children in her madness, or is she the only one to see the terrible truth? Is the evil to be situated in her or in the children and their complicity with Peter Quint and Miss Jessel? The ambiguity persists until the end, and we are never certain what is actually going on. We see only through the governess's eyes, and we never get unequivocal additional information. The persisting fascination of the story is based on the fact that James does not provide us with a clue to interpretation; he does not dissolve the mystery. Both interpretations remain possible, and he only sends us back to our own oscillating status of the subject without offering us support. It is either a ghost story about the link between childish innocence and radical evil, or a psychological thriller about the delusions of an obviously 'sexually frustrated' young woman (remember the mystical relationship with her employer, etc.). To decide for one or the other would be to miss the point: instead of determining the sense, James shifts the dilemma on to the reader. For that reason, this short story has remained a stimulus to 'interpretative delirium', an inexhaustible source of fascination.[7] It is not, perhaps, a coincidence that Hitchcock himself, at a certain point in his career, considered making a film based on 'The Turn of the Screw' (I am not quite sure whether one should be glad or sorry that he did not do it).

Hitchcock's solution with the ending in *Suspicion* seems, in comparison, rather unrefined and unconvincing, somehow patched up in the last minute of the film. Yet even as it is, it is less simple and more ambiguous than it seems. Although it clearly establishes sense and dissipates suspicion, it opens up another kind of ambiguity as to the status of the object. Since it turns out that suspicion was unfounded, the question arises what has been nourishing it in the first place. Factually unfounded, it is founded in something else.

Here, we have to go back to the beginning to remind ourselves that suspicion has been placed, from the very outset, in an Oedipal situation. Lina is overwhelmed with suspicions after the death of her father, General MacLaidlaw. She has married against his will and the only thing he bequeaths her is his portrait, which guarantees his massive presence after his death. And it is a portrait that actually moves when Johnnie addresses it, a father who is not quite dead. If Lina oscillates in her suspicions, she is on the other hand as though transfixed by the fatherly presence; her floating is conditioned by her transfixion. Borde and Chaumeton[8] had no hesitation in ranking *Suspicion* as a 'crime movie', a film centred around a murder, although technically there is no murder in sight. But the classification is quite appropriate: the murder in question is undoubtedly the murder of the father. It was easy to contradict the father while he was alive – the General who decrees at the beginning: 'Lina will never marry; she is not the type'; it was easy to falsify his verdict, but it is much harder to face his heavy absence, his silence, the absence of a decree; and this weight is the basis of suspicion.

Lina's passivity is symptomatic. She never seriously tries to convince somebody else, for example – in contrast to the governess in 'The Turn of the Screw', who constantly tries to persuade Mrs Grose, that microcosm of society and received opinion. Lina's suspicions are silent and private, confined to her solitude. But perhaps what she fears most is that they will turn out to be unfounded, that others will dissipate them (like her friend Isobel: 'Nonsense, Johnnie wouldn't hurt a fly'). So the ending retroactively offers another interpretation of suspicion: what Lina is most afraid of is Johnnie's innocence; her principal fear is that there is no reason for fear. Her anxiety is that she will have to accept Johnnie without the attenuating suspicion, without the benefit of the shadow of a doubt. Her anxiety is not anxiety over a possible loss, but rather that there will be no occasion for this loss. It stems not from a dreadful uncertainty but from a threatening loss of uncertainty. She fears the worst, and it happens.

The whole film could be summed up in the tenacious ambiguity of one sentence, but in French, since it does not work in English: '*Elle craint que Johnnie ne soit un assassin*'. The ambiguity is centred in one word: *ne*. The English equivalent could be either: 'She fears that Johnnie is a murderer' or : 'She fears that Johnnie is not a murderer'. Lacan has often pondered on the strange function of that French curiosity, the '*ne explétif*', the expletive negative particle which occurs with verbs of fear and has no real function – except that the subject of desire becomes strangely embodied in its ambiguity: what is it that s/he really fears?[9] That is where 'the desire which constitutes the ambivalence proper to the unconscious',[10] the presence of the subject of enunciation, comes to light.

The spectator and Lina are thus placed in an inverse symmetry: the spectator knows that the situation will be resolved in one of the two possible ways, although s/he doesn't know which and has to wait till the end; Lina plunges into suspicion knowing the solution, but postponing the moment of clarification as long as possible. The paradox of the scene with the glass of milk – one of Hitchcock's anthological shots – is that Lina could shake off the suspicions: if Johnnie were really a murderer, she could prove it only with her own death. She remains reduced to the anxious gaze, since any action would disturb her delicate balance, and she doesn't drink the milk because she is certain she will survive and will thus be left without an escape. In the end, the flight to her mother's house fails as well: Johnnie explains himself on the way and the happy future is unavoidable. In other words, if the ending seems disappointing, it is even more so for the heroine.

Suspicion thus develops two different logics of subjectivity. In the first, we deal with a floating, gliding, unplaceable subject which cannot be reduced to any global interpretation, with a constant in-between – with the subject of suspicion, uncertainty and suspense, present in the gaze. The second is the subject of certainty, the trans-fixed subject: here suspicion is the way to escape or postpone that certainty, to disavow the fixation. The subjectivity can be maintained as long as the floating persists, but in the first case in search of the certainty which would liberate her from suspicion, while in the second case fleeing the certainty which would be the end of in-between. On the one hand, the certainty appears as the remedy against the subject's predicaments; on the other, it appears as a catastrophe against which the subject's predicaments offer the best remedy. The second subjectivity is inserted in the first and thus casts a suspicious light on the whole. The suspicion itself becomes suspicious, not just the opacity of the events, and this ambivalence is shifted on to the spectator.

Notes

1. There is a traditional pattern where activity implies a certain blindness, and passivity makes it possible to see clearly – Fanny, the famous passive heroine of Jane Austen's *Mansfield Park*, is the only one to see clearly in the moral muddle, but at the price of her inactivity. Here, passivity does not help.

2. François Truffaut, *Hitchcock*, London: Panther 1969, p. 164.

3. See François Truffaut, 'Un trousseau de fausses clés', *Cahiers du cinéma* 39, 1954.

4. See Donald Spoto, *The Art of Alfred Hitchcock*, New York: Doubleday 1976, p. 116.

5. Raymond Durgnat, *The Strange Case of Alfred Hitchcock*, London: Faber & Faber 1974, p. 178. See also Stephen Heath, 'Droit de réponse', in Raymond Bellour, ed., *Le Cinéma américain* II, Paris: Flammarion 1980, pp. 87–93.

6. Spoto, p. 119.

7. Let me point out just O. Mannoni, 'Le tour de vis', in *Clefs pour l'Imaginaire*, Paris: Editions du Seuil 1969; and Shoshana Felman, 'Henry James: folie et interprétation', in *Folie et la chose littéraire*, Paris: Editions du Seuil 1978, where one can find an excellent overview of critiques.

8. Raymonde Borde and Etienne Chaumeton, *Panorama du film noir américain*, Paris: Editions de Minuit 1955, p. 38.

9. See Jacques Lacan, *The Four Fundamental Concepts of Psycho-Analysis*, Harmondsworth: Penguin 1979, pp. 56–7; also Jacques Lacan, *Ecrits: A Selection*, London: Tavistock 1977, p. 298.

10. Jacques Lacan, *Ecrits*, Paris: Editions du Seuil 1966, p. 664.

5

Notorious

PASCAL BONITZER

What matters in *Notorious* is not the fact that there are some bottles of wine filled with sand ('ore'), but that the wine is in the cellar; that the cellar door is locked; that the key is in the husband's possession; that the husband is in love with his wife; that she herself is in love with another; and that the third party wishes to know what is in the cellar.

Hitchcock claims that the McGuffin (in this case, the bottles of uranium) is in itself of no importance, a mere nothing. If one were then to ask what such a device were for, the answer would be that it serves to set the story going or, more precisely, to bring desire into play, and to make it circulate. A McGuffin may be defined as an object of desire – indeed, the quintessential object of desire, still more so because it traverses a space whose nature is architectural or, in other words, dramatized.

Anyone daring to go down to the cellar runs the most appalling risk. This is true of *Notorious*, and of *Psycho* likewise (perhaps to an even greater degree) – the two films by Hitchcock in which (it is worth noting in passing) the face of the mother is most terrible.

The majority of films made today disregard architecture. Scenarios are written, as is only to be expected, for actors, and are rarely based upon architectural factors. Hitchcock, however, used to request multiple photographs of the sets in which the action of his films was to unfold. He was a hyperrealist who had everything reconstructed, in the most minute detail, in the studio. What Hitchcock took seriously, what was deep, complex and disturbing in his work, was precisely that which limits depth in the theatre – namely, the set.

The set in Hitchcock is more than just a mere set; rather, it is a labyrinth in which everyone – characters, director and audience – loses and finds themselves, in the intensity of their emotions.

This is why the characters by themselves have a fabricated, conventional, often artificial quality. In my view, it is also why Hitchcock's films have tended to meet with such a poor critical reception when first released. An opinion expressed in 1948 by Eric Rohmer – in fact one of the most admiring interpreters of Hitchcock's *œuvre* – will probably strike today's readers as astoundingly inappropriate:

> The deliberate dryness of the treatment may well, in the last analysis, constitute the real originality of *Notorious* ... but one can also see why it should, in general, have proved such a deep disappointment to the critics, an expression that seems, in relation to the content of the film, so throwaway could not help but betray the fundamental weakness of Ben Hecht's scenario.[1]

Today, by contrast, we are impressed by the power and efficacy of the scenario, and by the mounting intensity bestowed upon it by the staging. We should, however, bear in mind that the European public in 1948 (which, in other respects, was undoubtedly more discriminating than that of today), not to speak of the critics, not only took Nazism more seriously than Hitchcock, but was just then discovering Italian neo-realism and immersing itself in existentialism. If Hitchcock's films were indeed characterized by a 'dryness', it was because his was an art of structures, which demanded that 'cinema' take precedence over all else, over any notion of realism, and certainly over any existentialist effusions on the part of the protagonists. Indeed, Bergman is the filmmaker furthest removed from Hitchcock.

Where the characters in Hitchcock's films love, suffer or die, they do so by virtue of a specific occupation of space. Cinema in this respect constitutes a supplementary, mobile architecture, which duplicates the trajectories of the characters and reorders – or, if you like, 'tricks out' – the space of the set in terms of the emotions that are in play. In the review quoted from above, Rohmer observed that the originality of *Notorious* consisted in the invention of the mobile close-up. The characteristic 'affect' of the film is, likewise, claustrophobia, and Alicia's gradual poisoning actually evokes that condition. Movement invariably proceeds in the same direction, from further away to closer up, as in the famous tracking shot on the key to the cellar, concealed by Alicia in the sequence at the reception.

Movement from further away to closer up is perhaps Hitchcock's characteristic device, and its erotic connotations are self-evident. If you set aside the concern with espionage, *Notorious* is ostensibly a love story. Sebastian loves Alicia, who loves Devlin. Yet love is clearly not the 'subject' of the film, but is rather the pretext for a perverse erotic situation in which Alicia, treated sadistically twice over, brushes against death, and in which she never stops – quite literally – agonizing: first with what is represented (of desire or of anxiety), and then with the actual, throughout the film. She agonizes erotically, *for* the cinema.

Suspense is therefore a kind of perversion, a form of sickness affecting not only cinematographic duration (with its compression and dilation) but also objects and modes of behaviour. *Notorious* thus constitutes the application of a law which, at the other extreme of American cinema, Nicholas Ray, in *Larger than Life*, was to carry to its ultimate conclusion. The more familiar or banal an object or act is, the greater its capacity to inspire terror. We are concerned here with the ambiguity between the *heimlich* and the *unheimlich*. Thus, the action in *Notorious* revolves entirely around the vortex constituted by the act of 'going to look for wine in the cellar'. Going to look for wine in the cellar – an innocent enough action, one might suppose – is the very thing that Sebastian must be prevented from doing at all costs. The wine is obviously fake and has, as it were, a false bottom. As spies, Sebastian, Alicia and Devlin are also beings with false bottoms. What is interesting about *Notorious* is not espionage as such – a topic of which everyone, starting with Hitchcock, makes fun – but the hypocrisy, pretence, splitting and perversion that espionage implies.

The *unheimlich*, or the uncanny, occurs when a known object suddenly presents an unfamiliar aspect. It is the same, yet it is other.

153

Thus, Alicia reveals herself to be other than what she was for Sebastian, just as the bottle of wine suddenly becomes something else for Alicia, Devlin and the audience. Likewise, Sebastian suddenly reveals himself to be someone else (no longer the loving husband but a cold-blooded murderer) for Alicia, when she realizes that she is being poisoned.

The *unheimlich*, or that quality of disturbing familiarity (if one had to describe the effect in concrete terms, one would describe it as *a familiarity which withdraws*, the implications for the figure of the mother being readily discernible here), is indeed Hitchcock's object, and this is undoubtedly why the family – indeed, the bourgeois family – is the only social machine which interests him. The familiar object (the family object) invariably contains the figure of the murderous mother – which is why, in spite of the intrigue and the superficial melodrama, *Notorious* reminds one above all of *Psycho*.

Notes

1. Eric Rohmer, *La Revue du cinéma*, 1948.

6

The Fourth Side

MICHEL CHION

I

One of the chief difficulties with the scenario of *Rear Window* was, I imagine, that of making the audience share, throughout the film, in the acts of outright voyeurism in which the protagonists indulge. For, right up until the end, they were not endangered by the suspected murderer whose behaviour they were watching, and they were not even coming to anyone's defence, since the crime had already been committed when they began to take an interest in the man.

However, in the opening scene between Jeff (James Stewart) and his masseuse and nurse, Stella (Thelma Ritter), this difficulty is tackled head-on, when an unambiguous condemnation of voyeurism serves to cut the ground from beneath the audience's feet. The condemnation – 'we become a race of Peeping Toms' – serves in fact as a kind of authorization, and when the time comes, Stella will prove the most willing of all to enter into the game, and the most fertile in morbid imaginings about the murder committed in the flat opposite.

Yet there is something which is neither mentioned nor represented in the course of the film, and which actually cannot feature, since the whole functioning of the story rests upon its foreclosure. I refer here to the fourth side of the courtyard, to which James Stewart's studio flat belongs, for this fourth side must by rights comprise several additional flats, from which other people could

155

equally well have noticed the doings of Thorwald, the murderer, and the dramatic events which sometimes unfolded *when the window was open* – such as when Thorwald seized hold of Lisa (Grace Kelly), after she had infiltrated his flat, and was about to attack her. That scene is itself shot as if, opposite the three walls of the courtyard that we see continually both overall and in detail, there was only one flat and one window, that of James Stewart.

We should also note that there are two places in the flat which we never enter, and which we see Grace Kelly enter without ever following her. These are the bedroom and the kitchen, whose doors lead into the living-room.

These restrictions are justified from the outset by the convention that has been adopted of always seeing things from James Stewart's point of view. Since his leg is in plaster, he cannot walk and can therefore never leave the single living-room. We are not supposed to see any more of the room than he sees himself, although we are able to see him too – given the rule governing identification in the cinema – inscribed in the space in which his gaze freely circulates – that is to say, that of his living-room.

Here, the application of the convention governing point of view serves as an invitation to the whole audience to share the protagonist's little flat with him, while at the same time causing it to forget, as the characters in the film do, that there could be other flats on the same side of the courtyard, which might provide an equally good – and perhaps a better – vantage point for observing what is happening in Thorwald's flat.

The convention is breached at at least four points in the course of the film, one of which is wholly explicit and is paraded as such, while the others are more discreet. Let us begin with the latter, which generally go unnoticed. The first occurs right at the beginning, when James Stewart is asleep in his wheelchair; his head, bathed in sweat, lolls beside the windowsill, and *his back is turned to the courtyard.* The courtyard itself is waking to a typical New York dog day, and we traverse it with our gaze much as James Stewart hears it in his sleep, with its echoing din of sound from the radio, children crying, car horns and boat sirens, although he is not yet able to see it. At the same time, it appears to be a sort of extension of his dream-filled cranium.

We seem to escape a second time from James Stewart's point of view a little later in the film, when he is once again asleep and in much the same position. We then see, from his window, Thorwald go out at night with a mysterious woman in black.

Films which begin with a man waking up, and then adopt his point of view, have a certain charm. I am thinking here of Orson Welles's *The Trial*, *City of Women* and the central section of *The Aviator's Wife*, all films where it is the real world which appears oneiric. In fact, it seems fair to say that there is not really a shift in the point of view when the character is asleep and the action starts or proceeds without him.

In *Rear Window*, space in fact assumes the wholly imaginary form of a cone, the apex of which is constituted by James Stewart's living-room (or, if you like, by his cranium, as he lies in a horizontal position with his back to the window) and which then opens out on to the courtyard and, beyond it, the world. The audience has always to forget that James Stewart's little flat cannot be all that there is facing the huge courtyard.

There are, however, two moments in the film when we leave the room, and therefore catch sight of the 'forgotten' fourth side. Indeed, we see it right at the end, when Stewart is thrown out of the window and falls into the courtyard, but the cutting is so fragmented and the situation so intense that we are unable to appreciate what its discovery implies (and, if my memory serves me well, there are no lights on, or other signs of occupation, on the fourth side).

The other 'sortie' – which has been much remarked upon, as Hitchcock had indeed intended – was the episode of the little dog's death. One evening, the retired, childless couple living on one of the upper storeys discovers the corpse of their 'beloved child', stretched out on the ground below. The old lady screams, weeps and anathematizes ('Why can't we love one another?'), bringing the whole microcosm of the courtyard to their windows and balconies – from the newly-weds, who for a brief moment forsake the conjugal bed, and 'Miss Lonely Hearts' on the ground floor, to the guests at the 'party' given by the young composer, and so on (in fact everyone with the sole exception, obviously enough, of Thorwald).

'It is the only moment in the film' – Truffaut observed to Hitchcock, who agreed – 'in which the staging changes point of view; we leave Stewart's flat, the camera is placed in the courtyard, seen from several different angles, and the scene becomes strictly objective.' It is in fact the first occasion upon which the occupants of the flats opposite are seen not from a distance, 'enlarged' and flattened out by a telephoto lens, but close up, in a 'normal' perspective, and from angles which, as far as height is concerned, are not those appropriate to James Stewart's window. There is also an extraordinary shot, extremely brief, which shows us *the whole courtyard*. In fact, we see only that part of the courtyard which faces Stewart's windows, but we are led to believe that we have seen it all, and this was the purpose of adopting this point of view which, though apparently objective, nevertheless forgot the fourth side. It is highly probable that this sequence's muddled feeling of unanimity – which is, moreover, very moving – was designed to convince us that the courtyard had gathered together and that we had seen all of it, and to leave us insufficient time to assemble and give substance to our awareness of a fourth side.

An exclusion that is so radical, and so crucial to the working of the film, may perhaps be related to the observations made by Jean-Pierre Oudart in his articles on 'Suture'[1] regarding the conjuring away of a fourth side, which serves to found the form of cinema which he terms 'subjective'.

I

The use of sound, a subject upon which we could say a great deal, obviously serves to focus our attention upon the courtyard. The sounds we hear from the radio, from muffled snatches of conversation, from children's games, from a piano, from the street and the town, are all designed to be referred to what we see opposite. But there is at least one sound, which plays a role that is all the more secret and significant for having no connection to any tenant opposite and is therefore, in relation to the others, out of place: the scales sung by an invisible singer. I like to think that this feminine voice contributes to this everyday and localized musical and sonorous texture, which issues from the courtyard as if it were a huge ditch of sounds, a free element, which cannot be placed.

It is in fact one of the monotonous sequences of this invisible singer
that we hear on the first evening, before the arrival, silent and unexpected, of Grace Kelly, and immediately before the marvellous and
unsettling silence which literally *closes in* on the kiss of the two lovers, in
this astonishing and extremely well prepared reflux of sonorous waves
which have unceasingly broken below James Stewart's window since
the beginning of the film.

Just as Godard, in *Carmen*, 'opens' and 'closes' the sound of the sea
at will, so Hitchcock freely opens and closes the sound of the courtyard,
depending upon whether he needs to direct James Stewart's attention
(and that of the audience) towards the exterior, or, conversely, if he
wishes to 'close off' the stage on to the little theatre of living-room and
on to the stage of Lisa and Jeff's intimate household.

The reference to the theatre is by no means gratuitous, for
Grace Kelly, in order to compensate James Stewart for ruining his
'play', offers herself, in her capacity as a woman, as a 'coming
attraction'.

Jeff's flat was clearly built and filmed as a four-sided stage, if you
will excuse the paradox. This impression is reinforced by the structure of its space, for the room is often shown widthways, with two
doors on the 'courtyard side' (which is not the same courtyard) and
the 'garden side', two doors leading into rooms which one cannot
enter – to which James Stewart's enforced immobility adds a further
element of theatrical constraint. It is worth recalling that *Rear
Window* was filmed immediately after *Dial M for Murder* (also with
Grace Kelly) and a few years after *Rope*, both of which were studies in
filmed theatre.

If, for the sake of argument, one were to imagine a stage version of
Rear Window, the characters would be facing us, and we would not
see the courtyard, the existence of which would be realized through
sound effects alone, and through the observations and reactions of
the characters in the flat. This would no doubt seem somewhat
contrived, but it has sometimes occurred in the theatre, as when the
actors in the play observe and comment upon a vast space (of some
battle or ceremony) which they see, looking out at the audience, and
thereby creating a kind of imaginary cone which begins at the stage
and flares out to infinity.

There is a sense in which, in *Rear Window*, the conjuring of the fourth side *around* James Stewart's flat serves to effect the strange and magical grafting of a theatre flat on to a cinema courtyard.

Note

1. *Cahiers du cinéma* 211, 212.

7

The Man Behind His Own Retina

MIRAN BOŽOVIČ

To see you is to love you.
(Bing Crosby)

Amare tuum est videre tuum.
(Nicholas of Cusa)

Rear Window is a film about the lust of the eye, this 'appetite of the eye', as Lacan specifies it in his *Seminar XI*,[1] and about the gaze, the form of appearance of the object *a* – *petit a* – within the visual field, which functions as the object of the appetite.

The film opens with the camera directly approaching the window, stopping exactly above the windowsill – that is, when the middle frame of a casement window literally covers the screen. This is a moment of complete identification between the view from the room and the view from the audience: we see all that can be seen from the room; whoever was in the room is now, as it were, in the audience and we have, as it were, entered his room. Once the view from the room fuses with our view, the camera slowly surveys the courtyard from right to left – this shot could be said to correspond to our first eye movement as a giant eye which has opened and looked around.

The movement of the camera directly towards the window which results in the coincidence of the window as a giant eye with the 'eye' of the camera – our own eye – depicts, from behind, a fusion of two looks, ours and Jeff's, a fusion that can be seen – this time from the front – in *The Wrong Man*, when the face of the real offender, *the right man*, fuses with Henry Fonda's face, *the wrong man*; as well as in *Psycho*, when Norman's morbid smile reveals the clenched teeth – that is to say, the moment his dead mother comes to see through his eyes.

That the window we are looking through functions virtually as an eye is evident from the fact that the room itself functions as a *camera obscura* – what unfolds in the room on this side of the window is precisely the inverted image of what unfolds beyond the window of the flat on the opposite side of the courtyard – the Thorwalds' flat. As Hitchcock told Truffaut: 'On one side of the yard you have the Stewart–Kelly couple, with him immobilized by his leg in a cast, while she can move about freely. And on the other side there is a sick woman who's confined to her bed, while the husband comes and goes.'[2] Both invalids are likewise victims of their mobile partners: as Lars seals the fate of his wife, so Lisa weaves Jeff into her plans; also, it is Lisa who crosses the courtyard to enter Thorwald's flat, and it is Thorwald who has come from the opposite side to Jeff's.

As spectators we are placed behind the retina of the giant eye viewing the inverted images which appear on it – that is to say, along with Jeff, we are occupying the same place as that of the bearded man in Descartes's engraving from his *Optics*, placed in a totally darkened room. Inserted in the hole in the front wall is 'the eye of a newly dead person', and if a freshly dismembered human body – or at least a head – is unavailable, then 'the eye of an ox or some other large animal'[3] will suffice. The dead eye peers at various objects lit up by the sun. Light comes into the room only through this eye. Looking at the back of the eye, says Descartes, 'you will see there, not perhaps without wonder and pleasure, a picture representing in natural perspective all the objects outside'[4] – that is, in the external world.

This experiment confirms, states Descartes, that 'the objects we look at do imprint quite perfect images of themselves on the back of our eyes'[5] – that retinal images adequately represent objects in the external world. It is Descartes's firm belief that we can assure ourselves of this by our own eyes. How? Merely by stepping out of the darkened room and comparing objects in the external world

with the retinal images we
have just seen on the back of
the dead eye.

Needless to say, the experiment fails, since the retinal
image can never be com-
pared to the object, to the
thing itself – in short, since
an imitation, a copy, can
never be compared to the
original. We can merely
compare *our* retinal image of
the object to *our* retinal image
of the image of the object
from the dead eye's retina.
Descartes's wonder is therefore inane and his pleasure
entirely unjustified: strictly
speaking, we are constantly
in a room such as Descartes's
bearded man is in – our own
eye *is* such a darkened room.
We can never step out, but
are forever entrapped in a
room in which we deal with
our retinal images only and
never with things themselves:
any comparison of our retinal

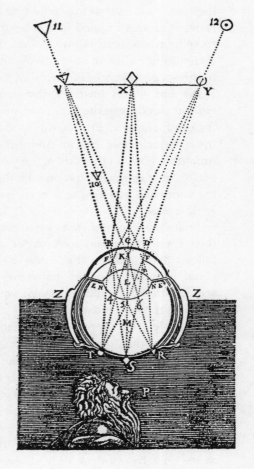

images to things themselves, to objects; of imitations, copies, to
originals; is illusory.

Precisely this impossibility of stepping out from the world of
imitations, copies and simulacra, is enacted in *Rear Window*. Jeff's
living-room, with its walls filled with photographs – imitations,
copies, simulacra – this room that Jeff cannot leave and is confined
to, corresponds to Descartes's room, to the eye as the darkened
room.

Condemned to this world of simulacra, Jeff is hence a man living
behind his own retina. The external world has become a spectacle in

his eyes. That everything unfolding beyond Jeff's window is a spectacle, is clearly implied in the beginning of the film, when we see three bamboo shades slowly raised, one after the other, revealing the scene, as in a theatre once the curtain is raised. Our understanding of the scene beyond Jeff's window as a spectacle is strengthened by Lisa's line whilst lowering the shades: 'show's over for tonight', cutting us off from the action on stage. What is the meaning of this theatre metaphor? For us, the spectators, the curtain has risen and the spectacle has begun: in our eyes the spectacle is what is unfolding both on this side of the window and on the other. For that reason, its meaning could only be that everything unfolding beyond the window *is also a spectacle in the eyes of the one in the room on this side of the window.*

Stella's suggestion that 'what people ought to do is get outside their own house and look in for a change', which immediately follows her statement that 'we've become a race of Peeping Toms', could be understood by Jeff merely as a demand to see himself seeing himself in the object viewed, the *tableau vivant*, which he observes through his window.

Since Jeff is trapped in his darkened room, in his own eye, he is, strictly speaking, occupying the absolute point of view – the point of view on which he can no longer take another, exterior point of view: from there one can go nowhere; it is simply not possible to step back and observe the point of view from which we have just been looking. The absolute point of view is a point of interiority which can never be externalized, a point from which we always look from inside out, a point we cannot possibly leave, a point from which we are unable to see ourselves but can only observe others – in a word, a point at which we can be nothing but voyeurs.

This intolerable condition of being entrapped in our own body, our own eye – or, as captured by another infamous voyeur, Norman Bates:

> 'I think that we're all in our private traps – clamped in them. And none of us can ever get out. We scratch and claw, but only at the air, only at each other. And for all of it, we never budge an inch.'

– that is, the unbearable experience of the absolute point of view – is strengthened by Jeff's being bound to his wheelchair because his leg is in a cast. Referring to his cast as a 'plaster-cocoon' from which he would like to escape, he perceives himself as a caterpillar trapped in a silky shell. The comparison to insects is definitely not incidental, since the absolute point of view is ultimately embodied by insects. Not only can insects not see themselves, their own bodies[6] – some can even not look straight ahead: owing to the structure of their compound eyes, they see an object – a candle, for example – only from a certain angle. This is the reason for their seemingly aimless flight: to reach the source of light they have to adjust their path to this constant angle, and it is only by way of the spiral pathway that they can eventually reach their destination.[7] It is obvious that these insects perceive the spiral pathway as 'straight', 'direct', as the

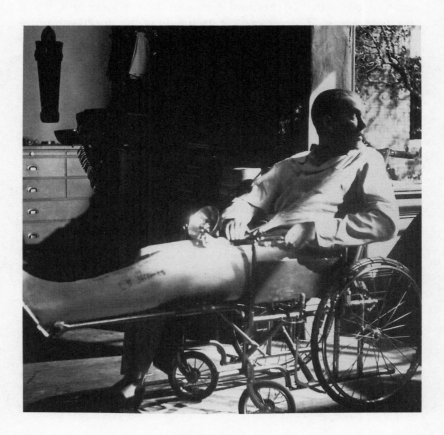

'shortest' way to the source of light, and one wonders if they would feel dizzy when flying straight ahead. Insects are surely those who most painfully experience the truth of Lacan's saying: 'I see only from one point, but in my existence I am looked at from all sides',[8] a saying which is merely a paraphrase of the unbearable experience of the absolute point of view.

Strictly speaking, Stella's suggestion is merely a Platonic paraphrase of the Delphic oracle, 'Know thyself': let us assume, says Plato, 'that instead of speaking to a man, it [i.e. the Delphic inscription] said to the eye of one of us, as a piece of advice – "See thyself"'.[9] How is that at all possible, since the eye cannot see itself?[10] An eye must look at an object, says Plato; by looking at it, it will see both the object and itself. That particular object is precisely the eye of someone else – that is, the third eye: once the eye looks at it, it will 'see itself seeing'. The eye can see itself only in the third eye's pupil – 'the thing wherewith *it* sees'. In Plato's words:

> if an eye is to see itself, it must look at an eye, and at that region of that eye in which the virtue of an eye [i.e. sight] is found to occur.[11]

It appears that Jeff has taken Stella's suggestion literally – as a Platonic paraphrase of the Delphic oracle: from that instant onwards he searches for that particular object, the third eye, in which he could, at the point from which the object itself, the eye, is gazing at him, 'see himself seeing'.

Thorwald's living-room window, functioning as an eye, offers itself as that particular object on the opposite side of the courtyard. How can a window function as an eye? How can a window gaze at us?

Let us recall the analysis of 'the split between the eye and the gaze' in Jean-Paul Sartre's *Being and Nothingness*. Sartre says that 'what *most often* manifests a gaze is the convergence of two ocular globes in my direction', and continues:

> But the gaze will be given just as well on occasion when there is a rustling of branches, or the sound of a footstep followed by silence, or the slight opening of a shutter, or a light movement of a curtain. During an attack men who are crawling through the brush apprehend as *a gaze*

to be avoided, not two eyes, but a white farmhouse which is outlined against the sky at the top of a little hill. . . . Now the bush, the farmhouse are not the gaze; they only represent the *eye*, for the eye is not at first apprehended as a sensible organ of vision but as the support for the gaze. They never refer therefore to the actual eye of the watcher hidden behind the curtain, behind a window in the farmhouse. *In themselves they are already eyes.* On the other hand neither is the gaze one quality among others of the object which functions as an eye, nor is it the total form of that object, nor a 'worldly' relation which is established between that object and me. On the contrary, far from perceiving the gaze *on* the objects which manifest it, my apprehension of a gaze turned toward me appears on the ground of the destruction of the eyes which 'gaze at me'. If I apprehend the gaze, I cease to perceive the eyes . . .[12]

Or, as Lacan, in his *Seminar I*, summarises Sartre:

I can feel myself under the gaze of someone whose eyes I do not see, not even discern. All that is necessary is for something to signify to me that there may be others there. This window, if it gets a bit dark, and if I have reasons for thinking that there is someone behind it, is straight-away a gaze.[13]

The scene evoked by both Sartre's and Lacan's words – but with a crucial difference between them: the window, according to Sartre, is an eye and not a gaze, whereas according to Lacan, it is a gaze – corresponds exactly to the scene in which Jeff stares into the darkness of Thorwald's window.

The idea of a window func-tioning as an eye or a gaze was not unknown to Hitchcock – he developed it in the 1920s in *The Lodger: A Story of the London Fog*. In a particular shot of a news van driving away, we see the heads of the driver and his mate through oval windows at the back of the car – that is, through *rear windows*. The two heads, the two dark blots, are silhouetted behind the illuminated oval windows, making them look like eyes. As the moving van sways, so do the heads in the oval windows – and since they sway more or less simultaneously, it appears as if eyeballs are moving in eye-sockets. Thus, the entire rear of the van resembles a face.[14]

Where is the gaze of the other, in the scene with a burning cigarette in the depth of Thorwald's window, according to Lacan, and where is it according to Sartre?

According to Sartre, this gaze is not on the object manifesting it, not on the window which is looking at us, and even less beyond the object, in the depth of the window, but *in front of it*. Sartre says: 'the other's gaze disguises his eyes; he seems to go *in front of them*'.[15] In a word, the gaze is upon us who have changed, the instant the window returns the gaze, from the subject of the gaze, from a voyeur, into the object of the other's gaze, into a voyeur seen. According to Sartre, we cannot see the gaze fastened upon us but can merely apprehend it upon ourselves – and we apprehend it at the expense of being blind to the object manifesting it, to the window/eye looking at us. An elementary reasoning lies behind the fact that for the gaze fastened upon us to be apprehended, blindness is required to the object manifesting it, to the window/eye looking at us: according to Sartre, we cannot simultaneously perceive the world and apprehend the gaze fastened upon us – we can do either one or the other. This is because, says Sartre, to perceive the world is to *gaze at* it, and to apprehend the gaze fastened upon us is not to apprehend the gaze-as-object; it is to be conscious of *being gazed at*.[16] As the subject of the gaze, I can also see the gaze of the other; the gaze of the other can also be the object – as long as the other's gaze is not directed upon me: once this occurs, it is no longer the gaze of the other which is the object, it is myself, the subject of the gaze, who becomes the object of the other's gaze. If it is true that once I apprehend the gaze I cease to see the eye looking at me – and vice versa: once I see the eye, the gaze disappears – then I have eyes so that I might not see that the other is gazing at me.

So, according to Sartre, Jeff would have to choose one of two alternatives – either he sees the window because it is not gazing back at him, or the window gazes at him and he cannot see it gazing – whereas according to Lacan, he can see both, the window and its gazing at him: the window is split into itself and the gaze *beyond*, *behind,* as a blot *in* the window. Rather than the Platonic illusion of perfect self-mirroring − that is, rather than Jeff 'seeing himself see himself' in the window, in this third eye − he sees − at the point of the gaze of the other, at the point from which the window itself looks back at him − the blot: the burning cigarette in the window.

Jeff sees the window − yet the window is already gazing at him; it is gazing back at him from the point from which he cannot see it, from the point to which he is, owing to the point of view he embodies, as it were, blind: 'I can never see properly, can never include in the totality of my field of vision, the point in the other from which it gazes back at me.'[17]

Thorwald's window is gazing back at Jeff, 'concerns him [*le regarde*]', in a different way from any other window in the courtyard. If any other window were to return a gaze, he would probably, the moment he apprehended the gaze, become an object − in the Sartrean terminology, his attitude towards all windows, *except Thorwald's*, is that of a 'nihilating subject'. Thorwald's window gazes back at him differently from any other because Jeff sees it in a different way: in it, there is something that intrigues him, something that all other windows lack, something that is 'in the window more than the window itself' and has always been of some concern to him − in short, the object-cause of his desire. *Faced with the window, Jeff can see himself only as the subject of desire.*

Jeff could have faced his desire earlier − when he fell into despair after the detective, Doyle, had persuaded him that Thorwald's hands were clean. At that moment he could have acknowledged his desire by way of elementary Cartesian 'mechanics of passions' according to which despair always reflects a desire, and by way of Lacan's formula 'man's desire is the desire of the Other'.[18] According to Descartes, despair is nothing but the extreme anxiety we experience when we realize that 'there is ... little prospect of our getting what we desire'.[19] How had Jeff had his desire in the palm of his hand? According to Lisa's words, he is 'plunged into despair' the moment it appears that 'the man didn't kill his wife': as man's desire is the desire of the Other, Jeff's despair that *there is little prospect of Thorwald's getting what he desires* − that is, of Thorwald's fulfilling his desire, killing his wife − reflects *Jeff's own* desire of ridding himself of Lisa, in one way or the other.

Rather than acknowledging his desire, Jeff persists in being a nihilating subject. As well as being blind to his desire, he moralizes even about voyeurism precisely as Sartre's voyeur does – the one who, when peeping through a keyhole, is surprised by the gaze of the other: it is probably not a coincidence that Stella refers to Jeff's long-focus lens as a 'portable keyhole'. How exactly does Sartre's *voyeur vu* moralize? What I have been doing to other people they can do to me too – as a voyeur I myself can be seen. Gazing at another subject, I endeavour to determine him/her as the object; yet that subject can also, in his/her turn, deny me my status of subject and determine me as object. Now it is I who am the object which the other is gazing at and judging – and appearing in the eyes of the other, as an object, makes me ashamed. In a word, 'being-seen-by-the-other' is the truth of 'seeing-the-other',[20] says Sartre.

And Jeff? 'I wonder if it's ethical to watch a man with binoculars and a long-focus lens.... 'Course, they can do the same thing to me, watch me like a bug under a glass if they want to.' Jeff has been watching his neighbours as an entomologist would observe insects with a magnifying glass, whereas he is now aware of the fact that they could have been doing the same to him – watching him like an insect under a glass. Hence, in this Sartrean perspective, Jeff is a predator aware of the fact that his prey can turn into a predator, and he into prey.

The instant the blot looks at Jeff from the window, however, he, as a predator, becomes *his own* prey: prey of his own gaze, like the entomologist who becomes prey of his own gaze when one of his specimens returns him the gaze from its eyespots. According to Lacan, mimicry is not only a spectacle that insects stage for the gaze of the other: by means of the eyespots on their wings, insects themselves *reproduce, as it were, the gaze of the other.*

So, although Jeff had his desire in the palm of his hand, he did not acknowledge it. As we have seen, he could easily have attained it working backwards from his despair. Thus, he must literally confront it when the window returns the gaze. This blot, this point from which the window is gazing back at him, is the cigarette burning in the darkness.

The Hitchcockian blot at its purest is to be found in the photograph of the car-race accident we are shown at the very beginning.

This photograph virtually epitomizes Holbein's 'The Ambassadors'. As in Holbein's painting, we see in the photograph a singular object  which is literally suspended, an object that 'does not fit', that 'sticks out'. Like Holbein's skull, this object is also oblique, extended and slightly blurred; yet Holbein's anamorphic skull can never be seen straight ahead but only from a specific angle – the skull therefore already presupposes the point of view of an insect – whereas in the photograph from *Rear Window*, the oblique, distorted object turns Jeff himself into an insect. That is to say, the blot in Holbein's painting can, from a certain angle, be captured as a death's-head, whereas Jeff, whilst eyeing the blot we see on the photograph, was literally confronted, eye to eye, with death itself: this blot could easily have been the last sight Jeff would ever see. Confronted with the blot – which is, of course, the spinning wheel flying directly into the camera, into the photographer – Jeff would probably have resembled a rat preying upon a moth which, by spreading its wings, returns the gaze of an owl – that is, reproduces the last sight the rat ever sees.

Just as the spinning wheel could not be observed from a safe distance, just as it undermined the photographer's position as a 'neutral', 'objective' observer – just as the wheel is the point at which Jeff is already caught in the photograph, the point at which he, as photographer, is himself photographed – according to Lacan, the gaze which is outside, on the side of the viewed object, is 'the instrument through which ... I am *photo-graphed*'[21] – so the burning cigarette is the point at which Jeff, as a voyeur, is already included in the viewed object, in the window. Just as the rat is already included in the gaze of the moth's eyespots – in the eyes of those predators that do not prey upon the moth these eyespots are, of course, 'blind' – so is Jeff already included in the gaze of Thorwald's window: in the eyes of those voyeurs – the occupants of the flats on the fourth, 'forgotten' side[22] – who, rather than prying upon an uninteresting old man, pry upon attractive, young 'Miss Torso', Thorwald's window is of course 'blind'. A moth's eyespots are therefore made to 'see' only in the eyes of the rat preying upon it; Thorwald's window is made to 'see' only in the eyes of Jeff's interested prying upon him – in a word, *the blot can return the gaze only to the subject of desire.* It is only the subject of desire, the desiring subject, who is able to see that the blot is gazing back at him, since the blot materializes precisely the object-cause of his desire – that is, the unfathomable X which 'concerns [*regarde*]' the subject, which animates his desire. The blot cannot be made to 'see' in the eyes of the Sartrean 'nihilating subject'; here, the confrontation, eye to eye, between the subject's viewing and the window's gaze is impossible: if the subject sees the window, the latter – *precisely because the subject sees it* – cannot gaze back at him, and vice versa.

We have already mentioned that Jeff, who is impatiently awaiting the day he will rid himself of his cast, sees himself as a caterpillar trapped in a cocoon. More precisely, Jeff sees himself as an insect undergoing the process of the transformation, the metamorphosis, into a fully grown insect, emerging out of the cocoon as a moth or a butterfly. This entomological metaphor is by no means coincidental. From the Ancient Greeks to this very day there has been something fascinating, yet ominous and uncanny, about the theme of the transformation of insects – in particular, the metamorphosis of a chrysalis into a butterfly. In Greek poetry, as D'Arcy W. Thompson said, 'allusions to the butterfly are scanty and rare'.[23] Even nowadays, entomologists – for example Pierre Louis[24] – are bewildered by the apparently inexplicable fact that the first entomologist, Aristotle, in his *Zoological Researches* – in which, as a rule, most species were given exhaustive, detailed description – when describing the metamorphosis of a chrysalis into a butterfly, found himself at a loss for words.

So what is it that is so fascinating, yet ominous and uncanny, about this theme? Let us look at Aristotle's description of the evolution of butterflies from a chrysalis, as interpreted by D'Arcy W. Thompson. On the one hand the chrysalis that does not eat, lies stiff and motionless, is, as it were, dead; in a word, the chrysalis is a corpse, which is evident from its Greek name, *nekydallos*, 'a little corpse'. On the other hand, however, the butterfly that emerges after a certain period is named *psyche*, the soul.[25] The thing that took Aristotle's breath away, whilst he observed the metamorphosis of the chrysalis into the butterfly, was that he witnessed the soul literally leaving the dead body.

Similar fascination with the metamorphosis of chrysalis into butterfly is found in Thomas Harris's *The Silence of the Lambs*, which cannot be fully grasped without reference to Aristotle's account. In this novel, a transsexual, having been denied transsexual surgery because of his criminal past, becomes a serial killer of women. Why? By being denied transsexual surgery, he is in fact denied *the transformation of the body* which would always be animated by one and the same soul – so he understandably chooses the only alternative available: *the transmigration of the soul* from one body to the other. He kills women with the intention of inhabiting their bodies. In the mouth of his flayed victims he inserts the chrysalis of an insect – the death's-head moth. In his eyes the victim is now only an apparently dead chrysalis which, after a certain period of time, will come alive again as a moth; whereas he, having clothed himself in her skin, will – the moment the moth flies out of the victim's mouth: the moment the soul leaves the dead body – come to inhabit her body: *transform himself into a woman.* Moreover, by intervening in the transformation cycle, the murderer has committed the 'perfect crime': the victim, as her soul, will live on as a moth marked by a skull on its back, whereas he, having renounced his own body, will thereafter animate her body.

How is this theme of the transformation, the metamorphosis of insects, to be understood in *Rear Window*? In at least three intertwined ways.

First: it can be understood as an allegory of the Resurrection. This is the way it has most often been understood. For example, in Malebranche: just as a caterpillar encases herself in her tomb and apparently dies, coming alive after a certain period without her body disintegrating, so has Christ died and been resurrected without his body being subjected to decay; just as a caterpillar no longer crawls on the ground but flies as a butterfly – according to Malebranche the caterpillar comes alive in 'an entirely spiritual body', a body which is in itself a soul: as a butterfly, *psyche* – so no longer is Christ 'crawling' around Judaea but ascends to heaven,[26] and so forth.

173

Judging by the photograph of the spinning wheel flying directly into the camera, by which the photograph was taken at the last moment, Jeff was literally eyeing death – he was, so to say, already dead – yet he survived miraculously. Even in Jeff's eyes it is obvious that, having rid himself of his cast, he will rise from the dead, for the cast is for him the same thing as a cocoon is for Malebranche: *a tomb* – at a given moment we are able to see, on the cast, the following 'epitaph': 'here lie the broken bones of L.B. Jefferies'.

Second: it has already been said that Jeff – who, because of his cast (his cocoon) is bound to a wheelchair, confined to his living-room, condemned to a fantasy world – represents a metaphor of man's entrapment in his own body, in his own eye: the objects in the external world can never be seen immediately, by themselves, but always by way of retinal images, and so on. In a certain philosophical tradition, the inaccessibility of objects in the external world was conceived along the same lines; let us again recall Malebranche: the reason our soul 'does not see [the objects] by themselves' lies in the fact that 'it is not likely, that [it] should leave the body to stroll about ... in order to behold all these objects'.[27] Just as in Malebranche's fantasy the soul, which would not be entrapped in the body, would stroll about and behold otherwise inaccessible objects in the external world as they are in themselves, so will Jeff, once rid of his cast – as the butterfly shuffles off its cocoon, or the soul its body – return from his sealed-off fantasy world: from the world of imitations, copies, simulacra, embodied in his room, into the previously inaccessible real world, amongst people, and so forth.

Third: the very theme of the transformation of insects reveals the clue to the Hitchcockian critique of voyeurism.

Once again – Jeff is a chrysalis, and 'the significance of the chrysalis is' – as remarked by Dr Hannibal Lecter, the psychiatrist from *The Silence of the Lambs* – 'change'.[28] A certain change is therefore awaiting Jeff – for now he is Gregor Samsa, who is going to bed and for whom an unpleasant surprise change is still waiting. What change? The change into an adult, sexually mature, winged insect – in a word, into an *imago*.

Both Gregor Samsa and Jeff will awaken as imagos. Gregor Samsa awoke as a giant insect, whereas Jeff 'awakes' as an image, a picture – which is precisely the original meaning of the Latin word *imago* – or, more precisely, will find himself *in* the picture, as a part of the *tableau vivant* he was viewing; as a spectator he will spot himself among the performers, he will become part of the spectacle he was previously following.

This transformation of the voyeur into the picture, of the spectator into the spectacle, will be accomplished with the help of somebody who himself has just stepped out of the picture, out of the spectacle: Thorwald, who will throw *Jeff* through the window. Even Jeff himself is aware of the fact that falling through the window actually means falling into the picture, into the spectacle: this is evident from his apparently senseless defence. He defends himself against the attacker by popping flashbulbs into his eyes, blinding him temporarily – therefore, *he does not want to be seen*, to become a part of the picture, of the spectacle, but desperately tries to maintain his position as a spectator. Simultaneously, he covers his eyes with his hand, so that he does not see – so that he does not see what? Precisely that Thorwald is nevertheless gazing at him, that *he is seen* – in short, that he is already part of the picture.

Thus Thorwald merely carries out what has already been the fact, although Jeff was not aware of it – if it is true that the picture was in his eye, then it is no less true that he himself was already in the picture.[29]

Therein consists the Hitchcockian critique of voyeurism, as articulated in *Rear Window*: *the voyeur himself is already in the picture*, he is searching for himself, for his own gaze in the picture; he is fascinated by his own presence, by his own gaze in it. That which attracts his attention in the picture is the blot that disrupts its consistency – and he is present in the picture precisely as the blot: 'if I am anything in the picture, it is always in the form of the screen, which I earlier called the stain, the spot',[30] says Lacan. If the picture were consistent, if it contained no blot, he would probably take no notice of it. Rather than by the picture itself, by its content, the voyeur is fascinated by his own presence, by his own gaze in it.

For the voyeur to exist at all, there must be some blot in the picture – if the blot were obliterated, the subject itself would be effaced. The Sartrean 'nihilating subject' exists in so far as the window *is not* gazing at him – the gaze of the other would objectivize him, would throw him back into an inert mass of the in-itself –

175

whereas the subject of desire exists in so far as the blot *is* gazing at him. This situation of the subject of desire facing the blot is perfectly rendered by the words of Nicholas of Cusa who, when placed in front of an icon of God, so craftily painted that wherever he placed himself it always gazed back at him, pronounced: 'I am because Thou dost look at me, and if Thou didst turn Thy glance from me I should cease to be'.[31]

The trap Hitchcock has set for Jeff, as well as for us, the spectators, could thus be epitomized by the formula of the Lacanian critique of voyeurism: *You want to see? Well, take a look – take a look at your own gaze!*

Notes

1. Jacques Lacan, *The Four Fundamental Concepts of Psycho-Analysis*, Harmondsworth: Penguin 1986, p. 115.
2. François Truffaut, *Hitchcock*, London: Panther 1969, p. 267.
3. *The Philosophical Writings of Descartes*, vol. 1, transl. J. Cottingham, R. Stoothoff and D. Murdoch, Cambridge: Cambridge University Press 1989, p. 166.
4. Ibid.
5. Ibid.
6. See Jean-Paul Sartre, *Being and Nothingness*, transl. H.E. Barnes, London: Methuen 1966, p. 358.
7. See D'Arcy W. Thompson, *On Growth and Form*, Cambridge: Cambridge University Press 1984, p. 178.
8. Lacan, *The Four Fundamental Concepts*, p. 72.
9. Plato, *Alcibiades I*, 132 d (transl. W.R.M. Lamb, The Loeb Classical Library, London: William Heinemann 1964, p. 209).
10. See Auguste Comte: 'The eye cannot see itself'; quoted from Sartre, p. 316.
11. Plato, *Alcibiades I*, 133 b (transl. Lamb, p. 211).
12. Sartre, pp. 257–8. Gaze/gazing substituted for look/looking (in the French original: *regard/regarder*).
13. Jacques Lacan, *The Seminar, Book I: Freud's Papers on Technique*, Cambridge: Cambridge University Press 1988, p. 215.
14. Truffaut, pp. 50–51.
15. Sartre, p. 258.
16. Ibid.
17. Slavoj Žižek, *Looking Awry: An Introduction to Jacques Lacan through Popular Culture*, Cambridge, MA: MIT Press 1991, p. 114.
18. Lacan, *The Four Fundamental Concepts*, p. 115.
19. René Descartes, *The Passions of the Soul*, in *Philosophical Writings*, p. 351.
20. Sartre, pp. 228, 257, 261.
21. Lacan, *The Four Fundamental Concepts*, p. 106.

22. See Michel Chion's chapter on *Rear Window* in this book, pp. 155–60.

23. D'Arcy W. Thompson, 'Aristotle the Naturalist', in *Science and the Classics*, Oxford: Oxford University Press 1940, pp. 62–3.

24. Pierre Louis, *Aristote: La découverte de la vie*, Paris: Hermann 1975, p. 117.

25. Thompson, 'Aristotle the Naturalist'.

26. Malebranche, *Entretiens sur la métaphysique et sur la religion*, ed. A. Robinet, *Oeuvres complètes*, XII–XIII, Paris: Vrin 1984, p. 274.

27. Malebranche, *The Search after Truth*, Book III, Part 2, ch. 1, transl. T.M. Lennon and P.J. Olscamp, quoted from *Berkeley*, Milton Keynes: Open University Press 1986, p. 79.

28. Thomas Harris, *The Silence of the Lambs*, London: Mandarin 1991, p. 157.

29. Lacan, *The Four Fundamental Concepts*, p. 96: 'No doubt, in the depths of my eye, the picture is painted. The picture, certainly, is in my eye.' The next sentence: *Mais moi, je suis dans le tableau* is incorrectly rendered by Alan Sheridan as 'But I am not in the picture', whereas it should read *But I, I am in the picture*.

30. Lacan, *The Four Fundamental Concepts*, p. 97.

31. Nicholas of Cusa, *The Vision of God*, transl. E. Gurney-Salter, in *The Portable Medieval Reader*, ed. J.B. Ross and M.M. McLaughlin, Harmondsworth: Penguin 1978, p. 686.

8

The Skin and the Straw

PASCAL BONITZER

Those who are professionally involved in cinema are only too aware of the fact that films nowadays enjoy increasingly brief runs. What title will still be up on the billboards when these lines appear in print? I am invariably preoccupied by this problem when I write my column, but there are precious few exceptions to the rule. Yet irrespective of the Cannes festival, Hitchcock, on the billboards for the last few months, will be there again in a few months' time, thanks to an endless stream of rereleases and fresh prints. It seems as if Hitchcock will always be with us.

Consider *The Man Who Knew Too Much*, a film which is usually regarded as a minor work. So it is, but let me state quite plainly – at the risk of seeming to be at odds with a relatively recent, but widely held view – that the whole of Hitchcock's œuvre is minor, and for this we should be thankful.

A Protective Surface

Hitchcock's work is minor in the sense that it is placed quite deliberately within the confines of a particular genre, that of the thriller, and does not pretend to do more than entertain. If in the last twenty years, since the publication of Truffaut's classic study of Hitchcock – which is a veritable *Ars poetica* of the cinema – the long-denied universality of his films has at last been acknowledged, it is because

178

the audience is aware that their minor status serves as the protective surface of a genuine metaphysics, much as the *trompe l'œil* genre in painting may in certain works establish a system with a false bottom, which turns the representation into a 'conceit' and surreptitiously places the spectator in front of an unfathomable and terrifying reality. The whole of Hitchcock's *œuvre*, which is itself astonishingly plastic, as is well known, is haunted by the anamorphic skull of the *memento mori*.

The Man Who Knew Too Much, in its second version (with James Stewart and Doris Day), appears to be a story whose joins are somewhat too visible and too flimsy, a thriller with slightly forced fresh developments tricked out with a sequence of technical bravado managed in Hitchcock's own inimitable fashion: the concert at the Albert Hall, with the famous clash of cymbals in the absurd 'Storm Cloud Cantata' conducted by Bernard Herrmann. It is certainly neither the most perfect nor the best constructed of Hitchcock's films – as is borne out by, for example, the red herring, the unduly emphasized false trail of the visit to the taxidermist, and the laboured picking-up of the story after the failed assassination in the Albert Hall, which should by rights have been a climax.

Yet Hitchcock's *œuvre* is exemplary even in its shortcomings, for they enable us to see what the notion of *auteur*, invented expressly by *Cahiers du cinéma* to honour Hitchcock, really means. This notion can be sustained only through a wager regarding the continuity of the *œuvre*, identifiable in the recurrences of a motif that is secretly woven from film to film, 'the image in the carpet'. Thus *The Man Who Knew Too Much* is already, in filigree, *Psycho*, which seems, in retrospect, to derive from the burlesque scene with the taxidermist and, above all, from the motif of the mother's voice, which acts upon the son at a distance, through the incongruous song '*Que sera, sera*'.

The vocal bond between mother and son in *The Man Who Knew Too Much* is the seemingly innocent expression of a normal, maternal and filial love, and also the sole safety line of a boy who has been kidnapped and whose life is in danger. In the light of *Psycho*, where the mother's voice has entered the son, tears him apart and possesses him in a murderous fashion, one cannot help but find even the normality of the ordinary, typical American family slightly disquieting.

This disquiet is reflected in the film, through a play of masks and mirrors, in which ordinary people invariably find other ordinary people disturbing; or, conversely, find disturbing people merely ordinary. The whole of the opening sequence of the film, from the encounter with Louis Bernard (Daniel Gelin), the agent of the Deuxième Bureau, up to the kidnapping of the child, is woven in this fashion. The two American couples, the tourists and the spies, are obviously doubles. In passing from one couple to the other, it is exactly as if the child were passing over from the other side of the mirror.

A Play of Mirrors

The film's structure is wholly specular. Regardless of whether we are in an interlude or in a sequence of pure action, everything takes place as if each character glimpsed his or her own reflection from the other side of an invisible surface, in a form that was unrecognizable, uncanny and monstrous. The only exception to this rule is the child, for he is what is at stake in the drama and cannot therefore be specularized. In the second scene, for example, Louis Bernard sees, from the depths of the parents' bedroom, his mortal reflection, in the form of the man with the disturbing face, who had supposedly entered the wrong room by mistake and who subsequently turned out to be the killer in the Albert Hall.

The sequence featuring the murder of Louis Bernard is constructed as a nightmare, in which a man would seem to be chasing his own reflection in order to stab it in the back. It is in fact impossible to distinguish pursuer from pursued, since they are identical silhouettes in burnouses, but Hitchcock deliberately accentuates this doubling effect by taking care not to show immediately that two men are involved. To begin with, one sees only a single burnous chased by policemen, and it is only later that one realizes that the burnous is not fleeing from the policemen but pursuing a second burnous – unless (for the ambiguity cannot be resolved) he had in reality fled not the policemen but the other burnous whom we had not seen.

A Comedy of Errors

This structure is still more explicit in two sequences which seem to be pure padding: the one which is set in a Moroccan restaurant and has James Stewart and Doris Day striking up an acquaintance with their doubles, the spy couple, and the one which features the taxidermist, Ambrose Chappell.

The first of these sequences is all the more noteworthy for the fact that everything that happens is banal in the extreme, except the entrance of Louis Bernard, accompanied by a young woman (who therefore make a third couple, a third reflection). Everything depends upon the fashion in which the protagonists had to be arranged in order to compose genuine reflections of each other. Thus, James Stewart begins by putting himself in the wrong place, in the sense that he is back-to-back with the *woman* from the other couple, but the exaggeratedly oriental softness of the sofa[1] forces him to change places with Doris Day, leaving him back-to-back with the *man*. A conversation can then begin, and the two couples, who had

initially been back-to-back, soon find themselves face-to-face. The sequence provides us with very little information, and serves simply to make sense of the swapping of places, the comedy of errors, the disturbing reduplication of faces that the film arranges so obsessionally.

The sequence at the taxidermist's shop, a false trail or 'red herring', serves clearly to show how the virtual reversibility of roles in the film functions. It is worth noting, in passing, that James Stewart's error – when he mistakes a chapel for Mr Chappell, only to have his confusion coincidentally reinforced by the telephone directory – turns upon an imaginary doubling of letters which transforms a common name into a proper name and a building into a human being.

A Red Herring

One is therefore led to suppose that Mr Chappell is a dangerous spy whose 'cover' is a taxidermist's workshop. Indeed, a disturbing man with a suspicious manner seems to be following James Stewart across an eerily deserted district, as he looks for the address of the man he believes himself to be seeking. We should note here that Hitchcock uses the dreamlike or nightmarish contrast between the desert of London and the throng in the souk at Marrakech to refer to the scene of Louis Bernard's murder. The man finally overtakes James Stewart and enters the workshop called Ambrose Chappell, thereby demonstrating that the follower was undoubtedly the followed. When James Stewart himself goes into the workshop, he does not suspect (any more than the audience does) that the disturbing man and Ambrose Chappell are one and the same.

This is a mistake, for the film invariably returns to the number two. James Stewart therefore finds himself face-to-face with two Ambrose Chappells, father and son. We then realize that the taxidermist's suspicious manner, which made him so suspect, arose simply from the fact that he himself had found James Stewart's behaviour very strange, and that in reality he was a harmless artisan. In other words, what James Stewart, and the audience, saw in him, *he* saw in James Stewart – that is, an uncanny being implicated in a mysterious and monstrous plot.

Likewise, it is not by chance that Hitchcock should have set the scene in a taxidermist's workshop rather than in, for example, a cabinet-maker's, and that the stuffed animals, although not yet birds, are all wild. His aim was to create, on the cheap, an effect of strangeness and latent cruelty verging on the burlesque. But it was also because the stuffed wild animals, being at once wild and harmless, symbolize the double meaning of the whole scene.

The Fingers of a Glove

Yet the meaning is eminently reversible, as in *Psycho*, where the honest lad at the motel – whose hobby is taxidermy, and who is apparently hounded by a mother as abusive as she is invisible – is in reality a madman who has stuffed his mother, and, being filled by her personality as if he were himself no more than an empty casing, commits murders under her influence.

We are the hollow men
We are the stuffed men
Leaning together
Headpiece filled with straw. Alas!

Such is Hitchcock's vision of man. Indeed, his films would seem to be structured like the fingers of a glove and, in their reversibility, represent the skin and the straw in turn. What haunts that structure, however, is the tearing blow of a beak; our anticipation of it creates the suspense. This sombre image is our own. It is as if we were led by a kind of go-between, a double who, on the screen-mirror, moves at random through a forest of deceiving or monstrous faces (the alignment of the singers in the Albert Hall characterizes this predicament to perfection), and as if we thought of ourselves as traversing with that double a domain of appearances, only to fall vertiginously into the void which constitutes us. It is because Hitchcock's films embrace this structure, which is that of the screen itself, so closely that they seem so often to epitomize the cinema, much as Holbein's 'The Ambassadors' and Velázquez's 'Las Meninas' seem to epitomize painting.

Notes

1. This crafty, engulfing softness is emphasized throughout this scene – being echoed, for example, in James Stewart's bread, which he has great difficulty in breaking, in the *tajine*, which has to be eaten with one's hands, without the use of knife, fork or left hand – to such an extent that one cannot help but think of the soft watches and edible structures of Salvador Dalí.

9

The Right Man and the Wrong Woman

RENATA SALECL

When explaining the failure of *The Wrong Man*, interpreters point out that Hitchcock, in this film, is not 'his usual self', that amusing, cynical narrator who does not hesitate to twist the story as he pleases, but a benevolent, sensitive and sympathetic observer. No doubt Hitchcock was deeply touched by the real-life adventure of an 'ordinary man', musician Manny Balestrero, who is mistakenly accused of robbery. This false identification drags him into a nightmarish battle with the state bureaucracy; although the actual robber is caught in the end, Manny's family life is ruined and his wife is hospitalized due to a psychotic breakdown. In order to emphasize this 'touch of the real', Hitchcock directed the film in a pseudo-documentary manner: black and white, realism of the *mise-en-scène*, repeating noise of the subway, images of descent and darkness, and so on. As Hitchcock announces in his cameo appearance at the beginning of the film, the story is 'dark, and frightening as much for its "truth", as for its gloom'. It is with the relation between the (objective) *truth* and the (subjective) *gloom*, however, that interpretive problems set in.

In order to achieve the atmosphere of gloom, Hitchcock situates the standpoint from which the story is told in the innocent Manny. In this way, the documentary character of the film is combined with Manny's subjective vision of the horrible circumstances he finds himself in. That is how Hitchcock's camera, in the first half of the film, creates the impression of the subject's helplessness in the face of bureaucratic machinery. Consider the scenes when Manny is taken to the police station: the camera first shows us Manny stepping out of the car, and then proceeds with the point-of-view shot in an extreme low-angle framing, thus rendering Manny's gaze at the threatening police building, forcing the spectators to experience vividly the weight of the institution which seems to be about to fall down on him. The same effect is achieved in the prison scenes: the camera first shows us the helpless expression on Manny's face and then cuts to the point-of-view shot, rendering his inquiring gaze at the narrow cell. Here, however, we come across the first enigma of the film: despite this use of the subjective camera – emphasized by the threatening music, the clashing of the handcuffs, the noise of the prison doors being slammed, and so on – *the story leaves us indifferent.* We are aware of Manny's innocence and should therefore identify ourselves with his point of view – yet *the identification fails.* In other words, in *The Wrong Man* Hitchcock does not succeed in arousing the feeling – so typical of the scenes in his films that are shot from a subjective point of view –

> that the person's gaze does not reveal things, that his step does not lead him *towards* things, but that things themselves stare at him, attract him in a dangerous way, grab him and are at the point of swallowing him, as it occurs in an exemplary way in *Psycho* when the detective Arbogast climbs the stairs. The will is never free, subjectivity is always under constraint and caught.[1]

In *The Wrong Man*, on the contrary, it is as if, in spite of the horrifying circumstances, Manny's will remains all the time free of constraint, for it is obvious that Manny is not in the least affected by the whole mishap; the subjective gaze thus *cannot* be 'his own'. This, then, is the discord aroused by the film: although Hitchcock uses the technique that is meant to effectuate the spectators' identification with the victim, the victim reacts as if the depicted horrors do not concern him, as if he were their indifferent observer. The subject (Manny) does not fit the mode of subjectivization the film's form proposes.

In Hitchcock's films which focus on the 'transference of guilt', the main character accused by mistake is never straightforwardly innocent. Although he is not guilty of doings mistakenly attributed to him, his false accusation poses the question of another guilt: whereas he is innocent as to the *facts*, he is guilty as to his *desire*. In *I Confess*, for example, Father Logan is not guilty of the murder; nevertheless, the real murderer realizes Logan's desire, since he kills the person who blackmailed Ruth because of her past relationship with Logan. The same goes for *Strangers on a Train*: obviously, Guy cannot be said to be guilty, in the legal sense of the term, of partaking in the murder of his wife; however, given the trouble his wife was causing him, he cannot be exempt from the accusation of subjective guilt either – in a sense, he could not but welcome Bruno's murder of his wife. On the contrary, in *The Wrong Man* the false accusation does not provoke a single shred of guilt – Manny simply maintains that he is innocent, and neither the following course of events nor his wife's madness can shake his stand or induce in him a feeling of self-reproach.

In short, Manny is as far as possible from a Kafkaesque hero whom some bureaucratic machinery performatively makes culpable: until the end of the story the guilt is imposed on him in an external way which does not affect him in the core of his being. Let us recall the scene at the police station: the repeated subjective shots of Manny's hands and feet seem to reflect his embarrassment and feeling of shame; then we see the ink-stains which remained on his hands after his fingerprints have been taken – which, of course, remind us of blood: 'The mark of guilt is on him; but it has been imposed and is no more deserved than the accusation of robbery with which he has also been stained.'[2] The odd effect of this scene is thus again that Manny is not the one who feels guilty and ashamed. Who, then, could that be? The answer is provided in the course of the film: the subject who willingly takes the guilt upon herself and, consequently, suffers mental illness is Manny's wife Rose. Now, what kind of mechanism could possibly provoke such a step? A seemingly convincing answer comes from Rose herself:

'It is my fault this happened to you, it's wisdom teeth. I know I shouldn't let you go down to the Insurance Office to borrow money for me and all this fell on you. We have been in debt before, because I haven't known how to handle things ... because I haven't known how to economize. Truth is I have let you down, Manny. I haven't been a good wife.'

Are we to believe this explanation? One of the fundamental lessons of Lacanian psychoanalysis is that the subject's admission of guilt always functions as a stratagem to lure the Other: the subject 'feels guilty' about the deeds he committed in order to mask another, far more radical guilt. 'Pleading guilty', then, is ultimately a ruse which aims at entrapping the Other:

> ... by sanctioning the fault proposed by the subject, the Other says nothing about the subject's real guilt. ... In order to be able to continue ignoring the truth of his guilt, the subject proposes to the Other a fault of which he does not have to be held responsible.[3]

One can easily recognize this kind of ruse in Rose's willingness to take the guilt upon herself − in her precipitate admission that the cause of all Manny's troubles was her being a bad wife and, specifically, her aching teeth (Manny was identified as a robber when she sent him on an errand to pick up a remedy for her toothache). The truth about her guilt must be sought elsewhere: *in her insight into what might lie behind Manny's perfection.*

Manny is depicted as an ideal husband: a loving father who works hard to make a living for his family and whom his children adore, a son deeply attached to his mother (whenever she calls him, he comes to help), a very reliable person who always comes home at the same hour, loves his wife and helps her as best he can (we see him washing up and occupying himself with children). This idyllic picture is reinforced by the scene of the children's squabble: the younger son's accordion disturbs his older brother, who wants to play the piano, yet as soon as Manny arrives, the matter is settled − he calms down his sons by promising to practise with each of them separately. After reconciling them, Manny professes something like his *credo* when he tells his sons that the way to success is the way of self-confidence; this scene and the scene with Manny praying in front of Christ's image, followed by the gradual superimposition of the face of the actual robber over Manny's face, are usually considered as tokens of Manny's strong faith in himself and in God. If he does not collapse and go mad, that is what saves him.[4]

At the very beginning of the film, however, when Manny comments on their life and points out that although they have no money for the dentist, 'we are pretty lucky people, darling', Rose expresses her doubts about their idyllic family life by retorting: 'Are we?' Without this smouldering doubt there would be no outbreak of Rose's psychiatric disorder: if the accidental false identification could lead to such disastrous consequences it was because within the apparent happiness of Manny's family a trauma already *insisted*, though it did not *exist*. As Lacan puts it, the Real of a trauma repeats itself '*by means of* reality':[5] for a trauma to break out, there must be an impulse from external reality, an accident that triggers it off, like the false identification in *The Wrong Man*. The irony of the film lies in the fact that its 'documentary', 'realistic' aspect is ultimately a lure: the *reality* of the story serves as a catalyst by means of which the traumatic core of the Real, structured in the suppressed *fiction*, breaks in. What is this fiction about?

One answer may be reached by comparing Rose's reaction to the typical behaviour of an obsessional neurotic: *Rose imposes guilt upon herself, because this is the only way she can save the appearance of Manny's perfection.* Only by blaming herself for all that went wrong is she able to turn herself away from the fact which became so intolerably blatant in the whole affair with Manny's false identification: the fact that Manny's perfection, industry, devotion ... are nothing but a mask for his impotence and passiveness:

> One wonders, indeed, if the idea of nervous strain such that the wife has to be hospitalized isn't a dilution of the domestic tension, and whether that might have been more particularized had the husband sensed that something passive in his personality, rather than his action, was partly responsible for her strain, and that only after his prayers for her does her breakdown become complete.[6]

Manny's passiveness, however, turns out to be much more radical: it must be conceived as the sign of his *psychotic* attitude. The truth behind his perfect image is not a simple weakness, but psychotic indifference manifested in the total absence of guilt – the ominous and uncanny character of his 'inner peace of mind' becomes palpable in the scenes where Manny, as indifferently as he reacted to his own misfortune, observes Rose's outbursts of madness with an impassive eye.[7] In this sense, the faith in himself and in God, usually interpreted as Manny's protection against his own breakdown, turns out to be precisely the expression of his madness: he is not marked by the fundamental, 'ontological' guilt which is constitutive of human existence – of the human being's existence as *parlêtre* (being-of-language)'. The Freudian name for this guilt is, of course, *parricide*: as Lacan rereads Freud, the mere fact that we speak implies our murdering the father; Father reigns only in so far as he is dead, in the guise of his Name. If the Kafkaesque nightmare of which Manny is a random victim does not end up inflicting guilt on him – that is, if he does not try to deceive the Other by offering, instead of the original guilt, a substitutional one – it is because Manny does not enter the dimension of guilt at all: he does not enter the relationship of symbolic debt. In other words, his guilt is not only repressed but *foreclosed*. This explains Manny's status as the perfect father, the focus of the family idyll[8] – in this very capacity, he is confined to psychosis. That is to say, the 'normal' functioning of a father implies that the family members fully take in the imperfections of the real father, that they notice the gap separating the empty symbolic function of the Name-of-the-Father from its empirical, contingent tenant. A father who does not take into account this gap and who, consequently, acts as a father who 'actually thinks he is a father', can only be a psychotic.[9]

How, then, does Manny's psychotic indifference precipitate Rose's fall into the delirium of self-inflicted culpability? Here, one should recall that this fall occurs as a reaction to her bursting into rage against Manny: 'You are not perfect yourself. How do I know you're not guilty? You don't tell me everything you do!' In this scene, Rose is sitting in a dark room, near the table lamp which sheds its light on her face and projects terrifying shadows all over the place. As she stands up and approaches Manny, we watch their large shadows deform into monstrous figures. Rose stops in front of a mirror, grabs the wire brush and flings it at Manny; the brush bounces off him and hits the mirror. At this point, the camera first shows the injured Manny and then cuts to the broken mirror, in which we can see the scattered image of his face, whose uncanny distortion recalls a Cubist portrait. In the next shot Manny's face

reappears, now with an innocent expression on it; he tries to touch Rose, who at first repels him and then sinks into lethargy, her face showing resignation. Her distant glance embraces Manny as she says: 'It is really something wrong with me. You will have to let them put me somewhere. People had faith in me and I let them down ... I was guilty.'

The throw of the brush designates the point when, for a brief moment, Rose is able to articulate her anger with Manny's impassive, impotent attitude, and thus to retain her own sanity. Yet she instantly breaks down and takes the guilt upon herself – why? The answer is provided by Manny's reflection in the broken mirror. What we see in it, for a moment, is *the reverse side of his perfect fatherly image: the cracked, clownish face of an obscene madman.*[10] Now, who – what gaze – can actually see this reflection? The gaze observing the image certainly cannot be Manny's, because in both this shot and the previous one Manny appears in front of the mirror, with his head in profile. Consequently, he cannot face the mirror. Neither is Rose turned in the direction of the mirror; because if she were, and could actually see the monstrously deformed face in the mirror, she should also be able to see her own reflection in it, which is not the case. For this reason, the only standpoint where the gaze could come from is *the standpoint of the table lamp.*

According to the Lacanian theory, every screen of reality includes a constitutive 'stain', the trace of what had to be precluded from the field of reality in order that this field can acquire its consistency; this stain appears in the guise of a void Lacan names *objet petit a.* It is the point that I, the subject, cannot see: it eludes me in so far as it is the point from which the screen itself 'returns the gaze', watches me: the point where the gaze itself is inscribed into the visual field of reality.

In psychosis, however, *objet a* is precisely *not precluded*: it materializes itself, it receives full bodily presence and becomes visible − for example, in the form of a pursuer who 'sees and knows everything' in paranoia. In *The Wrong Man*, this kind of object which materializes the gaze is exemplified by the table lamp, the source of light. As Lacan says in his *Seminar XI*: 'that which is light looks at me'.[11] The image of Manny the lamp sees in the broken mirror is

the image of his wounded face which turns into a disgusting caricature, and what Rose cannot integrate in the Symbolic order is
precisely this unbearable image. Here one must recall Lacan's
classic definition of psychosis: in psychosis, 'that which does not
come to light in the Symbolic order appears in the Real, the realm
outside the subject, for instance as a hallucination'.[12] Thus, since
Rose cannot stand looking at Manny's deformed image and cannot
integrate it in the Symbolic order, *this gaze materializes in the lamp as a
hallucinatory object.*[13]

Despite the fact that Rose ends up in psychosis, whereas Manny
remains sane, *The Wrong Man* confirms Bellour's thesis that in
Hitchcock's films male characters always suffer from psychosis,
while females become psychotic only by default or by reflection.[14]
Rose's psychosis is ultimately a reflection of Manny's: by taking the
guilt upon herself and going mad, she makes it possible for Manny
to preserve his attitude of psychotic indifference – since she takes the
role of the wrong woman, of a being burdened with guilt, he is able
to keep on living as the right man freed from guilt. Since she
assumes the role of a 'public' madwoman, *his* madness can continue
to wear the public mask of normality.

There is a famous Soviet joke from the time of so-called 'real
socialism', telling how Radio Erevan answered the question: 'Is it
true that Rabinovitch won a car in the lottery in Moscow?' – 'In
principle, he did, it's just that it wasn't a car but a bicycle. Besides,
he didn't win it, he had it stolen!' Our suggestion is that the usual
reading of *The Wrong Man* must make a similar turn in a feminist
direction: to the interpretation that the film is about a hero who got
trapped in the wheels of the Kafkaesque machinery, is then accused
by mistake and, owing to the steadiness of his morals, manages to
survive the whole affair, while his wife, because of the feminine
weakness of her character, cannot stand the pressure and goes mad,
one should answer: in principle, this is true; it is just that the man
survives only because he was mad from the very start. Besides, what
his wife cannot stand is not the pressure of the situation but the look
at the obscene caricature which is in fact the real image of her
husband.

Notes

1. Jean Narboni, 'Visages d'Hitchcock', in *Cahiers du cinéma, hors-série 8: Alfred Hitchcock*, Paris 1980, p. 33.

2. Lesley Brill, *The Hitchcock Romance*, Princeton, NJ: Princeton University Press 1988, p. 115.

3. Michel Silvestre, *Demain la psychanalyse*, Paris: Navarin Editeur 1988, p. 24.

4. On this particular point, Hitchcock considerably altered the 'true story', published in *Life* magazine: in the film Manny is a brave man, able to face reality, whereas the actual Manny was such a timid man that his lawyer feared he might suffer a breakdown during the trial, much like his wife.

5. Jacques Lacan, *The Four Fundamental Concepts of Psycho-Analysis*, Harmondsworth: Penguin 1986, p. 58.

6. Raymond Durgnat, *The Strange Case of Alfred Hitchcock*, London: Faber & Faber 1974, p. 277.

7. Note that psychosis is defined precisely by the discord between subject and subjectivization: in it, the subject is not integrated into the symbolic network which structures his/her mode of subjectivization, his/her symbolic identity – and, as we have already seen, this same discord is at work in our reception of the film.

8. Note that the father of the President Schreber – the famous psychotic whose memoirs were analysed by Freud – was also a kind of perfect father: the author of bestsellers about physical exercise for children and their correct bodily discipline, he was well known all over Germany.

9. As Lacan put it, not only a beggar who thinks he is a king is mad, but also a king who thinks he is a king – who unreservedly identifies himself with the symbolic mandate of a king.

10. When we recall his screen-persona in other films, the choice of Henry Fonda for Manny becomes significant. In his previous films Fonda was given positive characters to play; however, because of their very perfection, these characters radiated a sort of insensibility, coldness and monstrosity. (This aspect of Fonda's screen-persona was first pointed out by the collective authors of *Cahiers du cinéma* in their well-known analysis of Ford's *The Young Mr. Lincoln*; see ' "Young Mr. Lincoln" de John Ford' (texte collectif], *Cahiers du cinéma* no. 223, 1970.) Retrospectively, what Fonda's later success with playing the negative character in Sergio Leone's *Once Upon a Time in the West* reveals is precisely this trait which smouldered in his screen-persona from the very beginning and flashed for a moment in *The Wrong Man* as Manny's face in the broken mirror.

11. Lacan, *The Four Fundamental Concepts*, p. 96.

12. Jacques Lacan, *Ecrits: A Selection*, London: Tavistock 1977, p. 388.

13. This lamp, the materialization of the gaze which sees that which was foreclosed, reappears in the scene with the psychiatrist. The camera shows Rose sitting at the table; in front of her, on the table, is a big table lamp encircling her head with a bright light. Off screen we hear the voice of the psychiatrist asking Rose about her fear. Occasionally, we see the psychiatrist's figure standing behind the lamp – that is, precisely behind the standpoint of the gaze which here again becomes visible and, as such, projects, as the psychiatrist says, 'monstrous shadows that say hateful things'.

14. Raymond Bellour, 'Psychosis, Neurosis, Perversion', in Marshall Deutelbaum and Leland Poague, eds, *A Hitchcock Reader*, Ames: Iowa State University Press 1986, p. 321.

10

The Impossible Embodiment

MICHEL CHION

Psycho is concerned with the impossibility of attaching a voice to a body or, in other words, with the impossibility of embodiment. It is no coincidence that the French word for 'embodiment' [*mise-en-corps*] recalls the word for 'coffining' [*mise-en-bière*] or 'burial' [*mise-en-terre*], for something akin to interment is indeed involved. Interment is, as is well known, a symbolic act; some hold that it was the first of such acts to lead humankind towards a form of evolution distinct from that of other species. To bury someone is not merely to be rid of a decomposing body; it is also to assign a place to his or her soul, his or her double – or, if one does not believe in such things, to everything that remains *in us* or *for us* of his or her person. This is done by means of rites and marks such as stones, crosses or inscriptions, which tell the dead person: 'you will remain there', so that he or she does not return to haunt the living like a soul in torment. A ghost is traditionally one who went unburied or was badly buried. Precisely the same is true of the *acousmêtre*,[1] when the voice of a person not yet seen is involved, for here too there is something which can neither enter the frame in order to attach itself to one of the bodies which revolve there, nor occupy the withdrawn position of the shower of images, and is therefore doomed to wander on the surface. This is precisely the concern of *Psycho*.

Although much has already been written on this film, none of these often pertinent commentaries – unless I am much mistaken – discusses the part played in it by the voice of the mother as *acousmêtre.* In *Psycho*, the mother is first of all a voice. One catches a fleeting glimpse of a kind of dumb and bestial giantess, wielding a knife. One also catches sight, equally fleetingly, of a shadow-theatre silhouette behind the curtain of her room (like that of Mabuse behind the curtain). We are again allowed a fleeting glimpse, in the landing scene analysed below, of a body carried by Norman. Yet the voice – which is cruel, nagging and by no means fleeting – is heard all the time, at great length, off frame.

The voice of the mother is heard on three different occasions in *Psycho*, and each time it features in a key, linking scene:

- The first occasion is when Marion, having arrived at the motel, overhears an argument between the mother and her son, Norman.

- The second occasion (the 'landing scene') is when we hear another, almost equally stormy discussion between Norman and his mother, when he is trying to persuade her to go down to the cellar. It ends with the voice of the mother apparently becoming embodied.

- The third occasion, at the end of the film, is when Norman is shown in his cell, wholly possessed by the mother.

The Argument

Norman (Anthony Perkins), the young man keeping the motel where Marion (Janet Leigh), who is on the run, is stranded, invites her to dine in the old house beside the motel which he shares with his mother. As he goes back up towards the house, Marion settles into her room. She then overhears, from the house alongside, a heated exchange off frame between Norman and an old woman with a voice which is loud and harsh, but fairly distant and surrounded by a halo of reverberation. The acousmatic mother (the *Acousmère*) is enraged at the presumption shown by her son, a lecherous good-for-nothing, in introducing a strange woman into 'her' house. Norman comes back down again shortly afterwards and offers his apologies, explaining that his mother is unwell and defenceless, and that he is all she has in the world.

This scene obviously serves to set the acousmatic machinery in motion – or, in other words, even before the murder, *to create the desire to go and see it*. It is in fact a rule that any voice that is off frame arouses, simply through its acousmatic position, a desire to go and see who is speaking, even if it were the most harmless person in the world (but on condition that the voice could conceivably be included in the image, and is not the uncommitted voice of a commentator).

Once this key, linking scene has occurred, the fiction is propelled by the *idée fixe* of entering the house in order to see the mother. The violation of a family house by a woman is, as is well known, a characteristic scene in Hitchcock's films, and the consequences of such an action are generally very dramatic. Consider in this respect *Rebecca, Notorious, Rear Window, The Man Who Knew Too Much* (the 1956 version), *The Birds*, and so on. But in *Psycho*, entering the house also entails finding the site of the voice, bringing the mother into the frame, and attaching her voice to a body. So it is that, shortly after the first involvement of the *Acousmère*, a tall, mute, wild creature – whose features we never see, although we are led to suppose that it is the mother – rises up and stabs Marion in her shower. We later see the same silhouette emerge on to the landing outside its room, on the first floor, to eliminate the detective in the same fashion.

Here one could well object: 'But that is embodiment! no matter how briefly, we see your *Acousmère*!' Yet quite the reverse is true, for embodiment certainly does not consist of showing us here a mute body (which anyway is never facing us) and elsewhere a voice that is supposed to belong to it, with it being up to the audience to assemble these disjointed elements in their own minds. Embodiment is realized through the simultaneous assembly of a visible body and an audible voice. The body has to testify, in a particular fashion, 'this is my voice'; or the voice likewise has to testify, 'this is my body', through a sort of marriage contract consecrating the re-assuring fixation of the voice in the residence of the body, drawing off or dispelling the acousmetric powers. This is not the case here.

The Scene on the Landing

The second occasion upon which we hear the voice of the mother in *Psycho* occurs when, during the hunt for the mother, Norman goes up to her room on the first floor to take her away to a safe hiding-place. The whole scene revolves around our combined anticipation and fear of the imminent embodiment of the *Acousmère*.

At first, the camera follows Norman from behind and climbs the stairs with him. But when Norman enters the room through a door that has been left ajar, the camera does not enter, because it has already broken away and remained *outside*, on the stairs, effecting through the continuity of the shot a complicated movement of elevation and swing-back, which brings it vertically above the landing, when Norman leaves the room with his mother in his arms. Before that, we hear an off frame conversation from inside the room, between Norman and the mother. Her voice is still offensive, but closer, less shrill, duller and without any reverberation. This voice, which we have approached, in some sense brushes against the edge of the frame, leading us to expect an imminent embodiment, in which we fear that we may have to face what Pascal Bonitzer has termed a 'bad encounter'. Here is the off frame dialogue:

Norman: Well, Mother. I ...
Mother: I am sorry, boy, but you do manage to look ludicrous when you give orders.
Norman: Please, Mother!
Mother: No, I will not hide in the fruit cellar. Ha! You think I'm fruity, ha! I'm staying right here. This is my room and no one will drag me out of it, least of all my big, bold son!
Norman: Now come now, Mother! He came after the girl and someone will come after him! Mother, please! It's just for a few days. Just for a few days so they won't find you.
Mother: Just for a few days! In that dark, damp fruit cellar! No! You hid me there once and you won't do it again. Not ever again! Now get out! I told you to get out, boy!
Norman: I'll carry you, Mother.
Mother: Norman, what do you think you're doing? Don't you touch me! Don't! Norman! Put me down, put me down! I can walk with my own
...

With this, Norman leaves the room, but the camera is already fixed in its bird's-eye view, so that in the brief instant in which Norman appears and starts going down the stairs, and in which we hear the mother, we can see only an indistinct body that he holds in his arms. Very rapidly, a *fade to black* obscures the image and obliterates this vision, accompanied by a *fade to silence* of the mother's voice as she is speaking her last line. There should be no need to remind the reader that it is a relatively rare event in the talking cinema for lines spoken by an important character at the end of a scene to be cut in this fashion, and so returned to silence.

Hitchcock both offers and retracts the anticipated embodiment. The retraction is achieved by means of a distorting and distant point of view, but also through the brevity of the image and through its disappearance, into a fade to black affecting both sound and image, body and voice, at the same time, at the very moment at which we had supposed that we were holding them together. When the scene is over, the mother seems still to be awaiting a body.

There is a very strong reference here to the primal scene, as suggested by the words used by the mother off frame, with their terrifying double meaning of aggression and of desire ('Don't touch me! Don't touch me!') and their evocation of a bodily contact which we both expect and fear to see. Narratives in cinema have often posited a close relationship between those moments at which characters, though terrified, are drawn to go and see what they can only hear, and the primal scene. And, as Raymond Bellour has observed, the effect of the scene is reinforced by a 'shivering full stop' created by the revelation, at the end of the previous scene, that the mother was in reality *dead and buried,* and by the sheriff's words, which cleverly displace the question: 'Well, if the woman up there is Mrs Bates – who's that woman buried out in Greenlawn Cemetery?'

I know of few moments in cinema as disturbing as the retracting of this imminent embodiment. Marguerite Duras ventured upon this same territory in *India Song,* in which we are just about to see the dumb ghosts who are represented on screen, and those we hear off frame, synchronized and speaking. This accounts for the particularly fascinating and deadly effect of this film which, as its author realized, derives its power from *leaving off in the middle of something.*

Undoubtedly, *Son nom de Venise*, where the very same soundtrack is used for images of sets without their characters, reflected a need to dispel the ghostly wandering of *India Song*, by providing it with its symbolic closure: a prohibition upon voices to come on frame.

In *Psycho*, the fascination arises from the fact that what is given is withdrawn in one and the same movement, what is lost is lost through the very same mechanism by which it had been apprehended, the whole of this process unfolding in the course of a single, uninterrupted shot. Hitchcock explained why:

> I didn't want to cut, when he carries her down, to a high shot because the audience would have been suspicious as to why the camera has suddenly jumped away. So I had a hanging camera follow Perkins up the stairs, and when he went into the room I continued going up without a cut. As the camera got up on top of the door, the camera turned and looked back down the stairs again. Meanwhile, I had an argument take place between the son and his mother to distract the audience and take their minds off what the camera was doing. In this way the camera was above Perkins again as he carried his mother down and the public hadn't noticed a thing. It was rather exciting to use the camera to deceive the audience.[2]

We learn why Hitchcock chose a high-angle shot when he discusses the scene featuring the death of the detective:

> If I'd shown her back [the mother's back, in reality Norman in disguise], it might have looked as if I was deliberately concealing her face and the audience would have been leery. I used that high angle in order not to give the impression that I was trying to avoid showing her.[3]

It is clear that Hitchcock need not have adopted so subtle a procedure in order to keep his audience in a state of suspense. It seems to me that it was the actual functioning of belief that he wished to push as far as it would go, by applying a law of 'no editing' (the principle of which is 'don't cut!'), which others – for example, Bazin (and after him, to construct a critical analysis of such practices, Bonitzer) – had seen as a touchstone for the reality effect in the cinema.

When Hitchcock in effect attributes to the audience the question 'Why does the camera suddenly withdraw?', his formulation seems to imply a reference to *coitus interruptus*, and it is worth noting that those scenes in which Hitchcock refrains from cutting or editing often feature a kiss. To cut such a scene would, in his view, amount to separating the couple: 'I believe', he said, 'there is a lot that can be done with love scenes' (consider, in this context, the continuous shot of the kiss in *Notorious*), and he then goes on to recount a curious love scene, which was never shot, and which he imagined as he was conversing with Truffaut. For present purposes, we need recall only that this slightly smutty scene also rests on a disjunction between dialogue and situation. Here words were supposed both to distract from and to reinforce what one saw. Equally instructive for us is the nature of the personal memory which, he said, had remained very intense in his mind, and which he brought up in order to explain his preference for *not cutting*. Travelling in a French train, he saw a young couple arm in arm against a factory wall: 'The boy was pissing against the wall; the girl never once let go of his arm; she was looking at what he was doing, looking at the train as it passed by and then once more looked at the boy.'[4] Once again, this was, as Hitchcock observed, a kind of *ménage à trois*, between the two partners, and the gaze from the train to which the girl's gaze was a response. In all these scenes, the onlooker's gaze was implicated as third party in relation to the fused couple.

The 'no editing' rule which Hitchcock had imposed upon himself here had in fact been theorized by André Bazin in relation to a completely different kind of scene – fights between man and beast. Yet is there not something bestial about the image of the couple of Norman and his mother, especially if one recalls how the latter is shown – or rather not shown – in the two murder scenes? Bazin's text, which was originally published in 1953, raised the problem of *belief* in the cinema, and this too is wholly pertinent to the matter under discussion, for what Bazin is concerned with is 'the reality effect' when one simulates a fight between man and beast through trick editing. It is clear, observes Bazin, that the audience will not believe in the sequence if man and beast are shown in separate shots, and at least one shot showing them together will therefore be necessary for us genuinely to believe in what we see. He goes on to mention Chaplin, who, in *The Circus*, is 'actually in the lion's cage, and both are shut up in the cage of the screen'. The law is therefore formulated as follows:

> When an event in its essence depends upon the simultaneous presence
> of three or four factors in the action, editing is prohibited. It recovers its
> rights whenever the meaning of the action no longer depends upon
> physical contiguity.[5]

The landing scene could be analysed equally satisfactorily either in terms of Hitchcock's principle of 'not separating the couple' or in terms of Bazin's principle of 'showing man and beast together' (in this case, the living and the murderous dead, here body-to-body) – for in the case of both the human couple and the man and the beast, we are concerned with a primitive horror of sex.

Even as he allows us to see man and beast, son and mother, body and voice, together, Hitchcock has to retract them, since the beast is one half of what man is, the mother is a mummy, and the voice issues not from the body of the mother (unless by a kind of macabre ventriloquism) but from Norman's body playing both parts. It is as if what was designated here were the ultimately unfilmable – namely, the monstrous, fused couple, the two-backed beast of the primal scene, the impossible couple of body and voice.

The landing scene is constructed in such a way as to culminate in this final *brushing effect* of the body against the voice, where one verges upon the limits of the reality effect in cinema far more than one does with the convention of synchronization. It is worth remarking, in passing, that if Marguerite Duras often uses the voice *entirely liberated from the body* to sublime effect in her films, in the work of others the same device quickly goes stale. If it is true that where the voice is attached to the body there is a conventional couple that one may wish to sunder, *once it is far from the body, it quickly grows bored*. In *Psycho*, as in *India Song*, voice and body brush against each other at the end of a long, asymptotic trajectory. One then has to ask why there is something horrible about this contact, as if it were the wing of death which seemed at the same time to touch the audience.

The Cell

We have already mentioned the third occasion upon which the mother's voice features. It arises after Lila, Marion's sister, has found the real mother, in the form of a mummy, and after the psychiatrist has carefully unravelled the entire affair and given a logical explanation entirely consistent with the whole film. Everything would then seem to be resolved. Yet when someone comes to tell us that the prisoner is cold, and a policeman brings a blanket in order to take it to his cell, the camera follows the policeman just as it had followed Norman up the stairs. The audience still hopes to see the incestuous marriage between the voice of the mother and the body of Norman. Here too, we first of all hear the voice of the mother off frame saying 'Thank you', and we then enter the cell. But the voice that we then hear issuing from Norman's lips, the mother's monologue, is the sort of tight-lipped voice characteristic of spirit possession or ventriloquism.

Finally, the voice has not found a body which will assume it by speaking it and by assigning it a place, just as the mother's interment did not obey the rules, since she has been exhumed and stuffed. For the narrative to have come full circle, the body found in the cellar would undoubtedly have to have been given a symbolic reburial. As it happens, the closing shot in the film is one of disinterment, that of Marion's car (which is both her coffin, and that of the money she had stolen). Other allusions to interment − or to its opposite, stuffing − testify to the importance of this motif in *Psycho*. We should not be surprised to find that the voice of the ghost rules over the final image, which consecrates the triumph of the *acousmêtre*.

The same is true of *The Testament of Doctor Mabuse*, a film with which *Psycho* has much in common. Both films revolve around a being who is hidden from us, and whose existence and power are borne out and manifested by its voice (Mabuse, the mother). In either case, we are concerned with the impossibility of reattaching a voice to a body so as to give it a location, the body being that of an unburied person (a dissected and dispersed body in the case of Mabuse, a stuffed body in the case of the mother). Both films are similarly concerned with a man possessed by the voice of an *acousmêtre* that is more powerful than he is (Baum by Mabuse, Norman by the mother). In either case, there is a silhouette behind a curtain lit *contre-jour*, thus testifying to the presence of the Master, as well as a man who assumes the voice of his mother (Hofmeister in his madness, when he wishes to dispel the horror; Norman in his episodes of doubling). Both films feature the intrusion of a woman into a closed space (Lily enters the curtained room, while Lila – a similar name – ventures into the cellar), where she receives a revelation, in either case of something that is not human (not Mabuse but a mechanical contraption; not the living mother but a mummy). Finally, both stories end with the total identification of the weaker with the stronger being, who seems thus to have paid the price of terminal madness and confinement (Baum with Mabuse; Norman with his mother).

We know that Hitchcock had seen Lang's film, but I do not believe that he had consciously modelled the plot of *Psycho*, so different in many other respects, upon it. It is simply that both films revolve around the same myth of the *acousmêtre*, with the same rigour and the same concern to take cinema as far as it will go. With *The Testament of Doctor Mabuse*, as with *Psycho*, the talking cinema engages with its own structure, which is based upon an off frame inhabited by the voice, which is the necessary corollary of the frame. Finally, these films also touch upon the power of making the dead live through sound and image. They both revolve around the illusion of seeing and hearing, upon which cinema depends, and in them cinema is brought up against its own impossibilities, which are identified as such. Thus, voice and image may feature in it only as sundered one from the other, and can consummate rediscoveries only in a mythical unity that is for ever lost. The talking cinema is simply a sort of tying up, and this may indeed constitute its claim to greatness – when, instead of denying this tying up, it turns it into its subject, thereby going, under the sign of the impossible, to the very heart of the reality effect.

Notes

1. An old dictionary defines *acousmatic* as 'a sound one hears without seeing what causes it'. No praise can be too great for Pierre Schaeffer, who unearthed this rare word in the 1950s to refer to a situation in which listeners are very often placed nowadays, owing to the routine use of radio, telephone and records – a situation which has long existed, primarily because of these new media, but which, because it had never been pinned down by a specific term, was not even identifiable in itself,

still less in its consequences. On the other hand, since his specific concern was with concrete music, he had not bothered to coin a specific word for another, seemingly banal situation in which we do actually see the source, and therefore spoke in such case of 'direct' listening. Since this phrase is somewhat ambiguous, I have preferred to speak of 'visualized' listening.

The talking cinema naturally began with 'visualized' sound (which is often called 'synch' or 'in'), but it was not long before it took to making experiments in acousmatic, not only with music but also with the human voice. The example of Fritz Lang's *M*, made in 1930, is often quoted, where the shadow of the child-murderer is cast across his 'Wanted' poster, while his voice off frame says to the little girl (who is also off frame at that particular moment, in spite of what the well-known still suggests): 'You've got a fine balloon there!' The combination in this shot of voice and shadow, together with the use of the acousmatic voice for its disturbing effect, are very telling. Yet it is not long before the voice gets rid of the shadow, or of superimposition, in order to impose its own acousmatic personality.

It is important to realize that as one moves from one situation, which is visualized, to the other, which is acousmatic, the nature, presence, distance and 'colour' of the sound do not change. What alters is simply the relationship between what one sees and what one hears. M's voice, when he is nowhere to be seen, is just as much present and clearly defined as in the shots when he is actually visible. Thus, when we listen to the soundtrack of any film whatsoever without the frame, it is impossible, on the basis of sound alone, to differentiate between acousmatic sounds and visualized sounds. Only our visual perception of the film, or our memory of its images after we have seen it, enables us to decide. Listening without images may be said to 'acousmatize' all sounds regardless, without them preserving, in this acousmatized soundtrack (which then becomes a genuine soundtrack, a totality), any perceptible trace of their original relationship to the image.

To grasp what is at stake in this distinction, it is worth considering the ancient meaning of the term 'acousmatic', which was, it would seem, the name given to a Pythagorean sect whose adepts used to listen to their Master speaking from behind a hanging, so that, it was said, the sight of the sender would not distract them from the message (just as, on television, one may easily be distracted from what a person is saying by the way they knit their brows or play with their hands, details which the cameras often delight in capturing). But this rule prohibiting seeing, which turns Master, God or Spirit into an acousmatic voice, may of course be found in a large number of rites and religions, especially in Islam and Judaism. It is also to be found in the apparatus of the Freudian cure, in which the analysand does not see the analyst, who in turn does not look at the analysand. Finally, it features in the cinema, where the voice of the acousmatic Master who is hiding behind a door, a curtain or off frame lies at the heart of a number of major films – for example *The Testament of Doctor Mabuse* (the voice of the evil genius), *Psycho* (the voice of the mother) and *The Magnificent Ambersons* (the director's voice).

When an acousmatic presence consists of a voice – and above all when that voice has not been visualized, and one cannot therefore yet put a face to it – one is dealing with a being of a particular sort, a kind of talking, acting shadow, which I have named an *acousmêtre* – that is, an acousmatic being. A person who talks to you on the telephone, whom you have never seen, is an *acousmêtre*. But if you have already seen him/her – or, to speak in cinematic terms, you go on hearing him/her when he/she has just left the frame in which he or she was visible, is he/she still an *acousmêtre*? Such a person is obviously an *acousmêtre*, but one belonging to a different category, that of the 'visualized' *acousmêtres*. It is easy enough, of course, to multiply neologisms, if only to distinguish at least two different varieties, depending upon whether a face is or is not put to an invisible voice.

However, I would prefer to keep the definition of *acousmêtre* open, thereby avoiding the fabrication of necessarily more or less academic subdivisions. I shall leave this notion vague and general. What really counts, I would argue, is what one might term the *integral acousmêtre*, who is not-yet-seen but is able to enter the frame at any moment. A more familiar, reassuring phenomenon is the *acousmêtre* who is already-seen [*déjà-vu*], who has temporarily left the frame; whereas in the dark regions of the acousmatic frame, which surrounds and subsumes the visible frame, this *acousmêtre* may acquire, by contagion, some of the powers of the integral *acousmêtre*. Still more familiar is the kindly *acousmêtre* commentator, who never makes an appearance, but has nothing of himself to risk in the image.

2. François Truffaut, *Hitchcock*, London: Panther 1969, pp. 346–8.

3. Ibid., p. 343.

4. Ibid., p. 328.

5. André Bazin, 'Montage interdit', in *Qu'est-ce que le cinéma?*

PART III

The Individual:
Hitchcock's Universe

'In His Bold Gaze My Ruin Is Writ Large'

SLAVOJ ŽIŽEK

What's wrong with *The Wrong Man*?

To comply with the dialectical axiom that the only way to reach the underlying law of a universe is through its exception, let us begin with *The Wrong Man*, one of those films which clearly 'stick out' from the totality of Hitchcock's *œuvre*:

- on the one hand, *The Wrong Man* is Hitchcock at his purest. His special attachment to it is attested by the exceptional character of his cameo appearance: in a prologue, Hitchcock directly addresses the viewers, reminding them that what they will see is a tragedy taken from real life. This prologue sounds like some kind of implicit apology: sorry, but you will not get the usual comic-thriller stuff – here, things are for real, I shall lay my cards on the table and deliver my message directly, not wrapped up in the usual comedian's costume . . .[1]

- on the other hand, it is no less clear that there is something fundamentally wrong with the film: it is deeply flawed. In consequence, there are two questions to be answered: *What* is the 'message' that Hitchcock endeavoured to articulate 'directly' in *The Wrong Man*, and why did he *fail* in it?

The answer to the first question is contained in what is usually referred to as the *theological* dimension of Hitchcock's *œuvre*. The

211

story of the musician, Balestrero, whose quiet life is suddenly thrown off balance by an unforeseen accident – he is falsely identified as a bank robber – epitomizes the Hitchcockian vision of a cruel, unfathomable and self-willed God who sadistically plays with human destinies. Who is that God who, for no apparent reason, can turn our daily life into a nightmare? In their pathbreaking *Hitchcock* (1957), Rohmer and Chabrol[2] sought the key to 'Hitchcock's universe' in his Catholicism; although this approach seems largely discredited today – overshadowed as it is by the great semiotic and psychoanalytic analyses of the 1970s – it is still worth returning to, especially when one bears in mind that the Catholic tradition to which Rohmer and Chabrol refer is not Catholicism in general but Jansenism. The Jansenist problematic of sin, of the relationship between virtue and grace, in fact delineates for the first time the relationship between subject and Law which characterizes 'Hitchcock's universe'.

In the Preface to the English edition of *The Movement-Image*,[3] Gilles Deleuze locates the link that connects Hitchcock with the tradition of English thought in the theory of external relations, in the name of which English empiricism opposed the continental tradition of conceiving the development of an object as the explication of its inherent potential: is not 'Hitchcock's universe' where some wholly external and accidental intervention of Fate, in no way founded in the subject's immanent properties, all of a sudden radically changes his/her symbolic status (the wrong identification of Thornhill as 'Kaplan' in *North by Northwest*, the wrong identification of Balestrero as the bank robber in *The Wrong Man*, and so on, up to the couple in *Mr and Mrs Smith*, who suddenly learn that their marriage is void) – is it not inscribed into the tradition of English empiricism according to which an object is embedded in a contingent network of external relations? Yet what this tradition lacks is the subjective dimension, the tension, the absurd discord between the subject's self-experience and the external network which determines his/her Truth – in short, the determination of this network of external relations not as a simple empirical composite but as a *symbolic* network, the network of an intersubjective symbolic structure. This further specification is provided by the Jansenist theology of Port-Royal.

The starting point of Jansenism is the abyss separating human 'virtue' from divine 'grace': in terms of their immanent nature, all people are sinful, sin is something that defines their very ontological status; for that reason, their salvation cannot be dependent on the virtue that pertains to them as persons, it can only come from outside, as a divine grace. So, grace necessarily appears as something radically contingent — it bears no relation to the person's character or his/her deeds: in an inscrutable way, God decides in advance who will be saved and who will be damned.[4] The relation which, in our everyday life, we perceive as 'natural', is thus inverted: God does not decide on our salvation on the basis of our virtuous deeds, we accomplish virtuous deeds because we are saved in advance. The tragedy of leading characters in the plays of Jean Racine, the dramatist of Port-Royal, is that they personify the utmost aggravation of this antagonistic relationship between virtue and grace: it was Arnauld, Racine's contemporary, who characterized Phaedra as 'one of the just to whom grace was not vouchsafed'.

The consequences of this Jansenist split between immanent virtue and transcendent grace or damnation are far-reaching — Jansenism exerted a fascination on French Communists in their most 'Stalinist' period, since it was easy for them to recognize, in the split between virtue and grace, the forebear of what they called 'objective responsibility': as an individual, a person can be beyond all praise, honest, virtuous, and so on, yet if s/he is not touched by the 'grace' of insight into the historical Truth embodied in the Party, s/he is 'objectively guilty' and as such condemned to damnation. Jansenism thus contains *in nuce* the logic which, in the Stalinist monster trials, impelled the accused to acknowledge their guilt and to demand the harshest punishment for themselves: the fundamental paradox of Racine's *Athalie* is that in this drama on the conflict between the partisans of Jehovah — the true God — and the pagan Baal, *everybody*, including Mattan, the high priest of Baal, *believes in Jehovah*, as with the accused in the Stalinist trials, who knew themselves to be the 'scum of history' — knew, that is, that Truth is on the side of the Party.[5] The attitude of Racine's evil-doers thus announces the paradox of the Sadeian hero who reverses Pascal's motto 'even if you don't believe, kneel down and pray, act as if you believe, and the belief will come by itself': the Sadeian hero is somebody who – although deep in himself he knows that God exists – *acts as if God does not exist* and breaks all His command-ments.[6]

If this insertion of Hitchcock into the lineage of Jansenism seems far-fetched, it is sufficient to recall the crucial role played by *gaze* in Hitchcock's films as well as in Racine's plays. *Phaedre*, his most famous play, pivots on the misinterpretation of a look: Phaedre, the wife of King Theseus, reveals her love to Hippolytus, the king's son from a previous marriage, and is cruelly rebuffed; as her husband enters, she mistakes Hippolytus's grim expression – actually a sign of his distress – for an insolent determination to betray her to the king, and takes vengeance on him, the outcome of which is her own ruin.[7] Verse 910 of *Phaedre*, which enunciates this misreading ('In his bold gaze my ruin is writ large.'[8]), could serve as an appropriate epithet to Hitchcock's universe, where the Other's gaze – up to Norman Bates's final look into the camera in *Psycho* – epitomizes lethal threat: where suspense is never the product of a simple physical confrontation between subject and assailant, but always involves the mediation of what the subject *reads into the other's gaze*.[9] In other words, Hippolytus's gaze exemplifies perfectly Lacan's thesis according to which the gaze I encounter 'is, not a seen gaze, but a gaze imagined by me in the field of the Other':[10] the gaze is not the Other's glance as such, but the way this glance 'concerns me [*me regarde*]', the way the subject *sees him/herself affected by it as to his/ her desire* – Hippolytus's gaze is not the mere fact of his casting a glance at Phaedre, but the threat Phaedre sees in it, 'reads into it', from the position of her desire.[11]

The mysterious link that connects the two features enumerated – the pure 'machine' (the set of external relations which determine the subject's fate) and the pure gaze – in Lacanian terms: the signifier's structure, its *automaton*, and the *objet petit a*, its contingent leftover, *tuche* – is a key to Racine's as well as to Hitchcock's universe. A first hint as to the nature of this link can be obtained through a closer analysis of the scene from *Phaedre*: its crucial feature is the presence of a *third* gaze, that of the king, Theseus. The interplay of gazes between Phaedre and Hippolytus implies a Thirdness, an agent under whose watchful eye this interplay takes place and who, at any price, must be kept in ignorance as to the true nature of the affair. It is not by accident that this role is attributed to the king – who but the king, the ultimate guarantor of the social texture, is more apt to epitomize the blind mechanism of the symbolic order as such? The configuration here is homologous to that in Poe's 'The Purloined Letter', where we also witness the duel of two gazes (the queen's and the minister's) against the background of the third (king's) gaze, which must be kept ignorant of the affair. And do we not encounter a homologous configuration in *The Thirty-Nine Steps* as well as in Hitchcock's two later variations of the same formula (*Saboteur, North by Northwest*): namely in the scene of the duel between the hero and his adversaries in front of the ignorant crowd (the political rally in the first film, the charity dance in the second, the auction in the third)? In *Saboteur*, for example, the hero tries to snatch his girlfriend from the hands of the Nazi agents and to escape with her; yet the scene takes place in a great hall, in full view of hundreds of guests, so both sides have to observe the rules of etiquette – that is to say, the actions each of them undertakes against the adversary have to accord with the rules of the social game; the Other (epitomized by the crowd) has to be kept ignorant as to the true stakes.[12]

This, then, is the answer to our first question: *The Wrong Man* stages at its purest the theological background of 'Hitchcock's universe' where the heroes are at the mercy of '*Dieu obscur*', of the unpredictable Fate epitomized by the gigantic stone statues which appear regularly in his films (from the Egyptian Goddess in the British Museum – *Blackmail* – via the Statue of Liberty – *Saboteur* – to the Presidents' heads at Mount Rushmore – *North by Northwest*). These Gods are blind in their blessed ignorance; their mechanism runs irrespective of petty human affairs: Fate intervenes in the guise of a contingent coincidence which radically changes the hero's symbolic status.[13] Indeed, only a thin line separates this notion of '*Dieu obscur*' from the Sadeian notion of the 'Supreme-Being-of-Evil'.[14]

As to our second question, the answer is provided by another statue which, precisely, does *not* appear in any of Hitchcock's films: the Sphinx. What we have in mind here is a photograph of Hitchcock in front of the Sphinx, both of their faces in profile, emphasizing their parallelism – it is ultimately Hitchcock himself who, in his relationship to the viewer, assumes the paradoxical role of a

'benevolent evil God', pulling the strings and playing games with the public. That is to say, Hitchcock as *auteur* is a kind of diminished, 'aestheticized' mirror-image of the unfathomable and self-willed Creator. And the trouble with *The Wrong Man* is that in this film, Hitchcock *renounced* this role of a 'benevolent evil God' and endeavoured to transmit the message in a 'direct', 'serious' way – with the paradoxical result that the 'message' itself lost its persuasiveness. In other words, there is no meta-language: the 'message' (the vision of a universe at the mercy of the cruel and unfathomable '*Dieu obscur*') can be rendered only in the artistic form which itself mimes its structure.[15] The moment Hitchcock succumbed to the temptation of 'serious' psychological realism, even the most tragic moments depicted in the film somehow leave us cold, in spite of Hitchcock's tremendous effort to affect us . . .

The Hitchcockian allegory

Here one touches the question of Hitchcock's 'original experience', of the traumatic kernel around which his films circulate. Today, this problematic may seem outdated, a case of naive 'reductionist' search for the 'effective' psychological foundation of the artistic fiction on account of which psychoanalytic art criticism acquired such a bad name – yet there is another way to approach it. Let us take three widely disparate works: J.G. Ballard's *Empire of the Sun*, John le Carré's *A Perfect Spy*, Ridley Scott's *Black Rain* – what have they in common? In all three, the author – after a series of works which established a certain thematic and stylistic continuity delineating the contours of a specific artistic 'universe' – finally tackles the 'empirical' fragment of reality which served as its experiential support.

Following a series of science-fiction novels obsessed by the motif of wandering around in an abandoned, decaying world, full of the debris of a defunct civilization, *Empire of the Sun* gives a fictionalized account of Ballard's childhood when, at the age of eleven, he was torn by the Japanese occupation of Shanghai from his parents, so that he found himself alone in the rich foreigners' quarter of the town, free to wander around among the abandoned villas with dried, cracked pools. . . . Le Carré's 'Circus' is the ultimate depiction of the spy universe of betrayal, manipulation and double deception; in *A Perfect Spy* – written immediately after his father's death – le Carré revealed the source of his obsession with betrayal: his ambiguous relationship with his father, a corrupted impostor. Ridley Scott's films display a vision of a corrupted and decaying megalopolis (as one critic viciously noted, Scott is unable to shoot a street without 'atmospheric' litter and sordid mist); in *Black Rain*, he finally stumbled upon an object whose reality itself gives body to this vision: today's Tokyo – no need, there, to take refuge with dystopian visions of Los Angeles in 2080, as in *Blade Runner* . . .

It should be clear, now, why what we have here is not 'psychological reductionism': the unearthed fragment of experience (childhood in occupied Shanghai; obscene paternal figure; today's Japanese megalopolis) is not simply the 'actual' point of reference enabling us to reduce fantasy to reality but, on the contrary, the

217

point at which *reality itself touches fantasy* (one is even tempted to say: infringes upon it) – that is to say, the point of short-circuit by means of which the fantasy-trauma invades reality – here, in this unique moment of encounter, reality appears 'more dreamlike than dreams themselves'. Against this background, the reasons for the failure of *The Wrong Man* become somewhat clearer: the film does render the experiential foundation of 'Hitchcock's universe', yet this foundation simply lacks the fantasy-dimension – the miraculous encounter does not take place, reality remains 'mere reality', fantasy does not resound in it.

To put it another way: what *The Wrong Man* lacks is the *allegorical* dimension: its filmic enunciated (the diegetic content) does not index its process of enunciation (Hitchcock's relationship with the public). This modernist notion of allegory is, of course, opposed to the traditional one: within the traditional narrative space, the diegetic content functions as the allegory of some transcendent entity (flesh-and-blood individuals personify transcendent prin-ciples: Love, Temptation, Betrayal, etc.; they procure external clothing for suprasensible Ideas), whereas in the modern space, the diegetic content is posited and conceived as the allegory of its own process of enunciation. In his *Murderous Gaze*,[16] William Rothman deciphers Hitchcock's entire *œuvre* as such an allegorical staging of the 'benevolent–sadist' relationship between Hitchcock and his public; one is even tempted to say that Hitchcock's films ultimately contain only two subject positions, that of the director and that of the viewer – all diegetic persons assume, by turns, one of these two positions.

The clearest case of such an allegorical self-reflective structure is found in *Psycho*: far more convincing than the traditional allegorical reading (the interpretation of the policeman who stops Marion just before she reaches the Bates motel as the Angel sent by Providence to stop her on her way to perdition, for example) is the reading which interprets the diegetic content as the stand-in for the viewer (his voyeurism) or the director (his punishing the viewer's voyeurism).[17] To avoid the enumeration of well-known examples which attest to Hitchcock's playing with the ambiguous and split nature of the viewer's desire (the suspended sinking of Marion's car in *Psycho*; numerous allusions to the viewer's voyeurism from *Rear*

Window to *Psycho*; the hand of Grace Kelly reaching for help towards the camera – i.e. the viewer – in *Dial M for Murder*; the 'punishing' of the viewer by fully realizing his/her desire and depicting the malefactor's death in all its repulsive details, from *Saboteur* to *Torn Curtain*; etc.), let us confine ourselves to the second scene from *Psycho*: Marion (Janet Leigh) enters her office, followed by her boss and the oil millionaire who displays, in a boastful-obscene way, 40,000 dollars. The key to this scene is Hitchcock's cameo appearance at its very beginning:[18] for a brief moment, we see him through the windowpane standing on the pavement; when, seconds later, the millionaire enters the office from the very place occupied by Hitchcock, he wears the same stetson – he is thus a kind of stand-in for Hitchcock, sent by him into the film to lead Marion into temptation and thus propel the story in the desired direction.... Although *The Wrong Man* and *Psycho* are alike in many ways (the black-and-white bleakness of the everyday life they depict; the rupture in their narrative line; etc.), their difference is insurmountable.

The classical Marxist reproach here would be, of course, that the ultimate function of such an allegorical procedure, by means of which the product reflects its own formal process, is to render invisible its social mediation and thereby neutralize its sociocritical potential – as if, in order to fill out the void of social content, the work turns to its own form. And indeed, is not this reproach confirmed *per negationem* by *The Wrong Man* which, because of its suspension of the allegory, among all Hitchcock's films comes closest to 'social criticism' (dreary everyday life caught in the irrational wheels of judicial bureaucracy ...)? Yet one is tempted to defend here the exact opposite of this line of argument:[19] the strongest 'ideologico-critical' potential of Hitchcock's films is contained precisely in their allegorical nature. In order for this potential of Hitchcock's 'benevolent–sadistic' playing with the viewer to become manifest, one must take into account the strict concept of 'sadism' as it was elaborated by Lacan. In his 'Kant avec Sade', Lacan proposed two schemes which render the matrix of the two stages of the Sadeian fantasy[20] – here is the first scheme:

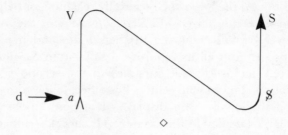

V [for *Volonté*] designates the Will-to-Enjoy, this fundamental attitude of the 'sadist' subject, his endeavour to find enjoyment in the pain of the other; while S is precisely this other subject suffering and – therein consists Lacan's point – as such, 'non-barred', full: the 'sadist' is a kind of parasite in search of the corroboration of his being. By means of his/her suffering, the other – his victim – confirms him/herself as resisting solid substance: the live flesh into which the sadist cuts authenticates, so to speak, the fullness of being. The upper level of the scheme, V → S, thus denotes the manifest 'sadistic' relationship: the sadistic pervert gives body to the Will-to-Enjoy which torments the victim in order to obtain the fullness of being. Lacan's thesis, however, is that this manifest relationship conceals another, latent relationship which is the 'truth' of the first one. This other relationship is contained in the lower level of the scheme, $a \diamond \mathbf{S}$: the relationship of the object-cause of desire to the split subject.

In other words, the sadist as aggressive Will-to-Enjoy is nothing but a semblance whose 'truth' is *a*, the object: his 'true' position is that of an *object-instrument of the Other's enjoyment*. The sadist does not act for his own enjoyment; his stratagem is, rather, to elude the split constitutive of the subject by means of assuming the role of the object-instrument in service of the big Other (a historico-political example: the Stalinist Communist who conceives himself as the tool of History, as the means of carrying out historical Necessity). The split is thereby transposed on to the other, on to the tormented victim: the victim is never a mere passive substance, a non-barred 'fullness of being', since the sadistic performance relies on the victim's split (his/her shame about what is going on with him/her, for example) – the sadist enjoys only in so far as his activity brings about such a split in the other. (In Stalinist Communism, this split provides for the obscene 'surplus-enjoyment' that pertains to the Communist's position: the Communist acts *in the name of the People* – that is, his lacerating the people at will is for him the very form of 'serving the People' – the Stalinist acts as a pure mediator, as an instrument by means of which the People, so to speak, tortures itself. . . .) The true desire of the sadist (d – *désir* – in the lower left-hand corner of the scheme) is therefore to act as an instrument of the enjoyment of the Other as 'the Supreme-Being-of-Evil'.[21]

Here, however, Lacan takes a crucial step further: the first scheme in its entirety renders the structure of the Sadeian fantasy; yet Sade was not a dupe of this fantasy of his – he was well aware that its place is within another frame that determines it. We can produce this second frame by simply rotating the first scheme by a quarter-turn:

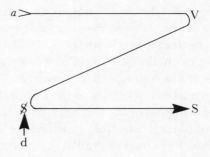

Such, then, is the 'actual' site of the subject who dreams the sadistic fantasy: an object-victim, at the mercy of the 'sadistic' Will of the big Other which, as Lacan puts it, here 'passes over into moral constraint'. Lacan exemplifies it by Sade himself, in whose case this constraint took the form of the pressure exerted on him by his environment, by his mother-in-law, who again and again arranged his imprisonment, up to Napoleon himself, who committed him to an asylum.

Sade – the subject who produced 'sadistic' scenarios in frantic rhythm – was thus 'actually' the victim of endless harassment, an object upon which state agencies lived out their moralistic sadism: *the real Will-to-Enjoy is already at work in the state-bureaucratic apparatus which handles the subject.* The result of it is $, the barred subject, which one must read here literally as erasure, the wiping out of the person from the texture of symbolic tradition: Sade's expulsion from 'official' (literary) history, so that there are almost no traces left of him as a person. S, the pathological-suffering subject, appears here as the community of those who, during Sade's lifetime, stood by him in spite of all hardship (his wife, sister-in-law, servant), and above all as the community of those who, after his death, never ceased to be fascinated by his work (writers, philosophers, literary critics ...).

At this precise point, the reasons for reading the scheme of the Sadeian fantasy retroactively – from the matrix of the four discourses – become clear: the scheme gains consistency if one reads its fourth term – S – as S_2, (university) knowledge endeavouring to penetrate the mystery of Sade's work. (In this sense, *a* in the second scheme could be said to stand for what remained of Sade after his death, for the object-product by means of which Sade provoked the moralistic-sadistic reaction of the Master: *a* is ultimately his work, his legacy as a writer.)

The quarter-turn in the scheme thus places the sadist in the position of victim: the transgression which at first appeared to subvert the Law turns out to pertain to the Law – *the Law itself is the ultimate perversion.* (In Stalinism, this shift designates the moment when the Stalinist himself turns into a victim – is forced to sacrifice himself to the higher interests of the Party, to confess his guilt in a political trial ... $ stands here for his erasure from the annals of history, for his transformation into a 'non-person'[22].) This quarter-turn also translates the logic of Hitchcock's 'sadist' playing with the viewer. First, he sets a trap of sadistic identification for the viewer by way of arousing in him/her the 'sadistic' desire to see the hero crush the bad guy, this suffering 'fullness of being'.... Once the viewer is filled out with the Will-to-Enjoy, Hitchcock closes the trap by simply realizing the viewer's desire: in having his/her desire fully realized, the viewer obtains more than he/she asked for (the act of murder in all its nauseous *presence* – the exemplary case here is the murder of Gromek in *Torn Curtain*) and is thus forced to concede that, in the very moment he/she was possessed by the Will to see the bad guy annihilated, he/she was effectively manipulated by the only

true sadist, Hitchcock himself. This acquiescence confronts the
viewer with the contradictory, divided nature of his/her desire (s/he
wants the bad guy to be crushed without mercy, yet at the same
time s/he is not prepared to pay the full price for it: as soon as s/he
sees his/her desire realized, s/he draws back in shame), and the
result, the product, of it is S_2: knowledge – that is, the endless flow of
books and articles on Hitchcock.

From I to *a*

The shift – the rotation – at work here could also be defined as the
passage from I to *a*: from gaze as point of symbolic identification to
gaze as object. That is to say, before he/she identifies with the
persons from diegetic reality, the viewer *identifies with him- or herself
as pure gaze* – that is, with the abstract point which gazes upon the
screen.[23] This ideal point provides a pure form of ideology in so far
as it pretends to float freely in an empty space, not charged by any
desire – as if the viewer were reduced to a kind of absolutely invisible, substanceless witness of events which take place 'by themselves', irrespective of the presence of his or her gaze. By means of
the shift from I to *a*, however, the viewer is forced to face the desire at
work in his/her seemingly 'neutral' gaze – here, it suffices to recall
the well-known scene from *Psycho* where Norman Bates nervously
observes the car containing Marion's body submerging in the
swamp behind his mother's house: when the car stops sinking for a
moment, the anxiety that automatically arises in the viewer – a
token of his/her solidarity with Norman – suddenly reminds him or
her that his/her desire is identical to Norman's: that his impartiality
was always-already false. At this moment, his/her gaze is de-ideal-
ized, its purity blemished by a pathological stain, and what comes
forth is the desire that maintains it: the viewer is compelled to
assume that the scene he witnesses is staged for his eyes, that his/her
gaze was included in it from the very beginning.

There is a well-known true story about an anthropological expe-
dition trying to contact a wild tribe in the New Zealand jungle who
allegedly danced a terrible war dance in grotesque masks; when
they reached this tribe, they begged them to dance it for them, and

the dance did in fact match the description; so the explorers obtained the desired material about the strange and terrible customs of the aborigines. Shortly afterwards, however, it was shown that this wild dance did not actually exist at all: the aborigines had only tried to meet the wishes of the explorers; in their discussions with them they had discovered what they wanted and had reproduced it for them.... This is what Lacan means when he says that the subject's desire is the desire of the other: the explorers received back from the aborigines their own desire; the perverse strangeness which seemed to them uncannily terrible was staged for their benefit. The same paradox is nicely satirized in *Top Secret* (Zucker, Abrahams and Abrahams, 1978), a comedy about Western tourists in the (now former) GDR: at the railway station at the border, they see a terrible sight through the window: brutal police, dogs, beaten children – when the inspection is over, however, the entire Customs post shifts, the beaten children get up and brush the dust from themselves – in short, the whole display of 'Communist brutality' was laid on *for Western eyes.*

What we have here is the inverse-symmetrical counterpoint to the illusion that defines the ideological interpellation: the illusion that the Other always-already looks at us, addresses us. When we *recognize* ourselves as interpellated, as the addressees of an ideological call, we *misrecognize* the radical contingency of finding ourselves at the place of interpellation – that is, we fail to notice how our 'spontaneous' perception that the Other (God, Nation, etc.) has chosen *us* as its addressee results from the retroactive inversion of contingency into necessity: we do not recognize ourselves in the ideological call because we were chosen; on the contrary, we perceive ourselves as chosen, as the addressee of a call, because we recognized ourselves in it – *the contingent act of recognition engenders retroactively its own necessity* (the same illusion as that of the reader of a horoscope who 'recognizes' him/herself as its addressee by taking contingent coincidences of obscure predictions with his/her actual life as proof that the horoscope 'is talking about *him/her*').

The illusion involved in our identification with a pure gaze, on the other hand, is far more cunning: while we perceive ourselves as external bystanders stealing a furtive glance into some majestic Mystery which is indifferent to us, we are blinded to the fact that the entire spectacle of Mystery is staged *with an eye to our gaze*: to attract and fascinate our gaze – here, the Other deceives us in so far as it induces us to believe that we were *not* chosen; here, it is the true addressee him/herself who mistakes his/her position for that of an accidental bystander.[24]

Therein consists Hitchcock's elementary strategy: by means of a reflexive inclusion of his/her own gaze, the viewer becomes aware of how this gaze of his/hers is always-already partial, 'ideological', stigmatized by a 'pathological' desire. Here, Hitchcock's strategy is far more subversive than it may appear – that is to say, what, exactly, is the status of the viewer's desire realized in the above-mentioned example of Gromek's murder in *Torn Curtain*? The crucial fact is that this desire is experienced as a 'transgression' of what is socially permitted, as the desire for a moment when one is, so to speak, allowed to break the Law in the name of the Law itself – what we encounter here is again perversion as a socially 'constructive' attitude: one can indulge in illicit drives, torture and kill for the protection of law and order, and so on. This perversion relies on the split of the field of Law into Law as 'Ego-Ideal' – that is, symbolic order which regulates social life and maintains social peace – and into its obscene, superegotistical reverse.

As numerous analyses from Bakhtin onwards have shown, periodic transgressions are inherent to the social order; they function as a condition of the latter's stability. (Bakhtin's mistake – or, rather, the mistake of some of his followers – was to present an idealized image of these 'transgressions': to pass in silence over lynching parties, and so on, as the crucial form of the 'carnivalesque suspension of social hierarchy'.) The deepest identification which 'holds a community together' is not so much identification with the Law which regulates its 'normal' everyday circuit as, rather, *identification with the specific form of transgression of the Law, of its suspension* (in psychoanalytic terms, with the specific form of enjoyment).

Let us recall small-town white communities in the American South of the 1920s, where the reign of the official, public Law is accompanied by its shadowy double, the nightly terror of Ku Klux Klan, the lynchings of powerless blacks, and so on: a (white) man is easily forgiven at least minor infringements of the Law, especially when they can be justified by a 'code of honour'; the community still recognizes him as 'one of us' (legendary cases of solidarity with the transgressor abound in Southern white communities); yet he will be effectively excommunicated, perceived as 'not one of us', the moment he disowns the specific form of *transgression* that pertains to this community – say, the moment he refuses to partake in the ritual Ku Klux Klan lynchings, or even reports them to the Law (which, of course, does not want to hear about them, since they exemplify its own hidden reverse).

The Nazi community relied on the same solidarity-in-guilt adduced by the participation in a common transgression: it ostracized those who were not ready to assume the dark reverse of the idyllic *Volksgemeinschaft*, the night pogroms, the beatings of political opponents – in short, all that 'everybody knew, yet did not want to talk about aloud'. And – therein lies our point – the identification which is 'extraneated', whose functioning is suspended, as a result of Hitchcock's allegorical playing with the viewer, is this very identification with transgression. Precisely when Hitchcock appears at his most conformist, praising the rule of Law, and so on, the ideologico-critical mole has already done its work, the fundamental identification with the 'transgressive' mode of enjoyment which holds a community together – in short: the stuff of which the ideological dream is effectively made – is contaminated beyond cure ...

Psycho's Moebius band

Psycho carries this Hitchcockian subversion of the viewer's identification to its utmost, forcing him/her to *identify with the abyss beyond identification*. That is to say, the key that enables us to penetrate the film's mystery is to be sought in the rupture, in the change of modality, that separates the first third from the last two-thirds (in accordance with the 'golden section' whereby the ratio of the smaller to the larger part coincides with the ratio of the larger part to the whole). During the first third of the film we identify with Marion, we experience the story from her perspective, which is why her murder derails us, causing us to lose the ground from under our feet – up to the end of the film, we are in search of a new footing, clinging to the point of view of the detective Arbogast, of Sam and

Lila ... yet all these secondary identifications are 'empty' or, more precisely, supplementary: in them, we identify not with subjects but with a pure, flat, investigative machine on which we rely in our effort to reveal the mystery of Norman, the 'hero' who replaces Marion as the film's focal point and dominates the last part, and who is in a sense nothing but her mirror-negative (as is indicated by the very mirror-relationship of their respective names: Marion – Norman). In short: after the murder of Marion, identification with the personality who dominates the diegetic space becomes impossible.[25] Where does this impossibility of identification come from? In other words, wherein consists the change of modality generated by the passage from Marion to Norman? At its most obvious, Marion's world is the world of contemporary American everyday life, whereas Norman's world is its nocturnal reverse:

> Car, motel, policeman, road, office, money, detective, etc. – these are signs of the present, actual positivity and renunciation; villa (= haunted castle), stuffed animals, mummy, stairs, knife, false clothes – these are signs from the stock of terrifying figurations of the forbidden past. It is only the dialogue of the two sign-systems, their mutual relationship brought about not by analogies but by contradictions, which creates the visual tension of this thriller.[26]

We are therefore a long way from the usual Hitchcockian subversion of the idyllic everyday surface with its dark reverse: the 'surface' subverted, literally turned inside out, in *Psycho* is not the idyllic image one encounters at the outset of *Rear Window*, or *The Trouble with Harry*, but a dreary, grey 'leaden time', full of 'banal' worries and anxieties. This American alienation (financial insecurity, fear of the police, desperate pursuit of a piece of happiness – in short, the *hysteria* of everyday capitalist life) is confronted with its *psychotic* reverse: the nightmarish world of pathological crime.

The relationship between these two worlds eludes the simple oppositions of surface and depth, reality and fantasy, and so on – the only topology that suits it is that of the two surfaces of the Moebius band: if we progress far enough on one surface, all of a sudden we find ourselves on its reverse. This moment of passage from one surface to its reverse, from the register of hysterical desire to that of psychotic drive, can be located very precisely: the fade-in,

227

after the murder of Marion, of the close-up of the drain which swallows water and blood, into the close-up of her dead eye. Here, the spiral first *enters* the drain, then *exits* the eye,[27] as if passing through the zero-point of an eclipse of time, a 'night of the world', to quote Hegel – in terms of science fiction, one can say that we 'pass the doors of time' and enter another temporal modality. A comparison with *Vertigo* is revealing here: in *Psycho*, we enter precisely that abyss which draws Scottie in *Vertigo*, yet which he is still able to resist.

As a result, it is not difficult to discern Lacanian names for the two surfaces of this Moebius band – to propose an elementary formula which regulates Marion's and Norman's universe:

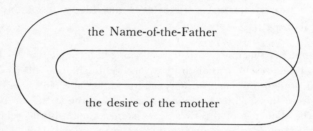

Marion stands under the sign of the Father – that is, of the symbolic desire constituted by the Name-of-the-Father; Norman is entrapped into the mother's desire not yet submitted to the paternal Law (and as such not yet a desire *stricto sensu*, but rather a pre-symbolic drive): the hysterical feminine position addresses the Name-of-the-Father, whereas the psychotic clings to the mother's desire. In short, the passage from Marion to Norman epitomizes the 'regression' from the register of *desire* to that of *drive*. In what does their opposition consist?

Desire is a metonymic sliding propelled by a lack, striving to capture the elusive lure: it is always, by definition, 'unsatisfied', susceptible to every possible interpretation, since it ultimately coincides with its own interpretation: it is *nothing but* the movement of interpretation, the passage from one signifier to another, the eternal production of new signifiers which, retroactively, give sense to the preceding chain. In opposition to this pursuit of the lost object which remains for ever 'elsewhere', drive is in a sense *always-already satisfied*: contained in its closed circuit, it 'encircles' its object – as

Lacan puts it — and finds satisfaction in its own pulsation, in its repeated failure to attain the object. In this precise sense, drive — in contrast to symbolic desire — appertains to the Real-Impossible, defined by Lacan as that which 'always returns to its place'. And it is precisely for this reason that identification with it is not possible: one can identify with the other only as desiring subject; this identification is even *constitutive* of desire which, according to Lacan, is by definition a 'desire of the Other' — that is to say intersubjective, mediated by the other: in contrast to the 'autistic' drive, contained in its circuit.

Norman thus eludes identification in so far as he remains prisoner of the psychotic drive, in so far as access to desire is denied him: what he lacks is the effectuation of the 'primordial metaphor' by means of which the symbolic Other (the structural Law epitomized by the Name-of-the-Father) supplants *jouissance* — the closed circuit of drive. The ultimate function of the Law is to confine desire — *not the subject's own, but the desire of his/her (M)Other*. Norman Bates is therefore a kind of anti-Oedipus *avant la lettre*: his desire is alienated in the maternal Other, at the mercy of its cruel caprice.

This opposition of desire and drive determines the contrasted symbolic economy of *Psycho*'s two great murder scenes, the shower-murder of Marion and the staircase-slaughter of the detective Arbogast. The shower-murder scene has always been a *pièce de résistance* for interpreters, its power of fascination diverting attention from the second murder, the film's truly traumatic point — a textbook case of what Freud called 'displacement'. Marion's violent death comes as an absolute surprise, a shock with no foundation in the narrative line which abruptly cuts off its 'normal' deployment; it is shot in a very 'filmic' way, its effect is brought about by editing: one never sees the murderer or Marion's entire body; the act of murder is 'dismembered' into a multitude of fragmentary close-ups which succeed one another in frenetic rhythm (the rising dark hand; the knife's edge close to the belly; the scream of the open mouth ...) — as if the repeated strikes of the knife have contaminated the reel itself and caused the tearing-up of the continuous filmic gaze (or, rather, the opposite: as if the murderous shadow stands in, within the diegetic space, for the power of editing itself ...).

How, then, is it possible to surpass this shock of the intrusion of the Real? Hitchcock found a solution: he succeeded in intensifying the effect by presenting the second murder as something *expected* – the rhythm of the scene is calm and continuous, long shots prevail, everything that precedes the act of murder seems to announce it: when Arbogast enters the 'mother's house', stops at the base of the empty staircase – this crucial Hitchcockian leitmotiv – and casts an inquisitive glance upwards, we immediately know that 'something is in the air'; when, seconds later, during Arbogast's ascent of the stairs, we see in close-up the crack in the second-floor door, our premonition is further confirmed. What follows then is the famous overhead shot which gives us a clear – so to speak geometrical – ground-plan of the entire scene, as if to prepare us for what finally arrives: the appearance of the 'mother'-figure which stabs Arbogast to death.... The lesson of this murder scene is that we endure the most brutal shock when we witness the exact realization of what we were looking forward to – as if, at this point, *tuche* and *automaton* paradoxically coincide: the most terrifying irruption of *tuche* which wholly perturbs the symbolic structure – the smooth running of *automaton* – takes place when a structural necessity simply realizes itself with blind automatism.

This paradox reminds one of the well-known sophism which proves the impossibility of a surprise: the pupils in a class know they will have to pass a written test within the next week, so how can the teacher effectively surprise them? The pupils reason as follows: Friday, the last day, is out, since on Thursday evening everybody would know that the test will have to take place the next day, so there would be no surprise; Thursday is also out, since on Wednesday evening, everybody would know that – Friday already being ruled out – the only possible day is Thursday, and so on.... What Lacan calls the Real is precisely the fact that, despite the irrefutable accuracy of this reasoning, *any day except Friday will still constitute a surprise*.

Behind its apparent simplicity, Arbogast's murder thus relies on a refined dialectic of expected and unexpected – in short, of (the viewer's) desire: the only way to explain this paradoxical economy, where the greatest surprise is caused by the complete fulfilment of our expectations, is to assume the hypothesis of a subject who is split, desiring – whose expectation is cathected by desire. What we have here is, of course, the logic of the fetishistic split: 'I know very well that event X will take place (that Arbogast will be murdered), yet I do not fully believe it (so I'm none the less surprised when the murder actually takes place).' Where, exactly, does the desire reside here, in the knowledge or in the belief?

Contrary to the obvious answer (in the belief – 'I know that X will take place, but I refuse to believe it since it runs against my desire ...'), the Lacanian answer here is quite unambiguous: in the knowledge. The horrifying reality that one refuses to 'believe in', to accept, to integrate into one's symbolic universe, is none other than the Real of one's desire, and the unconscious belief (that X could not actually happen) is ultimately a defence against the Real of desire: as viewers of *Psycho*, we desire the death of Arbogast, and the function of our belief that Arbogast will not be attacked by the 'mother'-figure is precisely to enable us to avoid the confrontation with the Real of our desire.[28] And what Freud calls 'drive' – in its opposition to desire, whose nature is by definition split – is perhaps precisely a name for the absolute 'closure' where what actually happens corresponds perfectly to what one knows exactly will happen....

Aristophanes reversed

What one should be attentive to in *Psycho* is how this opposition of desire and drive is far from being simply an abstract conceptual couple: a fundamental *historical* tension is invested in it, indicated by the different scenery of the two murders which relates to the way Norman is divided between the two locales. That is to say, the architectural locale of the two murders is by no means neutral; the first takes place in a motel which epitomizes anonymous American *modernity*, whereas the second takes place in a Gothic house which epitomizes the American *tradition*; it is not by accident that both haunted the imagination of Edward Hopper, an American painter if ever there was one – 'Western Motel' and 'House by the Railroad', for example (according to Rebello's *Alfred Hitchcock and the Making of 'Psycho'*, 'House by the Railroad' actually served as the model for the 'mother's house').

This opposition (whose visual correlative is the contrast between the horizontal – the lines of the motel – and the vertical – the lines of the house) not only introduces into *Psycho* an unexpected historical tension between tradition and modernity; it simultaneously enables us to locate *spatially* the figure of Norman Bates, his notorious psychotic split, by conceiving his figure as a kind of impossible 'mediator' between tradition and modernity, condemned to circulate endlessly between the two locales. Norman's split thereby epitomizes the incapacity of American ideology to locate the experience of the present, actual society into a context of historical tradition, to effectuate a symbolic mediation between the two levels. It is on account of this split that *Psycho* is still a 'modernist' film: in postmodernism, the dialectical tension between history and present is lost (in a postmodern *Psycho*, the motel itself would be rebuilt as an imitation of old family houses).

In consequence, the very duality of desire and drive can be conceived as the libidinal correlative of the duality of modern and traditional society: the matrix of traditional society is that of a 'drive', of a circular movement around the Same, whereas in modern society, repetitious circulation is supplanted by linear progress. The embodiment of the metonymic object-cause of desire which propels this endless progress is none other than *money* (one should recall that it is precisely money – 40,000 dollars – which disrupts Marion's everyday circuit and sets her on her fateful journey).

Psycho is thus a kind of hybrid of two heterogeneous parts: it is easy to imagine *two* 'rounded-off' stories, quite consistent in themselves, glued together in *Psycho* to form a monstrous whole. The first part (Marion's story) could well stand alone: it is easy to perform a mental experiment and to imagine it as a thirty-minute TV story, a kind of morality play in which the heroine gives way to temptation and enters the path of damnation, only to be cured by the encounter with Norman, who confronts her with the abyss that awaits her at the end of the road – in him, she sees a mirror-image of her own future; sobered, she decides to return to normal life.[29] From her standpoint, the conversation with Norman in the room with stuffed birds is therefore an exemplary case of a successful communication in the Lacanian sense of the term: she gets back from her partner her own message (the truth about the catastrophe that lurks) in a reversed form. So when Marion takes her shower, her story is – as far as narrative closure goes – strictly speaking over: the shower clearly serves as a metaphor of purification, since she has already made a decision to return and to repay her debt to society: that is, assume again her place in the community. Her murder does not occur as a totally unexpected shock which cuts into the midst of the narrative development: it strikes during the interval, the intermediate time, when the decision, although already taken, is not yet realized, inscribed into the public, intersubjective space – in the time which the traditional narrative can easily leave out (many films actually end with the moment of 'inner' decision).

The ideological presupposition behind it is, of course, that of a pre-stabilized harmony between Inside and Outside: once the subject really 'makes up his/her mind', the implementation of his/her inner decision in social reality ensues automatically. The timing of Marion's murder relies, therefore, on a carefully chosen ideologico-critical jest: it reminds us that we live in a world in which an insurmountable abyss separates the 'inner decision' from its social actualization; that is, where – in contrast to the prevailing American ideology – it is decidedly *not* possible to accomplish everything, even if one really resolves to do so.[30]

The film's second part, Norman's story, is also easy to imagine as a closed whole, a rather traditional unravelling of the mystery of a pathological serial killer – the entire subversive effect of *Psycho* hinges on putting together the two heterogeneous, inconsistent pieces.[31] In this respect, the structure of *Psycho* mockingly reverses Aristophanes' myth from Plato's *Symposium* (the split of the original androgynous entity into a masculine and a feminine half): the two constituents, taken in themselves, are fully consistent and harmonious – *it is their fusion into a larger Whole which denaturalizes them.* In contrast to the abrupt ending of Marion's story, the second part seems to accord perfectly with the rules of 'narrative closure': at the end, everything is explained, put in its proper place.... Yet on a closer look, the denouement proves far more ambiguous.

As Michel Chion has pointed out,[32] *Psycho* is ultimately the story of a Voice ('mother's voice') in search of its bearer, of a body to whom it could stick; the status of this Voice is what Chion calls *acousmatic* – a voice without a bearer, without an assignable place, floating in an intermediate space, and as such all-pervasive, the very image of the ultimate Threat. The film ends with the moment of 'embodiment' when we finally behold the body in which the Voice originates – yet at this precise moment, things get mixed up: within the traditional narration, the moment of 'embodiment' demystifies the terrifying phantom-like Voice, it dispels its power of fascination by enabling us – the viewers – to *identify* with its bearer. (This reversal whereby the unfathomable Phantom assumes shape and body – is reduced to a common measure – is far from being limited to horror movies: in *The Wizard of Oz*, for example, the Wizard's voice is 'embodied' when the little dog who follows the smell behind the curtain uncovers the helpless old man who creates the spectacle of the Wizard by means of a complicated apparatus of machinery).[33]

While *Psycho* also 'embodies' the Voice, the effect of it here is the exact opposite of 'gentrification' which renders possible our – the viewer's – identification: it is only now that we confront an 'absolute Otherness' which precludes any identification. The Voice has attached itself to the wrong body, so that what we get is a true zombie, a pure creature of the Superego, totally powerless in itself (Norman–mother 'wouldn't even hurt a fly'), yet for that very reason all the more uncanny.

The crucial feature with regard to the allegorical functioning of *Psycho* is that at this precise moment when, finally, the Voice finds its body, Norman – in the penultimate shot of the film which immediately precedes 'The End' – raises his gaze and looks directly into the camera (i.e. into us, the viewers) with a mocking expression which displays his awareness of our complicity: what is accomplished thereby is the above-mentioned reversal of our gaze from I to *a*, from the neutral gaze of the Ego-Ideal to the object. We look for the 'secret behind the curtain' (who is the shadow which pulls off the curtain and slaughters Marion?), and what we obtain at the end is a Hegelian answer: we always-already partake in the absolute Otherness which returns the gaze.

'A triumph of the gaze over the eye'

The uncanny gaze into the camera brings us back to Hitchcock's 'Jansenism': it bears witness to the 'triumph of the gaze over the eye', as Lacan puts it in his *Seminar XI*.[34] This 'triumph' can be epitomized by means of a formal procedure Hitchcock resorts to apropos of some traumatic object: as a rule he introduces it as an entity *dependent on gaze*. First, he shows the petrified gaze, 'thrown off the rails', attracted to some as yet unspecified X; only then does he pass to its cause – as if its traumatic character proceeds from the gaze, from the object's contamination by the gaze.

In *Suspicion*, for example, how does the film depict the first embrace between Cary Grant and Joan Fontaine? Two of Fontaine's friends are chatting at the church entrance, the atmosphere is idyllic and calm, totally windless, when, all of a sudden, the gaze of one of the girls is 'petrified', transfixed by what she sees – it is only then that the camera passes to the 'primordial scene' that fascinated her gaze: Grant forcing an embrace from Fontaine on a hill near the church, the two of them struggling, almost fighting, and then the first violent kiss, accompanied by a strong wind which starts to blow out of nowhere, against all the rules of 'realism'.... A somewhat less dramatic version of the same procedure is found in *The Wrong Man*: the lawyer explains to Balestrero and his wife the deadlock of his position; all of a sudden, his gaze is transfixed, as if shocked by something, and then the camera shows the object of his bewilderment, Balestrero's wife, who is absent-mindedly staring ahead of herself, losing contact with her environment.... In *Psycho* itself, we encounter the same procedure in the above-mentioned scene with Cassidy – Hitchcock's stand-in in the diegetic space – boastfully displaying 40,000 dollars in cash: the camera shows Marion's fellow-clerk (played by Patricia Hitchcock) who, in the midst of a sentence, gapes at something open-mouthed, as if she were witnessing an obscenity; what then follows is a shot of Cassidy flaunting a pile of banknotes ...

The transfixed gaze isolates a stain of the Real, a detail which 'sticks out' from the frame of symbolic reality – in short, a traumatic *surplus of the Real over the Symbolic*; yet the crucial feature of these scenes is that this detail has no substance in itself – it is, so to speak, 'substantiated', caused, created, by the transfixed gaze itself. The *objet petit a* of the scene is therefore the gaze itself, the gaze imposed on the viewer for a brief moment – in the case of *Suspicion*, for example, the point of view which allows us to see love-struggling on the windy hilltop where a 'normal' gaze sees nothing but placid countryside.[35] This procedure constitutes the exact opposite of the starting point of *North by Northwest*, where a signifier, 'George Kaplan', an empty symbolic place (the name of a nonexistent person), functions as a *surplus* of *the Symbolic* over reality.

The elementary feature of a symbolic order in its relation to 'reality' is that it always contains a surplus-signifier, a signifier which is 'empty' in the sense that there is nothing in reality which corresponds to it – this paradox was first articulated by Lévi-Strauss who, in his *Structural Anthropology*, pointed out how the division of a tribe into clans always produces the surplus-name of a clan which does not exist in reality. The function of the *Master* in the Lacanian sense of the term is closely related to this paradox: the master-signifier (S_1) is by definition 'empty', and the 'Master' is the one who, by mere accident, occupies this empty place. For that reason, a Master is ultimately – that is, constitutively – an impostor: the constitutive illusion of the Master is that his being a Master results from his inherent charisma, not from his accidental occupation of a certain place in the structure.

The two modalities of the outstanding surplus-element – S_1 or a – can be further specified by means of another Hitchcockian formal procedure: the dialectic of frame and its exterior – of the way a foreign body enters the frame. Let us recall the shower-murder in *Psycho* or any of the bird-attacks in *The Birds*: the tool of aggression (the hand with a knife; the birds) is not perceived simply as a part of diegetic reality; it is, rather, experienced as a kind of stain which from outside – more precisely: from an intermediate space between diegetic reality and our 'true' reality – invades the diegetic reality (in *The Birds* this holds literally, since the birds were often included in the shot afterwards, or even directly drawn as in cartoons). The famous 'God's-perspective' shot of Bodega Bay where, all of a sudden, birds enter the frame from behind the camera, is emblematic here: it works on the implicit assumption that before their entry into the frame the birds were not part of the diegetic reality,

but entered it from a space external to it.[36] Here Hitchcock mobilizes the feeling of threat which sets in when the distance separating the viewer – his/her safe position of pure gaze – from the diegetic reality is lost: the stains blur the frontier outside/inside which provides our sense of security.

Let us recall our attitude when, inside a car or a house, we observe a storm outside: although we are quite close to the 'real thing', the windowpane serves as a screen protecting us from immediate contact. The charm of a train journey resides precisely in this 'de-realization' of the world beyond the screen: it is as if we are at a standstill, while the world beyond runs past. . . . The intrusion of a stain disrupts this safe distance: the field of vision is invaded by an element which does not belong to the diegetic reality, and we are forced to accept that the pulsative stain which disturbs the clarity of our vision is part of our eye, not part of the reality we are looking at. No wonder, then, that in *The Lady Vanishes* – a film whose action takes place mostly in a train – the story pivots on such an apparition of a stain on the windowpane; yet the 'stain' which emerges here is a signifier, not an object. What we have in mind, of course, is the

scene in the dining-car where, in the midst of the conversation, the two crucial proofs of Miss Froy's existence (first her name written on a dusty glass, then the tea-bag with the name of Miss Froy's tea brand) appear on the 'screen' itself (on the dining-car's windowpane through which the hero and the heroine observe the countryside), only to be wiped out instantly.

This phantom-like apparition of a signifier on the screen follows the logic of symptom as return of the repressed, in a kind of reversal of Lacan's formula of psychosis: 'what is foreclosed from the Symbolic returns in the Real' – in the case of the symptom, what is excluded from reality reappears as a signifying trace (as an element of the symbolic order: a name, a tea brand) on the very screen through which we observe reality. In other words, the name 'Froy' and the empty tea-bag on the windowpane exemplify what Lacan, in his reading of Freud, conceives as *Vorstellungs-Repräsentanz*: the signifier which acts as a representative – a trace – of the excluded ('repressed') representation, in this case the representation of Miss Froy, excluded from the diegetic reality.

In contrast to this, the intrusion of the stain in the scenes from

Birds and *Psycho* is of a psychotic nature: here, the non-symbolized returns in the guise of a traumatic object-stain. *Vorstellungs-Repräsentanz* designates a *signifier* which fills out the void of the excluded representation, whereas a psychotic stain is a *representation* which fills out a hole in the Symbolic, giving body to the 'unspeakable' – its inert presence testifies that we are in a domain where 'words fail'. The surplus-signifier 'hystericizes' the subject, whereas the effect of the non-signifying stain is psychotic – we are thus again at the opposition hysteria–psychosis, the elementary axis of *Psycho*'s universe.

The asymmetry of these two returns (that of the stain of the Real where the word fails; that of the signifier to fill out the void that gapes in the midst of representational reality) is dependent on the split between reality and the Real. 'Reality' is the field of symbolically structured representations, the outcome of symbolic 'gentrification' of the Real; yet a surplus of the Real always eludes the symbolic grasp and persists as a non-symbolized stain, a hole in reality which designates the ultimate limit where 'the word fails'. It is against this background that *Vorstellungs-Repräsentanz* is to be conceived as an attempt to inscribe into the symbolic order the surplus that eludes the field of representation.[37] The success of what we call 'sublimation' relies on this reflexive reversal of the 'lack of the signifier' into the 'signifier of the lack' – that is to say, on this primordial metaphor by means of which the stain – the brute enjoyment for which there is no signifier – is replaced by an empty signifier, a signifier which does not signify any reality – that is to say: a stand-in for a representation which is constitutively excluded from reality, which must fall out if 'reality' is to retain its consistency:

$$\frac{\textit{Vorstellungs-Repräsentanz}}{\text{stain}}$$

The exemplary case of such a substitution is, of course, the passage from pagan to Jewish religion. Pagan gods still 'pertain to the Real', as Lacan puts it: they are gigantic stains of enjoyment, their domain is that of the Unnameable, which is why the only proper access to

239

them is via the ecstasy of sacred orgies. In Judaism, on the contrary, the domain of the 'divine' is purified of enjoyment: God changes into a pure symbol, a Name which has to remain empty, which no real subject is allowed to fill out – a kind of theological 'George Kaplan' surrounded by prohibitions which prevent any Thornhill from occupying its place. In other words, this substitution of the divine Name for the divine Thing entails a kind of reflection-into-itself of the prohibition: the Divine as the domain of the sacred Thing-Enjoyment was unnameable, it was prohibited from being contaminated by a name; whereas in the Judaic reversal, *the prohibition reverts to Name itself* – what is prohibited is not to name the Unnameable but to fill out the Name with positive content.[38] And the gigantic statues in Hitchcock's films (the Statue of Liberty, the four Presidents at Mount Rushmore, etc.), these monuments to petrified Enjoyment, are they not an indication of how today, the substitution of Name for the Thing is losing its edge – of how 'Gods' are reverting to the Real?[39]

The narrative closure and its vortex

The ultimate Hitchcockian dream was, of course, to manipulate the viewer directly, bypassing altogether the *Vorstellungs-Repräsentanz* (the intermediate level of representation and its reflective redoubling in the representative). Ernest Lehman, who wrote the scenario for *North by Northwest,* recalls the following remarks by Hitchcock from the time when they were working together on this film:

> 'Ernie, do you realize what we're doing in this picture? The audience is like a giant organ that you and I are playing. At one moment we play *this* note on them and get *this* reaction, and then we play *that* chord and they react *that* way. And someday we won't even have to make a movie – there'll be electrodes implanted in their brains, and we'll just press different buttons and they'll go "oooh" and "aaah" and we'll frighten them, and make them laugh. Won't that be wonderful?'[40]

What one should not miss here is the exact nature of the element excluded by this Hitchcockian fantasy: the 'mediating' element which would become superfluous if the fantasy of direct influence on the viewer were to be realized is none other than the *signifier*, the symbolic order. This dream of a drive that could function without its representative in the psychic apparatus is what one is tempted to baptize the psychotic core of Hitchcock's universe – a core strictly homologous to Freud's dream of a moment when the symbolic procedure of psychoanalysis will be replaced by pure biology. As long as we remain within the symbolic order, however, Hitchcock's relationship to the viewer is by necessity allegorical: the symbolic order (in the case of the film: the order of diegetic reality) always contains a kind of 'umbilical cord', a paradoxical element which links it to the excluded level of the interaction between Hitchcock and the public. In other words, it is true that what Hitchcock ultimately aims at is the so-called 'emotional manipulation of the public', yet this allegorical dimension can be effective only in so far as it is inscribed into diegetic reality itself by means of an element whose presence 'curves' the narrative space.

This element which enters the narrative space from the intermediate acousmatic domain is crucial if one is to conceive properly the problematic of 'narrative closure'. Narrative closure as a rule indexes the inscription of ideology into a text: the ideological horizon of a narrative is delineated by the borderline separating what can from what cannot take place in it – the extreme case is, of course, the so-called formulaic genres (the classic whodunit, for example, where one can rely absolutely upon the detective's capacity to solve the enigma). And according to Raymond Bellour, Hitchcock's films remain thoroughly within the closure that constitutes the 'Hollywood matrix': the 'machine for the production of the couple' where the final scene brings us back to the starting point, and so on.

The naive question 'Why couldn't the denouement be different?', although it extraneates the self-evident character of the closure, is, however, far less subversive than it may seem: it remains confined to the 'narrative closure' whose inherent condition is that it (mis)perceives itself as its opposite. Ideology is not the closure as such but rather the illusion of *openness*, the illusion that 'it could also happen otherwise' which ignores how the very texture of the universe precludes a different course of events – in this case, the universe itself would literally 'fall apart'. Contrary to the vulgar pseudo-

Brechtian version, the basic matrix of ideology does not consist in conferring the form of unavoidable necessity upon what is actually dependent on a contingent set of concrete circumstances: the supreme lure of ideology is to procure the illusion of 'openness' by rendering invisible the underlying structural necessity (the catastrophic ending of the traditional 'realist' novel or the successful final deduction in a whodunit 'works' only if it is 'experienced' as the outcome of a series of [un]fortunate contingencies).

What we necessarily overlook when we move within a narrative space is the way this space is 'curved': from within, the horizon always appears infinite and open. As is often the case, for a clear figuration of this one must look at a typical science-fiction narrative: the hero exerts himself to realize an 'impossible' goal (change into a different time-dimension – that is, into alternative history, as in Phillip Jose Farmer's *The Doors of Time*, or something of that order), yet when he finally seems to be on the verge of attaining it, strange things begin to occur, a series of accidents prevent him from fulfilling his plan and the world we know is thus saved . . .[41] It is almost superfluous to point out the psychoanalytic resonance of such a notion of 'narrative closure': what the fact of 'repression' ultimately amounts to is that *the space of 'what can be said', the subject's universe of meaning, is always 'curved' by traumatic blanks*, organized around what must remain unsaid if this universe is to retain its consistency. The subject necessarily misrecognizes the *constitutive* nature of these blanks – s/he perceives them as something that hinges upon pure contingency, as something that easily 'could not have happened' – yet when the thing *does* happen (when, for example, the meaning of a symptom is put in words), the entire universe falls apart. . . . And – to return to Hitchcock – the abovementioned dissolve in *Psycho* (into the drain, out of Marion's eye) is precisely such a passage through 'the door of time', from one closed-curved space into another.

One can see, now, how the narrative closure is closely linked to the logic of fantasy: the fantasy-scene stages precisely the irrepresentable X which curves the narrative space – which is, by definition, excluded from it. This X is ultimately the subject's birth and/or death, so the fantasy-object is the impossible gaze which makes the subject into a witness to his/her own conception or death (the entire wealth of fantasies can ultimately be reduced to a variation on two elementary scenes: that of the subject's conception – the parental coitus – and that of the subject's death).

The 'curvature' of the narrative space registers the fact that the subject never lives in 'his/her proper time': the subject's life is fundamentally barred, hindered; it elapses in a 'not-yet' modality, in the sense of being structured as the expectation and/or memory of an X, an Event in the full meaning of the term (Henry James's name for it was the jump of the 'beast in the jungle'), spent in preparation for a moment when things will 'really start to happen', when the subject will 'really begin to live'.... Yet when we finally approach this X, it reveals itself as its own opposite, as death – the moment of proper birth coincides with death.[42] The being of the subject is a being-towards ... structured in relationship to a traumatic X, a point of simultaneous attraction and repulsion, a point whose overproximity causes the eclipse of the subject. Being-towards-death is therefore, in its inherent structure, possible only with a being-of-language: the space curved is always a symbolic space; what causes the curvature of space is the fact that the symbolic field is by definition structured around a 'missing link'. [43]

The general lesson to be drawn from this is that a kind of fundamental 'narrative closure' is *constitutive* of reality: there is always an 'umbilical cord' which links the field of what we experience as 'reality' with its foundation which must remain unseen; this cord which 'curves' the narrative space links it to its process of enunciation. The narrative space is curved precisely in so far as its process of enunciation is always-already inscribed into it; in short: in so far as it is allegorical with regard to its process of enunciation. 'Narrative closure' is therefore another name for the *subjectivization* by means of which the subject retroactively confers meaning on a series of contingencies and assumes his/her symbolic destiny: recognizes his/her place in the texture of the symbolic narrative.

Rather than directly breaking these rules which guarantee the consistency of a narrative space (the usual strategy of the avant-garde authors), Hitchcock's subversion of it consists in dispelling the lure of its false 'openness' – in rendering visible the closure as such. He pretends to comply fully with the rules of closure – in *Psycho*, for example, both parts end with a closure (inner purification, catharsis, of Marion; Norman's embodiment) – yet the standard effect of closure remains unfulfilled: the surplus of the contingent real (Marion's senseless murder) emerges when, in terms of the inherent logic of the narrative, the story is already over, and saps the effect of closure; the final explanation of the mystery of the mother's identity changes into its opposite and undermines the very notion of personal identity ...

We can see, now, how the threads of our interpretation gather together. In the guise of the Other's gaze, Hitchcock registers a proximity beyond identification with *personae* from diegetic reality: its uncanniness fits perfectly the ambiguity which distinguishes the German term *das Unheimliche* – that is to say, its absolute Strangeness indexes its opposite, a threatening overproximity. This figure of 'absolute Otherness' is none other than the *Vorstellungs-Repräsentanz*: it stands in, within the diegetic reality, for a representation which is constitutively excluded from its space.

Therein consists the allegorical dimension of Hitchcock's universe: the *Vorstellungs-Repräsentanz* is the umbilical link by means of which the diegetic content functions as an allegory of its process of enunciation. The place of this figure is acousmatic: it never simply partakes in diegetic reality, but dwells in an intermediate space inherent to reality yet 'out of place' in it. As such, this figure 'curves' the narrative space: the space is curved at precisely the point at which we approach too close to the forbidden domain of the 'absolute Otherness'.... Hitchcock's entire universe is founded upon this complicity between 'absolute Otherness', epitomized by the Other's gaze into the camera, and the viewer's look – the ultimate Hegelian lesson of Hitchcock is that the place of absolute transcendence, of the Unrepresentable which eludes  diegetic space, coincides with the absolute immanence of the viewer reduced to pure gaze. The unique gaze into the camera which ends Norman's monologue and then dissolves into the mother's skull –

244

this gaze which addresses us, the viewers – separates us from the symbolic community and makes us Norman's accomplices.

Lacanian theory provides a precise notion for this 'absolute Otherness': the subject beyond subjectivization – beyond what Lacan, in his *Seminar* II, upon introducing the notion of the 'big Other', called 'the wall of language' – in other words: the subject *not* bound by the symbolic pact[44] and as such identical to the Other's gaze (from the uncanny look into the camera of the *Lodger*'s hero to Norman's final look into the camera in *Psycho*). In so far as this subject dwells 'beyond the wall of language', its correlative is not a signifier representing it, marking its place within the symbolic order, but an inert object, a bone which sticks in the subject's throat and hinders his/her integration into the symbolic order (let us recall the motif of a skull, of a mummified head, which runs from *Under Capricorn* – Ingrid Bergman's confrontation with the aboriginal head – to *Psycho* – Lila's confrontation with Mrs Bates's head).[45]

In *The Silent Scream*, Elizabeth Weis makes a perspicacious remark on how the status of horror in Hitchcock's films changes with *Psycho*: here, for the first time, horror (the high-note violin squeak that accompanies the two murders and the final confrontation) becomes transsubjective – that is, it can no longer be qualified as the affect of a diegetic personality.[46] From our perspective, however, this 'transsubjective' dimension is precisely the dimension of subject beyond 'subjectivity': in *Rear Window*, for example, the horror and tension are still 'subjectivized', located into a narrative universe, attached to a subjective point of view; whereas the 'impersonal' abyss we confront when we find ourselves face-to-face with Norman's gaze into the camera is the very abyss of the subject not yet caught in the web of language – the unapproachable Thing which resists subjectivization, this point of failure of every identification, is ultimately *the subject itself*.

This opposition between subjectivization as symbolic integration – the subject's subordination to the performative power of language – and the subject in so far as s/he dwells 'beyond the wall of language' is made into the axis around which the entire story turns for the first time in *Murder!*, in the form of the opposition between Sir John and Handell Fane, a direct forerunner of Norman Bates, the murderer who performs in a circus dressed as a woman. Sir John operates as a male Master endeavouring to 'dominate the play' by means of the forceful narrativization of events, while Fane is an intermediate, unfathomable figure who – when cornered by the Master's narrative manipulations – resolves upon public suicide and thereby commits the only act *stricto sensu* in the film. *Murder!* thereby subverts the traditional ideological cathexis of the sexual difference according to which man is defined by activity proper and woman by its fake substitute (masquerade, hysterical theatre): the film's ultimate achievement is to unmask man's act itself as the supreme form of performance, of theatrical imposture. Man's world presents itself as a world of the performative, of the Master-signifier, of the 'word which in itself constitutes an act', which pretends to overcome and devalue feminine theatricality, yet *this overcoming is in itself the supreme theatrical gesture* (like the elementary rhetorical device of self-disavowal, of feigning renunciation of rhetoric – 'What is now at stake is the thing itself, not cheap rhetorical trifling . . .').

Here, one should rectify the perspicacious insight of Tania Modleski, who discerns the fundamental strategy of Sir John in his '*risking feminization and hystericization* in order to achieve mastery and control':[17] the point is not only that Sir John regains mastery over the events through manipulated, controlled theatricality; the point, rather, is that this mastery of his is nothing but a self-sublation of theatricality and, as such, its supreme effect. Therein consists the traumatic message of Fane's suicide, of this 'paroxysm of poetic and patriarchal justice':[48] by carrying it out, Fane unmasks Sir John as an impostor – the shocking authenticity, the dignity of the act, changes Sir John's activity into mere performance and his discourse into mere semblance.[49]

The crucial index of the changed historical constellation between *Murder!* and *Psycho* is the shift from the Master to the Hysteric as his 'truth': in *Murder!*, Fane – the figure of Otherness – is opposed to a male Master (Sir John); whereas in *Psycho*, the counterpart to Norman is a hystericized woman. This shift also affects the character of the figure of Otherness: in *Murder!*, Fane's status is epitomized by an authentic *act* which reveals the imposture of the Master's performance, whereas in *Psycho*, Norman/Mother brings to its (psychotic) utmost the hysterical split of the subject ($). By his suicide, which confirms his refusal to compromise his desire, Fane attains the impossible self-identity 'beyond mask', the death drive's apogee, whereas at the end of *Psycho*, Norman irrevocably loses his identity in his mask: his desire is immediately identified with that of his (M)Other – that is to say, he changes into a mouth-piece of the paranoiac Other embodied in the maternal mask; for that reason, Fane's act is a *suicide* and Norman's is a *murder*.[50]

Sir John and Marion are ultimately beings of theatre: hysterical theatre is the 'truth' of the Master's imposture, of his performance – which is why the reverse of the Master's imposture is an authentic *act*, and the reverse of the hysteric's theatre a murderous *passage à l'acte*.[51] More precisely, in both cases the act is suicidal, only the direction is opposite: in *Murder!*, Fane annihilates himself (not for the sake of the symbol, of the signifier, but for the sake of what is 'in himself more than himself'); whereas in *Psycho*, Norman, by killing the other-woman, annihilates what is 'in himself more than himself'.

The gaze of the Thing

This dimension of the subject beyond subjectivization emerges in its purest in what is certainly the crucial shot in *Psycho*, perhaps even the quintessence of Hitchcock: the shot from above of the second-floor hall and staircase in the 'mother's house'. This mysterious shot occurs twice. In the scene of Arbogast's murder, the shot of Arbogast from the top of the stairs (i.e. from what is still a 'normal' perspective, accessible to human eyes) all of a sudden 'takes off', jumps back into the air and passes into the uppermost point from which the entire scene in its ground-plan is on view. The scene of Norman carrying the mother into the cellar also begins with an 'inquisitive' shot from the bottom of the same staircase – that is to say, with a shot which, although not subjective, automatically sets up the viewer in the position of somebody striving to overhear the conversation between Norman and his mother in the room upstairs; in an extremely arduous and long tracking shot whose very trajec-tory mimics the shape of a Moebius band, the camera then elevates and simultaneously turns around its axis, so that it reaches the same point of 'God's view' on the entire scene. The inquisitive perspective sustained by the desire to penetrate the secret of the house finds its accomplishment in its opposite, in the objective overview of the scene, as if returning to the viewer the message 'you wanted to see it all, so here you have it, the transparent ground-plan of the entire scene, with no fourth side (off-field) excluded . . .'.

The crucial feature of this tracking shot is that it does *not* follow the trajectory of the standard Hitchcockian tracking shot (from the establishing plan rendering the overview of the scene to the 'stain' which sticks out[52]) but obeys a different, almost opposite logic: from the ground-level gaze which invites the viewer's identification to the position of pure meta-language. At this precise moment, the lethal Thing ('Mother') enters through the right-hand door; its odd, 'unnatural' character is indicated by the way it moves: with slow, discontinuous, intercepted, cut movements, as if what we see is a doll revivified, a living dead, not a true living person.

The explanation offered by Hitchcock himself in his conversations with Truffaut is, as usual, deceptive in its very disarming persuasiveness; Hitchcock enumerates two reasons for including this 'God's view': (1) it makes the scene transparent and thus enables the director to keep the identity of 'Mother' secret without arousing the suspicion of cheating or hiding something; (2) it introduces a contrast between the serene, immovable 'God's view' and the next shot, the dynamic view of Arbogast falling down the stairs.[53]

What Hitchcock's explanation fails to provide is simply the *raison d'être* of the cut from the 'normal' ground-level view on Arbogast to the ground-plan view from above – that is, of the inclusion of 'God's view' (or, in the second case, the *raison d'être* of the long continuous tracking shot from the ground-level inquisitive view to 'God's view'). The cut which then follows in the murder of Arbogast is even more odious: it transposes us from the level of reality (i.e. from the standpoint  of pure meta-language making transparent the ground-plan of reality) into the Real, into the 'stain' which sticks out from the frame of reality: while we observe the scene from 'God's view', the 'stain'

(the murderous Thing) enters the frame, and the next shot renders precisely *the point of view of this stain*. This cut to the subjective view of the murderer himself (herself?) – to the impossible gaze of the Thing which has just entered the visual field of reality – accomplishes, in Hegelese, the reflection-into-self of the *objective gaze* into the *gaze of the object itself*; as such, it designates the precise moment of passing over into perversion.

The inherent dynamic of the entire scene of Arbogast's murder epitomizes *Psycho*'s trajectory from hysteria to perversion:[54] hysteria is defined by the identification of the subject's desire with the desire of the other (in this case, of the viewer's desire with the inquisitive desire of Arbogast as diegetic personality); whereas perversion involves an identification with the 'impossible' gaze of the object-Thing itself – when the knife cuts Arbogast's face, we see it through the very eyes of the 'impossible' murderous Thing.[55] In Lacanian mathemes, we thus passed from $\$ \lozenge a$ to $a \lozenge \$$: from the subject peering anxiously into the space in front of him/her, looking in it for the traces of 'more than meets the eye' – for the mysterious maternal Thing – to *the gaze of the Thing itself on the subject*.[56]

249

Hitchcock's explanation according to which the function of 'God's view' was to keep us, viewers, in ignorance (as to the mother's identity), without arousing suspicion that the director is trying to hide something from us, therefore imposes an unexpected yet unavoidable conclusion: if we are kept in ignorance by assuming God's view, then *a certain radical ignorance must pertain to the status of God Himself*, who clearly comes to epitomize a blind run of the symbolic machine. Hitchcock's God goes His own way, indifferent to our petty human affairs – more precisely, He is *totally unable to understand us, living humans*, since His realm is that of the dead (i.e. since symbol is the murder of thing). On that account, he is like God from the memoirs of Daniel Paul Schreber, who, 'being only accustomed to communication with the dead, *does not understand living men*'[57] – or, to quote Schreber himself:

> ... *in accordance with the Order of Things, God really knew nothing about living men* and did not need to know; consonantly with the Order of Things, He needed only to have communication with corpses.[58]

This Order of Things is, of course, none other than the symbolic order which mortifies the living body and evacuates from it the substance of Enjoyment. That is to say, God as Name-of-the-Father, reduced to a figure of symbolic authority, is 'dead' (also) in the sense that *He does not know anything about enjoyment*, about life-substance: the symbolic order (the big Other) and enjoyment are radically incompatible.[59] This is why the famous Freudian dream of a son who appears to his father and reproaches him with 'Father, can't you see I'm burning?' could be simply translated into '*Father, can't you see I'm enjoying?*' – can't you see I'm alive, burning with enjoyment? Father cannot see it, since he is dead, whereby the possibility is open to me to enjoy not only *outside* his knowledge – unbeknownst to him – but also *in his very ignorance.* The other, no less well known Freudian dream, the one about the father who does not know he is dead, could thus be supplemented with '(*I, the dreamer, enjoy the fact that*) father does not know he is dead'.[60]

To return to *Psycho*: the 'stain' (Mother) thus strikes as the prolonged hand of the blinded Deity, as His senseless intervention in the world. The subversive character of this reversal comes to light when we confront it with another, almost identical, reversal at work, among others, in Fred Walton's *When a Stranger Calls*, perhaps the best variation on the theme of anonymous phone menaces. The first part of the film is narrated from the point of view of a young girl babysitting in a suburban family mansion: the children are asleep on the first floor, while she watches TV in the sitting-room. After the first threatening calls repeating the demand 'Did you check the children?', she alerts the police, who advise her to lock all the doors firmly, not to allow anybody to enter the house, and to try to engage the molester in a long conversation, enabling them to trace the call. Soon afterwards, the police locate their source: another telephone within the same house.... The molester was there all the time, and has already killed the children. The killer appears thus as an un-fathomable object with whom no identification is possible, a pure Real provoking unspeakable terror. At this point in the story however, the film takes an unexpected turn: we are suddenly trans-posed into the perspective of the killer himself, witnessing the miser-able everyday existence of this lonely and desperate individual – he sleeps in an asylum, wanders around sordid cafés, and attempts in vain to establish contact with his neighbours; so that when the detective hired by the murdered children's father prepares to stab him, our sympathies are wholly on the poor killer's side.

As in *Psycho* itself, there is nothing subversive about the two points of view in themselves: if the story were narrated from the sole perspective of the young babysitter, we would have the standard case of a victim threatened by a phantomlike, bodyless and, for that reason, all the more horrifying menace; if we were limited to the murderer's self-experience, we would have the standard rendition of the murderer's pathological universe. The entire subversive effect hangs upon the rupture, the passage from one perspective to the other, the change which confers upon the hitherto impossible/ unattainable object a body, which gives the untouchable Thing a voice and makes it speak – in short, which *subjectivizes* it. The killer is first depicted as an untouchable, horrendous entity, as an *object* in the Lacanian sense, with all the transferential energy invested in him; then, all of a sudden, we are transposed into his own perspec-tive.[61] Yet the crucial feature of *Psycho* is that Hitchcock precisely does *not* accomplish this step towards subjectivization: when we are thrown into the 'subjective' gaze of the Thing, the Thing, although it 'becomes subject', *does not subjectivize itself*, does not 'open up', does not 'reveal its depth', does not offer itself to our emphatic compassion, does not open a crack which would enable us to take a peep into the wealth of its self-experience. The point-of-view shot makes it even more inaccessible – we look through its eyes, and this very coincidence of our view with the Thing's gaze intensifies its radical Otherness to an almost unbearable degree.

'Subjective destitution'

Another way to define this gaze of the Thing on the subject which subverts the usual opposition of 'subjective' and 'objective' is to say that it marks the moment when the subject is immediately entrapped in, caught into, the dream of the Other-Thing. In Hitchcock's films before *Psycho*, a similar shot occurs twice: in *Vertigo*, when, in his dream, Scottie (James Stewart) stares at his own head,

depicted as a kind of psychotic partial object located in the point of convergence of the running lines in the background; and, first of all, thirty years previously in *Murder!*, when, seconds before his suicidal jump, a series of visions appear to Fane during his flying on the trapeze; first the faces of the two main protagonists (Sir John and Nora), then the swinging void. This scene seems to rely on the standard shot/counter-shot procedure: the objective shot of Fane alternates with the subjective shot of his visions, which is why interpreters (Rothman, for example) concentrate on the content of his visions; the true mystery of the scene, however, is the uncanny 'objective' shots of Fane, who flies in the air and gapes into the camera with a strange, masochist-aggressive gaze.

The basic impression of this shot (and of the two similar shots

252

from *Vertigo* and *Psycho*) is that the 'natural' relationship between movement and the state of rest is *reversed*: it is as if the head which gapes into the camera (the point of gaze) is at a standstill, whereas the entire world around it runs dizzily and loses clear contours, in contrast to the 'true' state of things where the head dashes by and the background stands still.[62] The homology of this impossible gaze from the point of view of the Thing which 'freezes' the subject, reduces him to immobility, with ana-morphosis is by no means acci-

dental: it is as if, in the three above-mentioned shots, the anamorphic stain acquires clear and recognizable outlines, while all the rest, the remaining reality, becomes blurred. In short, *we look at the screen from the point of anamorphosis, from the point which makes the stain clear* – and the price we pay for it is the 'loss of reality'. (A more humorous, yet not so effective version of it occurs in *Strangers on a Train*, in the shot of the crowd on the platform of the tennis court: all the heads turn in the same rhythm, following the ball – except one, that of the assassin Bruno, who stares rigidly into the camera – that is, into Guy, who is observing the platform.)[63]

The gaze of the Thing thus concludes the 'triad' the terms of which form a kind of 'negation of negation': (1) the shot/counter-shot alternation of Arbogast and what he sees remains at the level of the standard suspense – the investigator enters a forbidden domain where an unknown X lurks – that is to say, where every object depicted is coloured by the subject's desire and/or anxiety; (2) the cut into an objective 'God's view' on the entire scene 'negates' this level – obliterates the stain of the subject's 'pathological' interests; (3) the subjective shot of what the murderer sees 'negates' the object-ivity of 'God's view'. This subjective shot is the 'negation of negation' of the subjective shot of what Arbogast sees at the beginning of the scene: it is a return to the subject, yet to the subject *beyond* subjectivity, which is why no identification with it is possible

– in contrast to our identifying with Arbogast's inquisitive glance at the beginning, we now occupy an impossible point of absolute Strangeness. We are brought face-to-face with this strangeness at the very end of the film, when Norman raises his eyes and looks straight into the camera: while we look at Arbogast's cut-up face, we see it through these same eyes.[64]

The crucial feature not to be missed here is the co-dependence between the objective shot from above ('God's view') and the point-of-view shot of Arbogast's cut-up face which immediately follows it (therein consists the contrast to which Hitchcock refers).[65] In order to elucidate it, let us perform a simple mental experiment and imagine the scene of Arbogast's murder *without* the 'God's view' – confined to the limits of the standard shot/counter-shot procedure: after a series of signs registering the imminent threat (a crack in the second-floor door, etc.), one gets a point-of-view shot of Arbogast as seen through the murderer's eyes ... in this way, the effect of the 'gaze of the Thing' would be lost, the subjective shot would not function as the gaze of the impossible Thing, but as a simple point-of-view shot of one of the diegetic *personae* with whom the viewer can easily identify.

In other words, *'God's view' is needed to clear the field of all subjective identifications*, to effectuate what Lacan calls *'destitution subjective'* – it is only on this condition that the subjective point-of-view shot which follows it is perceived not as a view of one of the diegetic subjects, but as the impossible gaze of the Thing.[66] Here, one should recall the remarks of Jean Narboni which refer precisely to Arbogast's climbing up the stairs, on how Hitchcockian shot/counter-shot procedure epitomizes the impossibility of a 'free, investigative, autonomous and active gaze not determined by things, belonging to the subject-investigator who is not himself part of the rebus, i.e. of what Hitchcock calls "tapissery"':

> ... why do we have, apropos of so many [Hitchcock] scenes shot from a subjective point of view, the feeling that the person's gaze does not reveal things, that his step does not lead him *towards* things, but that things themselves stare at him, attract him in a dangerous way, grab him and are on the point of swallowing him, as occurs in an exemplary way in *Psycho* when the detective Arbogast climbs the stairs? The will is never free, subjectivity is always under constraint and caught.[67]

Yet this tie that, so to speak, pins the subject to objects – the found-ation of Hitchcock's 'subjective *mise-en-scène*' – is not his last word: the view from above that procures the geometrically transparent ground-plan of the scene, and follows Arbogast climbing the stairs, is precisely the impossible gaze which is autonomous, not deter-mined by things, purified of all pathological identification, free of constraint (in the above-mentioned later scene of Norman moving his mother to the cellar, the camera accomplishes this self-purifi-cation of the gaze within a continuous tracking shot which begins as an inquisitive ground-level glance and ends with the same 'God's view' of the entire scene: by means of its round movement, the gaze here literally disengages from, twists off, the pathological constraints). The cut from this neutral-free gaze into the gaze of the Thing itself that follows is therefore an inherent subversion of its purity – not a relapse into subjectivity, but an entry into the dimen-sion of the subject beyond subjectivity.

The suicide scene in *Murder!* involves a homologous formal dynamic: the suicidal jump is immediately preceded by a subjective shot which renders Fane's view of the arena and the public from the top of the circus tent – that is, from a point which coincides with 'God's view'. This point-of-view shot registers Fane's purification: after enduring *destitution subjective*, after freeing himself of subjective identifications, he can throw himself downwards, back into terres-trial reality, becoming an object-stain in it. The rope on which he hangs is the umbilical cord linking 'God's view' – the position of a pure meta-language, the view freed from all close-to-the-ground subjective identifications – with the obscene Thing which stains reality.[68]

The collapse of intersubjectivity

The antagonism between the objective 'God's view' and the 'subjec-tive' gaze of the Thing repeats on another, far more radical level the standard antagonism between objective and subjective which regul-ates the shot/counter-shot procedure. This complicity between 'God's view' and the obscene Thing designates, not a simple complementary relationship of two extremes, but an absolute coincidence – their antagonism is of a purely *topological* nature; what we have is *one and the same* element inscribed on two surfaces, put on two registers: the obscene stain is nothing but the way the objective-neutral view of the entire picture is present in the picture itself. (In the above-mentioned 'God's-view' shot of Bodega Bay from *The Birds* the same topological reversal is effectuated within the same shot: as soon as the birds enter the frame from behind the camera, the neutral 'objective' shot turns into the 'subjective' shot rendering the gaze of the obscene Thing, i.e. of the killing birds.)

We thereby rejoin the starting point of our analysis, since we have already encountered a homologous complicity of the two opposing features apropos of Hitchcock's 'Jansenism': (1) the determinated-ness of subjective destinies by the transsubjective blind automatism of the symbolic machinery; (2) the priority of the gaze over what is seen, which makes the entire domain of 'objectivity' dependent upon the gaze. This same antagonism defines the notion of the 'big Other' at the moment when Lacan first elaborated it (in the early 1950s; i.e. in his first two Seminars): the 'big Other' is introduced as the unfathomable Otherness of the subject beyond the wall of language, and then unexpectedly reverts to the asubjective blind automatism of the symbolic machine which regulates the play of intersubjectivity.[69] And the same reversal constitutes the dramatic *tour de force* of Rothman's interpretation in *The Murderous Gaze*: after hundreds of pages dedicated to the figure of absolute Otherness in Hitchcock's films, epitomized by the gaze into the camera, the final outcome of the analysis of *Psycho* is that this Otherness ultimately coincides with the machine (camera) itself.

In order to experience this paradoxical coincidence in a 'living' form, it is enough to recall the two constituents of monsters, cyborgs, the living dead, and so on: they are machines which run blindly, without compassion, devoid of any 'pathological' consider-ations, inaccessible to our pleas (the blind insistence of Schwarzen-egger in *Terminator*, of the living dead in *The Night of the Living Dead*, etc.), yet at the same time they are defined by the presence of an absolute gaze. What is truly horrifying about a monster is the way it seems to watch us all the time – without this gaze, the blind insist-ence of its drive would lose its uncanny character and turn into a simple mechanical force. The final dissolve of Norman's gaze into the mother's skull epitomizes this undecidability, this immediate coincidence of opposites which constitutes what is perhaps the ultimate Moebius band: the machine produces a leftover – the gaze as stain – yet it suddenly turns out that this leftover comprises the machine itself. *The sum is contained in its leftover – this umbilical link that pins the Whole on its stain is the absolute paradox that defines the subject.*

This, then, is the last misapprehension to be clarified: the ultimate 'secret' of *Psycho*, the secret epitomized by Norman's gaze into the camera, does *not* amount to a new version of the platitude on the unfathomable, ineffable depth of a person beyond the wall of language, and so on. The ultimate secret is that this Beyond is in itself hollow, devoid of any positive content: there is no depth of 'soul' in it (Norman's gaze is utterly 'soulless', like the gaze of monsters and the living dead) – as such, this Beyond *coincides with gaze itself*: 'beyond appearance there is not the Thing-in-itself, there is the gaze'[70] – it is as if Lacan's proposition bears directly on Norman's final gaze into the camera; it is as if it was made to summarize the ultimate lesson of *Psycho*.[71] Now, we can also answer Raymond Durgnat's[72] ironic remarks on the false 'depth' of Hitch-cock's films ('Potemkin submarines – a fleet of periscopes without hulls'); rather than being refuted, this description must be trans-posed into the 'thing itself': the odious lesson of *Psycho* is that *'depth' itself (the unfathomable abyss which defines our phenomenological experience of the other as 'person') is a 'periscope without hull'*, an illusory effect of the surface-mirroring, like the veil painted by Parrhasius which brings forth the illusion of the content hidden behind it ...

This gaze which reveals the true nature of the Beyond is the hard kernel of the Cartesian *cogito*, the bone that stuck in the throat of the contemporary critics of 'Cartesian metaphysics of subjectivity'. That is to say, one of the recurrent anti-Cartesian themes in contem-porary philosophy from the late Wittgenstein to Habermas is that the Cartesian *cogito* allegedly failed to take into account the primacy of intersubjectivity: *cogito* – or so the story goes – is 'monological' as to its structure and as such an alienated, reified product that can emerge only against the background of intersubjectivity and its 'life-world'. In an implicit counter-movement, *Psycho* indexes the status of a subject which precedes intersubjectivity – a depthless void of pure Gaze which is nothing but a topological reverse of the Thing. This subject – the core of the allegedly 'outdated' Cartesian problematic of Machine and Gaze – that is, of the Cartesian double obsession with mechanics and optics – is what the pragmatic-hermeneutic intersubjective approach endeavours to neutralize at any price, since it impedes the subjectivization/narrativization, the subject's full integration into the symbolic universe.

Hitchcock's path from his films of the 1930s to *Psycho* thus, in a way, runs parallel to that of Lacan. In the 1950s, Lacan's theory was also, via the motif of intersubjectivity, inscribed into the traditional anti-scientist discourse: psychoanalysis must avoid objectivizing the patient; in the psychoanalytic process, 'truth' emerges as the result of intersubjective dialectic where the recognition of desire is inextricably linked to the desire for recognition.... The Seminar on Transference (1960–61) expressly abandons this problematic in favour of *agalma*, the 'hidden treasure', the non-symbolizable object ('surplus-enjoyment') which is 'in the subject more than the subject itself' and thereby introduces an irreducible asymmetry into the intersubjective relationship.[73] For Lacan in the 1950s the object is reduced to the role of the 'stake' in the intersubjective game of recognition (to desire an object is a means to desire the desire of the other who claims this object, etc.), whereas for the later Lacan, *the object is what the subject is looking for in another subject* – what bestows upon the subject his/her dignity. The nostalgia many interpreters of Lacan – above all in Germany and Britain – feel for the 'dialectical-intersubjective' Lacan of the 1950s, who fits so well the contemporary 'life-world' and/or speech-act problematic (and can even be conceived as its forerunner) is therefore nothing but a form of resistance against Lacan, a desperate endeavour to neutralize the hard core of his theoretical edifice.

We can now understand why Hitchcock – in this respect no less a Cartesian than Lacan himself[74] – resists the temptation of flashback/voice-over: this formal device still relies upon intersubjectivity as medium of symbolic integration. For this reason Hitchcock's universe is ultimately incompatible with that of the *film noir*, where the flashback/voice-over device found its apogee – it is enough to mention Anatole Litvak's *Sorry, Wrong Number* (1948), a textbook exemplification of the Lacanian thesis on how the subject's truth is constituted by the discourse of the Other. It tells the story of an arrogant rich woman, confined to bed by her paralysed legs, who accidentally overhears a phone conversation about a planned murder; she sets out to investigate the affair and, after a whole day of phoning, finally establishes that the victim of the intended murder is herself – too late, since the murderer is already on the way.... As J. P. Telotte pointed out,[75] the outstanding feature of this film is that it reverses – in Hegelese, 'reflects-into-itself' – the usual procedure of *film noir* whereby, by way of gradual reconstruction – that is, of a series of partial insights – the narrator endeavours to unearth the 'true image' of some mysterious person (the paradigm here, of course, is *Citizen Kane*): in *Sorry, Wrong Number*, this mysterious, unknown person *coincides with the narrator herself.* By means of a series of other-persons' narratives, visualized in flashbacks, the narrator gradually puts all the pieces together and (re)constructs the truth about herself, realizing that she was unknowingly the centrepiece of an intricate plot – in short, she finds her truth outside herself, in the intersubjective network whose effects elude her grasp.

Therein consists the 'testamentary' dimension of the voice-over/ flashback device: lying at death's door, when all there was to happen had already taken place, the subject endeavours to clear up his/her life's mess by organizing it into a consistent narrative (*Double Indemnity, DOA*, etc.). The ultimate lesson of it is that when we put all the pieces together, the message that awaits us is 'death': it is possible to (re)construct one's story only when one faces death. In other words, *film noir* is paradoxically all too 'trustful' on account of the very features which constitute its 'blackness' (its atmosphere of hopeless fatality where the game is over before it begins, etc.): it still relies on the consistency of the 'big Other' (the symbolic order). It remains entirely within the confines of 'narrative closure': its narrative forms a closed symbolic itinerary of Fate whose letter 'arrives at its destination' with implacable necessity.

Let us recall what is perhaps the darkest and most disturbing specimen of the genre, Edmund Goulding's unjustly under-estimated *Nightmare Alley* (1947), the story of 'The Great Stanton', a small-time carnival operator who obtains the secrets of a fake mind-reader and sets himself up as a spiritualist; just as he seems to be on the verge of riches through his exploitation of wealthy clients, his fraud is exposed and his fall is as swift as his success. Early in the film, Stanton (played by Tyrone Power) reveals his horror of and repugnance towards the 'geek', a freak-show attraction who eats live chickens, the lowest form of carnival life; at the film's end, he himself returns to the shoddy carnival as a geek.... The 'narrative closure' consists in this metaphorical loop: at the outset, the hero witnesses a scene of humiliation towards which he maintains an attitude of superiority – what he overlooks is that this scene is a metaphor of his own future: the dimension of *de te fabula narratur*, the fact that, at the end, inexorable Fate will force him to occupy this very despicable place.[76] It is easy to discern in this loop the ethical imperative at work in the Freudian motto *wo es war, soll ich werden* – where that despicable creature is, this is your true place, there you shall arrive. This is, ultimately, what the 'death drive' is about: the 'death drive' is the name for a compulsion which inexorably draws the subject towards that place ...

What escapes notice as a rule, however, is the radical incompatibility between the voice-over/flashback and *film noir*'s other characteristic device, the subjective camera: Telotte completely misses the point by discerning the same attitude in both of them (the emphasis on the 'point of view' – that is, on how social reality is distorted by a subjective perspective) – for him the subjective camera is a mere radicalization of what is already at work in the voice-over/flashback.[77] The discontinuity between the voice-over/flashback and the subjective camera is ultimately the discontinuity between the Symbolic and the Real: by means of voice-over/flashback, the subject integrates his/her experience into the symbolic universe and thereby into the public space of intersubjectivity (it is not by accident that the flashback-narrative as a rule has the form of a confession to the Other, the representative of social authority), whereas the effect of the subjective camera is its exact opposite – the identification with the other's gaze excludes us from the symbolic space. When, in a film, we suddenly 'see things through another's eyes', we find ourselves occupying a place that no symbolization can accommodate.

Nowhere is this discontinuity more pronounced than in Hitchcock, the director of the subjective camera *par excellence* who, for that very reason, experiences such difficulties in handling the flashback:

in those rare cases when he resorts to it (*Stage Fright, I Confess*), the result is deeply ambiguous and strange, and the flashback as a rule proves false. This discontinuity is brought to its extreme in *Psycho*: at the end, the result is the direct opposite of the placement of different subjective perspectives into a common field of intersubjectivity which brings about the 'truth-effect'. That is to say, at the end, the two levels whose coincidence defines the successful flashback-narrative drift apart: the flat 'objective' scientific public *knowledge* pronounced by the psychiatrist on the one side, Norman's/Mother's final monologue, his/her subjective *truth*, his final confinement to the psychotic universe, on the other – with all the links between the two cut off.

The constitutive split between knowledge and truth is, of course, a commonplace of Lacanian theory: the hysteric 'lies' about the factual, propositional, content of his utterances, yet this very lie on the level of the enunciated brings forth the truth of his desire, his authentic subjective position of enunciation – in contrast to the obsessional neurotic, who speaks 'the truth and nothing but the truth' in order to conceal the falsity of his/her subjective position. Let us recall the opposition of the American Left and the McCarthyist witch-hunters in the early 1950s: on the level of 'factual accuracy', the McCarthyists were undoubtedly closer to the truth, at least as far as the Soviet Union was concerned (is it necessary to point out the naive, idealized image of the Soviet Union in Leftist circles?), yet in spite of this an unmistakable sense tells us that, within that concrete social link, 'truth' (authenticity of the subjective position) was decidedly on the side of the persecuted Left, whereas the witch-hunters were scoundrels even when the propositional content of their utterances was 'accurate'. The paradox is that *intersubjective truth can be enunciated only in the form of a lie*, of the falsity of propositional content: there is no 'synthesis' by means of which it would be possible to articulate the (intersubjective) truth in the form of (propositional) truth, since, as Lacan puts it, truth always has the structure of a fiction.

The crucial point not to be missed here, however, is the opposition between this hysterical intersubjective truth – that is, authentic subjective position – and the *psychotic* truth which enunciates itself in the 'mother's' final monologue: what the latter lacks (and this lack makes it a psychotic delirium) is precisely the dimension of *inter-subjectivity* – Norman's 'truth' is not integrated into the intersubjective field.

The ultimate social-ideological lesson of *Psycho* is therefore the collapse of the very field of intersubjectivity as medium of Truth in late capitalism, its disintegration into the two poles of expert knowledge and psychotic 'private' truth. Does, however, this mean that today, in the late capitalist universe, psychoanalysis (which ultimately consists in the symbolic integration of our traumas, by way of narrating them to the analyst who epitomizes the big Other of intersubjectivity) is no longer possible? The public fascination with figures like Hannibal Lecter, the cannibal serial killer from Thomas Harris's novels, provides a ray of hope: this fascination ultimately bears witness to a deep longing for a Lacanian psychoanalyst. That is to say, Hannibal Lecter is a sublime figure in the strict Kantian sense: a desperate, ultimately failed attempt of the popular imagination to represent to itself the idea of a Lacanian analyst. The relation of Lecter to the Lacanian analyst corresponds perfectly to the relationship which, according to Kant, defines the experience of the 'dynamic sublime': between wild, chaotic, untamed, raging Nature and the suprasensible Idea of Reason beyond any natural constraints. True, Lecter's evil – he not only kills his victims but goes on to eat parts of their entrails – strains to its limits our capacity to imagine the horrors we can inflict on our fellow-creatures; yet even our utmost effort to represent to ourselves Lecter's cruelty fails to capture the true dimension of the act of the analyst: by bringing-about *la traversée du fantasme* (going-through our fundamental fantasy), he literally 'steals the kernel of our being', the *objet petit a*, the secret treasure, *agalma*, what we consider most precious in ourselves, denouncing it as a mere semblance. Lacan defines the *objet petit a* as the phantasmatic 'stuff of the I'; as that which confers on the $, on the fissure in the symbolic order, on the ontological void that we call 'subject', the ontological consistency of a 'person', the semblance of a fullness of being – and it is precisely this 'stuff' which the analyst 'swallows', pulverizes. This is the rationale of the unexpected 'eucharistic' element at work in Lacan's definition of the analyst, namely his repeated ironic allusion to Heidegger: 'Mange ton *Dasein*!' – 'Eat your being-there!' Therein

262

consists Hannibal Lecter's power of fascination: by its very failure to attain the absolute limit of what Lacan calls 'the subjective destitution', it enables us to get a presentiment of the Idea of the analyst. So, in *The Silence of the Lambs*, Lecter is truly cannibalistic, not in relation to his victims but in relation to Clarice Starling: their relation is a mocking imitation of the analytic situation, since in exchange for his helping her to capture 'Buffalo Bill', he wants her to confide – what? Precisely what the analysand confides to the analyst, the kernel of her being, her fundamental fantasy (the crying of the lambs). The *quid pro quo* proposed by Lecter to Clarice is therefore: 'I'll help you if you let me eat your *Dasein*!' The inversion of the proper analytic relation consists in the fact that in compensation Lecter helps her track down 'Buffalo Bill'. Lecter is not cruel enough to be a Lacanian analyst: in psychoanalysis we must *pay* the analyst to allow us to offer our *Dasein* on a plate ...

Notes

1. A further proof of Hitchcock's personal commitment is that despite his considerable interest in financial matters, he made *The Wrong Man* gratis, renouncing his director's fee.

2. Eric Rohmer and Claude Chabrol, *Hitchcock: The First Forty-Four Films*, New York: Frederick Ungar 1979.

3. 'Hitchcock produces a cinema of relation, just as English philosophy produced a philosophy of relation' (Gilles Deleuze, *Cinema 1: The Movement-Image*, London: The Athlone Press 1986, p. X).

4. Another crucial feature of Jansenist theology is that God never intervenes in the world by openly producing miracles – by breaking the laws of nature: grace appears as a miracle only to believers, while others perceive it as a coincidence. This circle points towards the *transferential* nature of Grace: I recognize a miracle – i.e. a sign of Grace – in a happenstance only in so far as I already believe.

5. One is even tempted to construct here a Greimasian semiotic square to account for the disposition of the main characters in Racine's *Athalie*:

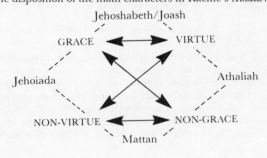

The fundamental opposition is that between Queen Athalie, who is virtuous yet not vouchsafed by grace, and the high priest Jehoiada, who is touched by grace yet clearly not virtuous (devoid of compassion, prone to furious outbursts of revenge, etc.). The place of Mattan is also clear and univocal (he is neither virtuous nor touched by grace, and as such an embodiment of Evil pure and simple), but difficulties arise as to its counterpoint, i.e. the ideal synthesis of grace and virtue. Neither of the two candidates – Jehoiada's wife Jehoshabeth and her nephew Joash, the legitimate pretender to the throne of Judah – really suits: the very feminine virtues of Jehoshabeth (compassion, readiness to compromise with the enemy) make her unfit for the role of God's instrument, while Joash's very perfection makes him monstrous, more an ideological automaton than a virtuous living being (and for that very reason susceptible to treason: later, he will effectively betray Jehovah, as is revealed in Jehoiada's nightmarish vision). What is indicated by this impossibility to fill out the upper place is the inherent limitation of the ideological space mapped by the semiotic square of virtue and grace: the relationship between grace and virtue is ultimately an antagonistic one, i.e. grace can find an outlet only in the guise of non-virtue.

6. And the specificity of the Humean philosophical *deism* is that it produces a third version of this split. A deist is in earnest about the radical alterity of God, about the inappropriateness of our human, finite notion to measure Him, and draws radical conclusions from it: every human worship of God actually entails His abasement, i.e. reduces Him to the level of something comparable to man (by venerating God, we impute to Him a self-complacent susceptibility to our flattery – consequently, the only attitude worthy of God's dignity is 'I know that God exists, yet for that very reason I *do not* venerate Him, but simply follow the elementary ethical rules accessible to everybody, believer or non-believer, by means of their innate natural Reason'. (Cf. Miran Božovič, 'Der Gott der Transvestiten', in *Gestalten der Autorität*, Vienna: Hora Verlag 1991.) By adding a fourth, atheist version ('I know that God does not exist, yet for that very reason I feel obliged to follow the elementary ethical rules accessible to everybody, believer or non-believer …') we again obtain a Greimasian semiotic square where the four positions can be arranged into two contradictory and two contrary couples.

7. As in the well-known story of 'appointment in Samarra', where the servant misinterprets Death's surprised look as a mortal threat; see Chapter 2 of Slavoj Žižek, *The Sublime Object of Ideology*, London: Verso 1989.

8. 'Ah! je vois Hippolyte;/Dans ses yeux insolents je vois ma perte écrite' (Jean Racine, *Phèdre*, 909–10).

9. See, as perhaps the supreme example, the intricate exchange of gazes between Ingrid Bergman, Cary Grant and Claude Rains during the reception scene from *Notorious*.

10. Jacques Lacan, *The Four Fundamental Concepts of Psycho-Analysis*, Harmondsworth: Penguin 1977, p. 84.

11. The death's-head moth offers perhaps the supreme case of this reflexivity of gaze at work in mimicry. That is to say, the usual notion of mimicry involves a simple deceitful appearance which lures the eye into taking the animal for what it is not (a locust looks like a splinter; a small powerless fish inflates and assumes threatening proportions …); yet in the case of the death's-head moth the animal deceives our eye by *mimicking the gaze itself*, i.e. by presenting itself to our eye as something that returns the gaze. Lacan often evokes the classical tale of the contest between the

two Greek painters, Zeuxis and Parrhasius: victory goes to Parrhasius, who paints a veil on the wall; Zeuxis turns to him and says: 'Well, now show us what you have painted behind it.' The deception of the death's-head moth is located on the same level: it lures our eye not by the convincing features of the imitated object, but by producing the illusion that it returns the gaze itself. And is not the lure of the 'rear window' in Hitchcock's film of the same name ultimately identical? The black window on the opposite side of the courtyard arouses James Stewart's curiosity precisely in so far as he perceives it as a kind of veil that he wants to pull off in order to see what lies hidden behind it; this trap works only in so far as he imagines in it the presence of the Other's gaze, since, as Lacan puts it, the Thing-in-itself beyond appearance is none other than the gaze. See Miran Božovič's chapter on *Rear Window* in this book, pp. 161–77.

12. For a more detailed account, see Chapter 4 of Slavoj Žižek, *Looking Awry: An Introduction to Jacques Lacan through Popular Culture*, Cambridge, MA: MIT Press 1991.

13. Here, of course, a structural homology immediately imposes itself: such radical externality of the symbolic network that determines the subject's fate with regard to his/her inherent properties is conceivable only against the background of the commodity-universe where the 'fate' of a commodity, its exchange-circuit, is experienced as radically external to its positive, inherent properties (its 'use value'). Yet the use of such abstract homologies is not to be overestimated – ultimately, they function as an excuse for postponing the elaboration of the concrete mechanisms of mediation.

14. This line is crossed, among others, by Captain Ahab in Melville's *Moby Dick*. Ahab is well aware that Moby Dick – this obscene Thing *par excellence* – is just a stupid gigantic animal; yet as such, it is a cardboard mask of the real Evil, God who created a world in which there is ultimately nothing for man but pain. Ahab's aim is therefore that, by striking Moby Dick, he should deal a blow at the Creator Himself.

15. *The Wrong Man* thus failed as a 'serious' film for precisely the same reason that *Mr and Mrs Smith* failed as a comedy: Hitchcock's mastery of comic detail remains unsurpassable as long as it is part of the encompassing thriller frame, yet as soon as he tackles a comedy directly, the magic touch is lost.

16. William Rothman, *The Murderous Gaze*, Cambridge, MA: Harvard University Press 1982.

17. Stephen Rebello's *Alfred Hitchcock and the Making of 'Psycho'* (New York: Dembner 1990) documents how Hitchcock, against all pressures, insisted on a series of points which, to a viewer unaware of the allegorical dimension of his work, cannot but seem an incomprehensible compliance with the worst commercial instincts: he insisted that Sam and Lila are not to develop into full-blooded characters, i.e. that they are to remain 'flat' tools of our probing into the mystery of Norman's mother; he cut from the final version an overhead shot of the slaughtered Marion lying naked near the running shower, although everybody around him agreed on the immense poetic power of this shot evoking the tragic nonsense of a wasted young girl's life. Within the diegetic narrative content, these elements would undoubtedly add to the film's texture; yet the moment one takes the self-reflective allegorical level into account, it becomes clear why they are superfluous: they would function as a kind of noise disturbing the dialogue between Hitchcock and the viewer. A further reason why the relationship between Sam and Lila must remain 'empty' is the antagonism between partnership and love in Hitchcock's films (see the Introduction to

this book): from the 1940s onwards, partnership increasingly precludes love or any other genuine emotional involvement. In other words, far from contributing to the psychological depth of the film, a 'full-blooded' relationship between Sam and Lila would effectively *flatten* its ideologico-critical sting.

18. See Leland Poague, 'Links in a Chain: *Psycho* and Film Classicism', in Marshall Deutelbaum and Leland Poague, eds, *A Hitchcock Reader*, Ames: Iowa State University Press 1986, pp. 340–49.

19. ... to which even Fredric Jameson succumbs, at least for a moment – see Fredric Jameson, 'Allegorizing Hitchcock', in *Signatures of the Visible*, New York; Routledge 1990, p. 127.

20. Jacques Lacan, 'Kant with Sade', *October* 51 (Winter 1990).

21. A connoisseur of Lacan can easily discern in this scheme a prefiguration of the 'discourse of the Master' from the matrix of the four discourses:

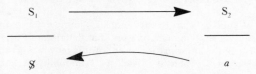

The Will-to-Enjoy (V) designates the attitude of the Master (S_1), assumed by the agent of the discourse – the sadist – on the manifest level, while its counterpart, S, is his other, the victim on to whom the sadist transposes the 'pain of being'; on the lower level, the terms exchange places ($a \diamond \math$, not $\math
diamond a$) because, as Lacan puts it, the Sadeian perversion reverses the formula of fantasy, i.e. the confrontation of the barred subject with the object-cause of his/her desire.

22. In his Seminar on Transference, Lacan pointed out this crucial difference between neurosis (hysteria) and perversion as regards their relation to the social order: in so far as hysteria designates resistance to social interpellation, to assuming the allotted social identity, it is by definition subversive, whereas perversion is in its structure inherently 'constructive' and can easily be put to the service of the existing social order. See Jacques Lacan, *Le Séminaire, livre VIII: Le transfert*, Paris: Editions du Seuil 1991, p. 43.

23. We refer here, of course, to Christian Metz's analyses from his 'The Imaginary Signifier', in *Psychoanalysis and Cinema*, London: Macmillan 1982.

24. It is easy to see how this brings us back to the Jansenist problematic of predestination. For a further elaboration of the way this illusion works in the ideological process, see Chapter 3 of Slavoj Žižek, *For they know not what they do*, London: Verso 1991.

25. Robin Wood formulated this change of modality clearly, yet his perspective remains that of subjectivization; for that reason, he is compelled to conceive it as a simple weakness of the film, i.e. as a lapse, a 'compromise' with the standard detective-narration formula of investigating a mystery – what eludes him is the *structural impossibility* of identifying with Norman. See Robin Wood, *Hitchcock's Films*, New York: A.S. Barnes 1977, pp. 110–11.

26. Georg Seesslen, *Kino der Angst*, Reinbek bei Hamburg: Rowohlt 1980, p. 173.

27. It was Robin Wood who pointed out this crucial detail: *Hitchcock's Films*, p. 112.

28. Hitchcock relied on a homologous dialectic of the (un)expected already in *Sabotage*; see Mladen Dolar's chapter on *Sabotage* in this book, pp. 129–36.

29. Such a forerunner of the first part of *Psycho* actually exists: many of its motifs can be discerned in Hitchcock's TV film *One More Mile to Go* (1957).

30. Another strategy of subverting the classic narrative closure is at work in Ulu Grosbard's melodrama *Falling in Love* with Meryl Streep and Robert de Niro, whose ending enacts, in a condensed form, the entire gamut of possible denouements of extramarital affairs in cinema history: the couple parts under the pressure of the environment; the woman is on the verge of committing suicide on the rails; after the break-up of the affair, they meet again by chance and realize that although they are still in love, they have missed the right moment; finally, they run into each other once again in a commuter train and (so it seems) reunite for good – the charm of the film consists in this playing with different codes, so that the viewer can never be sure if what he/she sees is already the final denouement.... What makes *Falling in Love* a 'postmodern' film is this reflected relationship to the history of cinema, i.e. its playing-over of the different variants of the narrative closure.

31. The narrative shift has a long and respectable tradition, starting from Mozart–Schikaneder's *Magic Flute*: after the first third (where the Queen of Night charges Tamino, the hero, to deliver her beautiful daughter Pamina from the clutches of the tyrannical Sarastro, the Queen's ex-husband and Pamina's father), Sarastro miraculously changes into a figure of wise authority, so that the accent now shifts on to the couple's ordeal under his benevolent supervision. In so far as *The Magic Flute*'s 'production of the couple' by means of the ordeal can serve as the paradigm of Hitchcock's 1930s films, one is almost tempted to say that *Psycho* passes through the way of *The Magic Flute* backwards, in the opposite direction.

A somewhat similar shift is often at work in contemporary popular culture, where it assumes the form of a sudden change of genre within the same work (Alan Parker's *Angel Heart*, for example, where the private-eye-investigation narrative changes into a tale of the supernatural). The appropriate use of narrative shift can unleash a tremendous ideologico-critical potential by rendering visible the necessity because of which the immanent logic of a narrative space throws us into discontinuous externality: say, the unexpected shift of an 'intimate' psychological drama into the sociopolitical dimension, *precisely in so far as it is experienced as 'unconvincing'*, reproduces, at the level of the conflict of genre codes, the discord between subjective experience and objective social processes, this fundamental feature of capitalist everyday life – here, as Adorno would put it, the very weakness of the narrative form, the 'unfounded' shift in the narrative line, functions as an index of social antagonism.

32. See Michel Chion's chapter on *Psycho* in this book, pp. 195–207.

33. One of the formulaic twists of thrillers is, of course, the adding, at the very end, of a supplementary 'turn of the screw' which belies the 'embodiment', as in a short story from Hitchcock's TV series where a woman finally kills her neighbour, whom she has identified as the anonymous molester threatening her by phone – yet when she sits down by his body, the phone rings again and the well-known voice bursts into obscene laughter...

34. Lacan, *The Four Fundamental Concepts*, p. 103.

35. See the excellent analysis of this scene by Stephen Heath, 'Droit de regard', in Raymond Bellour, ed., *Le Cinéma américain* II, Paris: Flammarion 1980, pp. 87–93.

36. Even in such a 'light-hearted' thriller as *To Catch a Thief*, we find the same effect towards the end when the shadowy contour of Cary Grant enters the 'God's-perspective' shot of the garden where the party is taking place. A similar effect occurs during the sexual act between Mickey Rourke and Lisa Bonet in Alan Parker's *Angel Heart*: the rain which trickles from the leaking ceiling changes all of a sudden into blood; the red stain which erupts from everywhere and overflows the field of vision is not perceived as part of diegetic reality, it is rather as if it comes from the intermediate space between diegetic reality and our (viewer's) 'proper' reality – i.e. *from the very screen that separates them*. In other words, it enters the frame of diegetic reality in the same way as the birds enter it in the course of their attacks in *The Birds*, or the mother's knife in the course of Marion's murder.

37. This reflexive redoubling is precisely what Lacan adds in his (obvious mis)reading of the Freudian concept of *Vorstellungs-Repräsentanz*. With Freud, *Vorstellungs-Repräsentanz* designates the simple fact that drive does not pertain to biology pure and simple, but is always articulated by means of its psychic represen-tatives (the fantasy-representations of objects and scenes which stage its satisfaction), i.e. *Vorstellungs-Repräsentanz* is the drive's representative within the psychic appar-atus (see Sigmund Freud, 'Repression', *Standard Edition* XIV, pp. 152–3, and 'The Unconscious', *Standard Edition* XIV, p. 177). With Lacan, on the contrary, *Vorstel-lungs-Repräsentanz* is a representative (a place-holder [*le tenant-lieu*]) of what the representational field excludes, it stands in for the missing ('primordially repressed') representation: 'Now, that is precisely what I mean, and say – for what I mean, I say – in translating *Vorstellungsrepräsentanz* by representative of the representation' (Lacan, *The Four Fundamental Concepts*, p. 218).

38. Such a prohibition defines, among others, the very notion of democracy as it was elaborated by Claude Lefort: in democracy, the locus of Power is by definition empty, i.e. Power is a purely symbolic place that no real subject is allowed to occupy.

39. The superficial index of it is perhaps the retreat of the Judaeo-Christian attitude in the face of so-called 'New Age consciousness'.

40. Donald Spoto, *The Dark Side of Genius: The Life of Alfred Hitchcock*, New York: Ballantine 1984, p. 440.

41. Let us just recall – among many products of this kind – a science-fiction film about an atomic aircraft carrier on a routine cruise near Midway in 1972; a strange cloud-vortex suddenly appears from nowhere and transfers it thirty years back, immediately before the Battle of Midway. After long hesitation, the Captain decides to follow his patriotic duty and to intervene – in other words, to enter the forbidden domain and thereby get involved in the time-snare, changing his own past – yet at this very moment, the mysterious vortex appears again and throws the aircraft carrier back into the present.

42. Biology offers here an almost perfect metaphor of this paradoxical status of the subject. What we have in mind is a species of worm – *Acarophenax tribolii* – mentioned by Stephen Jay Gould (see his 'Death before Birth, or a Mite's *Nunc Dimittis*', in *The Panda's Thumb*, Harmondsworth: Pelican 1983, pp. 63–4; for a Lacanian reading, see Miran Božovič, 'Immer Ärger mit dem Körper', *Wo Es War* 5–6, Vienna: Hora Verlag 1988): inside the mother's body, i.e. before his own birth, the male copulates with and fecundates his 'sisters', then passes away and is born dead – in other words, he skips the 'living body' and passes directly from the state of foetus to that of corpse. This limit-case of a foetus born as a corpse is the closest

biological correlative to the status of the 'barred' subject of the signifier ($), never living in 'its proper time', passing over 'real life' . . .

43. On this notion of the 'missing link', see Chapter 5 of Žižek, *For They Know Not What They Do*.

44. Besides Norman, there are two more brief apparitions of absolute Otherness in *Psycho*, yet – significantly – they are later 'domesticated', i.e. their Otherness proves a lure, since they are both an agency of Law: the policeman with dark glasses perceived by Marion as a threat to her escape (due to the hysterical distortion of her vision, Marion misperceives those who are actually trying to stop her flight to ruin as impediments on her way to happiness), and Arbogast's first appearance as the eavesdropping intruder in the conversation between Sam and Lila (his face, shot in extreme close-up, assumes unpleasantly obtrusive dimensions of a stain). One of the most striking appearances of this absolute Otherness in Hitchcock's films is found in *Murder!*: when Fane (the murderer) first enters, his outstanding feature is his fixed, quasi-hypnotic gaze into the camera . . .

45. One should recall here Lesley Brill's crucial insight into how the contours of Hitchcock's universe are delineated by the extremes of *romance* (where the movement runs 'from outside inwards': due to an external contingency which throws them together, the couple is forced to behave as if they were married or in love, and this imitation, this external ritual, begets, in a performative way, 'true' love – the matrix of Hitchcock's films of the late 1930s) and *irony* (where, on the contrary, communication fails, since we do *not* succeed in 'doing things with words'; i.e. where the word remains 'empty' and lacks the performative power to establish a new intersubjective link): the romance is undermined precisely by the presence of the 'absolute Otherness' (Lesley Brill, *The Hitchcock Romance: Love and Irony in Hitchcock's Films*, Princeton, NJ: Princeton University Press 1988).

46. Elizabeth Weis, *The Silent Scream*, London: Associated University Presses 1982, pp. 136–46.

47. Tania Modleski, *The Women Who Knew Too Much*, New York and London: Methuen 1988, p. 38.

48. Ibid., p. 40.

49. This innermost theatricality of Sir John's activity enables us to identify the role of the stage in *Murder!* with that of the courtyard in *Rear Window*: in the latter, James Stewart is able to relate to the woman (Grace Kelly) only in so far as she appears in the courtyard beyond the door and thus enters his fantasy-frame; like Sir John, who can relate to a woman only in so far as she enters the universe of the play he is about to write.

50. In consequence, one can say that *Psycho* presents the ultimate version of the 'transference-of-guilt' motif. The symbolic exchange which defines the Hitchcockian murder. i.e. the fact that, in Hitchcock's films, murder is as a rule accomplished for someone else – by means of it, the psychotic assassin realizes the hysteric's desire (Bruno realizes Guy's desire in *Strangers on a Train*, etc.) – is here localized in one and the same person, as an exchange between its two psychic agencies: Norman's maternal superego commits the murder and then transfers the guilt to his ego.

51. Considering that, according to Lacan, the status of the act is that of *objet petit a*, and that, at *Psycho*'s end, Norman becomes a medium through which the superego-*knowledge* of his Mother speaks, this double passage (from Sir John to Fane, from Marion to Norman) can easily be located in the diagonal cross of

Lacan's matrix of the discourse:

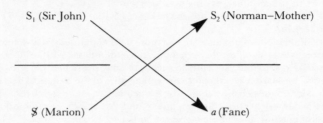

S₁ (Sir John)   S₂ (Norman–Mother)

$ (Marion)   a (Fane)

52. For a theory of Hitchcockian tracking shot, see Žižek, *Looking Awry*, pp. 93–7.

53. See François Truffaut, *Hitchcock*, London: Panther 1969, pp. 343–6.

54. See Raymond Bellour, 'Psychosis, Neurosis, Perversion', in Marshall Deutelbaum and Leland Poague, eds, *A Hitchcock Reader*, pp. 311–31.

55. Apropos of Jacob Boehme's mystical relationship to God as Thing, Lacan says: 'To confuse his contemplative eye with the eye with which God is looking at him must surely partake in perverse *jouissance*' ('God and the *Jouissance* of the Woman', in Juliet Mitchell and Jacqueline Rose, eds, *Feminine Sexuality: Jacques Lacan and the Ecole Freudienne*, New York: Norton 1982, p. 147).

56. This perverse gaze of the Thing emerges for the first time in Kant's *Critique of Practical Reason*; in the last paragraph of the first part, the question is raised of why God created the world in such a way that the Supreme Good is unknowable to us, finite humans, so that we cannot ever fully realize it? The only way to elude the hypothesis of an evil God who created the world with the express intention of annoying humankind is to conceive the inaccessibility of the Thing (God, in this case) as a positive condition of our ethical activity: if God as Thing were immediately to disclose Himself to us, our activity could no longer be ethical, since we would do Good not because of moral Law itself but because of our direct insight into God's nature, i.e. out of the immediate assurance that Evil will be punished. The paradox of this explanation is that – for a brief moment, at least – Kant is forced to accomplish what is otherwise strictly prohibited in his 'critical philosophy' – the reversal from $ ◇ a to a ◇ $ – and to view the world *through the eyes of the Thing* (*God*): his entire argument presupposes that we position ourselves within God's reasoning.

57. Sigmund Freud, 'Psychoanalytic Notes on an Autobiographical Account of a Case of Paranoia (Schreber)', in *Case Histories* II, Harmondsworth: Penguin 1979, p. 156.

58. Ibid.

59. Cf. Abraham Lincoln's famous answer to a request for a special favour: 'As President, I have no eyes but constitutional eyes; I cannot see you.'

60. Therein consists, according to Lacan, the asymmetry between Oedipus and Jocasta: Oedipus did not know what he was doing, whereas his mother knew all the time who her sexual partner was – the source of her enjoyment was precisely Oedipus's ignorance. The notorious thesis on the intimate link between feminine enjoyment and ignorance acquires thereby a new, intersubjective dimension: woman enjoys in so far as her *other* (man) does not know.

61. We encounter a homologous inversion in numerous hard-boiled novels and

films: the moment when the *femme fatale* subjectivizes herself. She is first rendered from the perspective of her (masculine) social environment and appears as a fatal object of fascination which brings perdition and leaves behind ruined lives, 'empty shells'; when we are finally transposed into her point of view, it becomes manifest that she herself cannot dominate the effects of 'what is in her more than herself', of the *object* in herself, upon her environment – no less than the men around her, she is a helpless victim of Fate.

62. It was of course the backwardness of film technique which was ultimately responsible for such an impression: at that time, it was technically impossible to conceal the discord between the figure and its background; yet the paradox is that this very discord engenders the crucial artistic effect.

63. One is even tempted to suggest that this shot reveals the secret of Platonism: the only way to isolate – to disconnect from the universal process of generation and corruption – the site of absolute standstill is the fixation upon the Other's gaze as the immovable point in the picture.

64. The similarity between this shot of Arbogast's face and the shot of Henry Fonda's face reflected in the cracked mirror in *The Wrong Man* is therefore fully justified: in both cases, the point of view is that of the Thing. See Renata Salecl's chapter on *The Wrong Man* in this book, pp. 185–94.

65. In *Whatever Happened to Baby Jane?* Robert Aldrich endeavoured to obtain a similar effect by shooting the scene where Bette Davis brings the starved Joan Crawford a rat on a tray from the same 'God's' perspective; the 'stain' here is the dead rat itself, which becomes visible when the tray is uncovered. What makes the crucial difference with *Psycho* is the absence of a cut into the gaze of the terrifying stain (Thing) responsible for the subversive effect of the scene of Arbogast's murder.

66. It is interesting to note how Hitchcock resorted to a homologous sequence of shots back in 1930, in the mousetrap scene in *Murder!*, at the crucial moment when Fane – the murderer – is on the verge of walking into Sir John's trap. Sir John and Fane rehearse a scene from Sir John's play; when Fane reaches the passage in the manuscript which was planned to induce him to divulge his guilt, Hitchcock abruptly abandons the standard shot/counter-shot procedure, the camera assumes 'God's perspective' and shows us both protagonists (Sir John and Fane) from far above; this strange shot is then quickly followed by an over-the-shoulder, quasi-subjective close-up of Fane, who nervously turns over the page in order to see what comes next in the manuscript (i.e. how much Sir John actually knows about the murder), and comes across a blank page. (On this scene, see Alenka Zupančič's chapter on theatre in this book, pp. 73–105.) Far from bringing relief to Fane (by confirming that Sir John does not know the entire truth about the murder), the blank page produces an uncanny shock, a kind of premonition of Fane's death. That is to say, this blank page is closely related to the void that Fane encounters in his third vision during his swinging on the trapeze, immediately before his suicide (first he sees Sir John, then Diana, and finally nothing – nothing which stands in for himself).

67. Jean Narboni, 'Visages d'Hitchcock', in *Cahiers du cinéma, hors-série 8: Alfred Hitchcock*, Paris 1980, p. 33.

68. There is a structural homology between this scene and the mousetrap scene in Laurence Olivier's *Hamlet*: in the latter, the invisible 'rope' connects its two nodal points, the stage and the king. The stage where the 'truth' about the death of Hamlet's father is revealed in the form of fiction materializes 'God's view', which is

THE INDIVIDUAL

why it functions as the first nodal point around which the camera swings in a long panning shot; the obscene stain in the picture is, of course, the murderous king in public – the moment he recognizes the truth about his crime on the stage, he becomes the second nodal point around which the camera swings. The homology is thus clear: in Olivier's *Hamlet*, the function of the rope (which reaches from the height of 'God's view' and strangles the assassin in *Murder*) *is taken over by the camera itself*, which encircles the king the moment he displays his guilt. (See also Alenka Zupančič's chapter on theatre in this book, pp. 73–105.)

69. For a more detailed elaboration of this constitutive duplicity of the Lacanian notion of 'big Other', see Chapter 6 of Žižek, *For They Know Not What They Do*.

70. Lacan, *The Four Fundamental Concepts*, p. 103.

71. A film which was known to Lacan, as is proved by a passing reference to it in the Seminar on Transference (Lacan, *Le Séminaire, livre VIII: Le transfert*, p. 23).

72. Raymond Durgnat, *The Strange Case of Alfred Hitchcock*, London: Faber & Faber 1974.

73. Lacan, *Le Séminaire, livre VIII: Le transfert*, pp. 20–22.

74. For whom, as it is well known, the subject of psychoanalysis is none other than the Cartesian *cogito*.

75. J.P. Telotte, *Voices in the Dark: The Narrative Patterns of Film Noir*, Chapter 4 ('Tangled Networks and Wrong Numbers'), Urbana: University of Illinois Press 1989.

76. One encounters the same loop in Josef von Sternberg's *Morocco*: at the beginning, Marlene Dietrich, the *femme fatale*, scornfully observes the band of women who follow on foot the caravan of legionaries on its march into the desert in order to stay with their lovers; at the end, she herself joins the band, since her only true love is in the caravan.

77. See, for example, Telotte, p. 17: 'Far more than the voice-over/flashback, the subjective camera emphasizes point of view . . .'.

272

Notes on the Contributors

Pascal Bonitzer is a French film theorist associated with the journal *Cahiers du cinéma*; in recent years he has also become known as a screenplay writer. His works include *Le Regard et la voix* (Paris 1976) and *Le Champ aveugle* (Paris 1982).

Miran Božovič is Professor of the History of Philosophy at the University of Ljubljana, Slovenia, and author of *Descartes, Cogito and Madness* (in Slovene, Ljubljana 1990).

Michel Chion is a French film theorist associated with *Cahiers du cinéma*; he is also a composer of *musique concrète*. His publications on film include *La Voix au cinéma* (Paris 1982), *Le Son au cinéma* (Paris 1985) and *La Toile trouée* (Paris 1988).

Mladen Dolar is Professor of Social Philosophy at the University of Ljubljana and author of *The Structure of the Fascist Domination* (in Slovene, Ljubljana 1982) and *Hegel's 'Phenomenology of Spirit'* (in Slovene, Ljubljana 1991).

Fredric Jameson is Professor of Comparative Literature at Duke University, North Carolina. His most recent publications include *Late Marxism: Adorno, or, The Persistence of the Dialectic* (Verso: London 1990) and *Postmodernism, or, The Cultural Logic of Late Capitalism* (Verso: London 1991).

Stojan Pelko is a Slovene film theorist and editor-in-chief of the journal *Ekran*.

Renata Salecl is a Researcher at the Institute for Criminology at the

University of Ljubljana and author of *Discipline as a Condition of Freedom* (in Slovene, Ljubljana 1991).

Slavoj Žižek is a Researcher at the Institute of Social Sciences at the University of Ljubljana. His publications in English include *The Sublime Object of Ideology* (Verso: London 1989) and *For they know not what they do* (Verso: London 1991).

Alenka Zupančič is a Researcher at the Institute for Philosophical Studies at the Slovene Academy of Sciences and Arts, Ljubljana.

Index

Films directed by Hitchcock are followed by (AH)

absolute Otherness 244–5, 256, 269 n44
accidental encounters 41–3
acousmêtre 195–205, 206–7 n1, 233–4
act, structure of 90–103, 246–7
Aldrich, Robert, *Whatever Happened to Baby Jane?* 271 n65
allegory 218–19, 241, 244–5, 265 n17
Angel Heart (Alan Parker) 267 n31, 268 n36
Antonioni, M. 40, 45
Arbuckle, Fatty 16
architecture 151–3
Arendt, Hannah 52
Aristophanes 233
Aristotle, *Zoological Researches* 172–3
Arnauld, Antoine 213
Austen, Jane, *Mansfield Park* 150
Avery, Tex 18
The Aviator's Wife 157
Awakenings 11 n3

Bakhtin, Mikhail 225
Ballard, J.G., *Empire of the Sun* 217
Bazin, André 201, 202–3
Bellour, Raymond 2, 11 n3, 29 n3, 60, 107, 119, 193, 200, 241
Bentham Jeremy 144
Bergman, Ingmar 152
Bergson, Henri 86
big Other 256
The Birds (AH) 5, 7, 37, 48, 63, 197, 236–7, 239, 256
Blackmail (AH) 7, 25–6, 28, 135, 215

Black Rain (Ridley Scott) 217
blindness, figures of 106–19
blot, *see* stain
Blow-Up (Antonioni) 40, 45
Blue Velvet (David Lynch) 11 n1
Bogdanovich, Peter 130
Bonitzer, Pascal 132–3, 198, 201
Brill, Lesley 269 n45

Cahiers du cinéma 3, 179
Carmen (Jean-Luc Godard) 159
Casablanca 137
Catholicism, *see* Jansenism
Cavell, Stanley 58
Chabrol, Claude 132
    Hitchcock 212
Chandler, Raymond 40, 56
    Farewell, My Lovely 56
Chaplin, Charlie 16, 202
    The Circus 202
The Cheat (C.B. DeMille) 17
Chion, Michel 233
Citizen Kane (Orson Welles) 259
City of Women (Federico Fellini) 157
Conrad, Joseph, *The Secret Agent* 129–30
crime 18, 19–20, 82–9, 94–5

Dances with Wolves 11 n3
Dead Poets' Society (Peter Weir) 98–102
death
    and narrative 259–60
    in *Sabotage* 130–2
    stage as place of 79–82

275

INDEX

deep shot 58
deism 264 n6
Deleuze, Gilles 82, 86, 87, 107, 109,
    110–11, 113, 115, 117, 133
    The Movement-Image 212
    The Time-Image 116
DeMille, Cecil B. 17
de Palma, Brian 28
Derrida, Jacques 2, 111, 113
    Mémoires d'aveugle 108
Descartes, René 169
    Optics 162–3
desire
    and drive 228–32
    and the gaze 169–72, 225
    and suspense 132
    and theatre 97–8
destitution subjective 254–5
Dial M for Murder (AH) 6, 45, 60, 73, 131,
    159, 206 n1, 219
Dishonoured (von Sternberg) 137–8
doubling effects 31–41, 96–8, 180–4
Duras, Marguerite 200, 203
Durgnat, Raymond 135, 145, 257

editing, and suspense 15–16, 23–4, 28,
    201–3
Eliot, T.S. 1
endings 145–7, 149
episodic structure 59–60
eroticism 24–8, 153

Falling in Love (Ulu Grosbard) 267 n30
Family Plot (AH) 5, 60
fantasy 242–3
Farmer, Philip Jose, *The Doors of Time* 242
Fatal Attraction 11 n1
Ferry, Odette 27
film, as concept 74–8
Foreign Correspondent (AH) 4, 6, 9, 21, 44,
    109, 133
Foucault, Michel 2, 144
Frenzy (AH) 5, 25
Freud, Sigmund 93, 119, 126, 190, 229,
    231, 238, 241, 268 n37
Fried, Michael 113

gaze, the 16–21, 26–8, 74–6, 102, 109,
    113–14, 132–4, 143–9, 161–72, 175–6,
    186, 214–15, 223–5, 234–7, 244–5
    of the Thing 248–58, 270 n56
    see also point-of-view
Godard, Jean-Luc 19, 159
Godfather films 10 n1

'God's view' shots 247–56, 268 n36,
    271 n65, 271–2 n68
Gould, Stephen Jay 268 n42
Goulding, Edmund 259–60
Griffith, D.W. 15, 16, 28, 74, 132
Grosbard, Ulu, 267 n30
guilt 84–90, 186–93, 269 n50

Habermas, Jürgen 257
Hamlet (Laurence Olivier) 87–90,
    271–2 n68
Harris, Thomas, *The Silence of the Lambs*
    173, 174, 262–3
Hayakawa, Sessue 17, 18
Heath, Stephen 58, 121 n20
Heidegger, Martin 262
Holbein, Hans, 'The Ambassadors' 171
Hopper, Edward 231

I Confess (AH) 73, 79, 80–1, 187, 261
identification
    in film 115–16, 226–8, 234
    with forms of transgression 225–6
    and guilt 186
ideology 241–2
Iles, Frances, *Before the Fact* 145
images, kinds of 107–9, 118
India Song (Marguerite Duras) 200, 203
initiation, narratives of 138
interpellation 224
interpretation, kinds of 1–3, 47–9, 126–7
intersubjectivity 257–62

James, Henry 243
    'The Turn of the Screw' 146–7, 148
Jameson, Fredric 2
Jansenism 211–16, 256

Kant, Immanuel 50, 90–5, 262
    Critique of Practical Reason 270 n56
    Metaphysics of Morals 94
    Metaphysical Foundations of Morality 92
Kouleshov 17

Lacan, Jacques 2, 46, 82, 148, 166, 168–9,
    170, 171, 175, 189, 190, 193, 214, 224,
    229, 230, 238, 239, 254, 256, 257, 261,
    262, 263, 266 n21, 266 n22, 268 n37
    Encore 7
    The Ethic of Psychoanalysis 91, 95
    and intersubjectivity 258
    'Kant avec Sade' 219–22
    Seminar I 167
    Seminar II 245

Seminar XI 161, 192, 235
The Lady Vanishes (AH) 3, 4, 6, 8, 9, 12 n6, 22, 23, 34, 44, 115, 137–42, 237–8
Lang, Fritz 42, 204–5, 206 n1
Larger than Life (Nicholas Ray) 153
Le Carré, John, *A Perfect Spy* 217
Lefebvre, Henri 50
Lefort, Claude 268 n38
Lehman, Ernest 240
Lévi-Strauss, Claude, *Structural Anthropology* 236
Litvak, Anatole 258–9
The Lodger (AH) 3, 167, 245
Louis, Pierre 172
Lumière brothers 16, 18–19

M (Fritz Lang) 42
The Magnificent Ambersons (Orson Welles) 206 n1
Malebranche, Nicolas 173, 174
The Man Who Knew Too Much (AH) 6, 22, 45, 67, 73, 119, 127, 178–84, 197
Marnie (AH) 5, 7, 25, 37
Méliès, Georges 16
Melville, Hermann, *Moby Dick* 265 n14
metamorphosis 172–5
Millar, Gavin 33
Miller, Jacques-Alain 93, 95
mimicry 264 n11
Mr and Mrs Smith (AH) 112, 212
modernism and postmodernism 1–5, 10–11 n1, 48, 58–60, 232
modernity and tradition 232
Modleski, Tania 246
Morin, Edgar 16
Morocco (von Sternberg) 272 n76
mother
  desire of 36–9, 228
  and the uncanny 154
  voice of 179, 194–205, 233–4
motifs, study of 125–7, 179
Mozart, W.A., *The Magic Flute* 4, 34, 138, 267 n31
Mozhukin experiment 17, 18
Murder! (AH) 73, 74–7, 79, 82, 83, 84–7, 90, 96–8, 103–4, 245–7, 252–3, 255, 269 n44, 271 n66
musical themes, as messages 137–42

Narboni, Jean 133, 254
narrative closure 241–6, 259–60
nature 21–2, 61
Nicholas of Cusa 176

Nightmare Alley (Edmund Goulding) 259–60
The Night of the Living Dead 256
North by Northwest (AH) 5, 7, 20–1, 24, 27, 28, 43, 44, 45, 47–71, 73, 126, 212, 215, 236, 240
Notorious (AH) 4, 6, 8, 9, 25, 26, 27, 37, 45, 53, 60, 126, 151–4, 197, 202

objects
  types of 6–9
  perverse 25–7, 28, 33–46, 239
  see also the Thing
Oedipus complex 147–8
Olivier, Laurence, *Hamlet* 87–90, 271–2 n68
One More Mile to Go (AH) 267 n29
Oudart, Pierre 158

Parker, Alan 267 n31, 268 n36
perversion 249, 266 n22
  see also under objects
Plato 166
  Symposium 233
play-within-a-play 82–90
Poe, Edgar Allen 114, 215
point-of-view 155–8, 164–6
  see also subjective camera
politics 22–3
primal scene 200, 203
Prix de beauté 137
Psycho (AH) 3, 10, 24, 28, 37, 39, 125, 129, 130, 131, 135, 151, 154, 162, 164, 179, 183, 195–205, 214, 218–19, 223, 226–34, 235, 236, 239, 242, 243–52, 256–8, 261–2, 265 n17, 269 n44
psychoanalysis, Lacanian 262–3
psychotic attitude 189–93, 227–9, 239, 261–2
public and private 52–5, 66–71

Racine, Jean 213
  Athalie 213, 263–4 n5
  Phaedre 214
Ray, Nicholas 153
Real, surplus of 239–40
  see also stain
Rear Window (AH) 5, 6, 18, 20, 21, 23, 25, 26, 111, 132, 133, 143–4, 155–76, 197, 218–19, 227, 245, 265 n11, 269 n49
Rebecca (AH) 4, 109, 110–11, 197
Rebello, Stephen, *Alfred Hitchcock and the Making of 'Psycho'* 231, 265–6 n17
reciprocity 41–3

Regnault, François 25
religion 239–40
Renoir, Jean 133
repetition 110–11, 112, 126
Reville, Alan 27
Rohmer, Eric 132, 152, 153, 212
Rope (AH) 4, 73, 77–8, 115, 159
Rothman, William 97, 252
    Murderous Gaze 218, 256

Sabotage (AH) 4, 24, 129–32, 134–5
Saboteur (AH) 7, 25, 28, 56, 70, 109,
    111–16, 117, 118, 125, 215, 219
Sade, Marquis de 221–2
sadism 219–23
Sadoul, Georges 3
Sartre, Jean-Paul 71, 170
    Being and Nothingness 166–7, 168
Sato, Tadao 16
Schreber, Daniel Paul 250
Scott, Ridley 217
The Secret Agent (AH) 4, 9, 73, 129
Sennett, Mack 15, 16
The Seventh Seal (Ingmar Bergman) 49
sexual relationships 9–10
Shadow of a Doubt (AH) 4, 6, 8, 9, 24, 31–9,
    41, 45, 106, 109, 117, 118, 125, 135
Shakespeare, William, *Hamlet* 73, 82, 84,
    87–90, 129, 271–2 n68
sinthoms, motifs as 126
Something Wild (Jonathan Demme) 11 n1
Son nom de Venise 201
Sorry, Wrong Number (Anatole Litvak)
    258–9
sound, use of 158–9
space 49–71, 152–3, 159
Spellbound (AH) 61, 64, 125, 126
Spoto, Donald 33, 37, 145, 146
Stage Fright (AH) 10, 20, 39, 73, 79–80, 83,
    261
stain, as inducing the gaze 20–9, 33,
    133–4, 169–72, 175–6, 192, 235–40,
    248–9, 257
    see also object, perverse; the Thing
Stalinism 213, 220–1, 222
Sternberg, Josef von 137–8, 272 n76
Strangers on a Train (AH) 5, 6, 7, 25, 39–44,
    45, 62, 125, 127, 187, 253
subjective camera 260
    see also the gaze
subjectivity
    types of 5–9, 149
    and the gaze 134
    subject beyond 245–58

suicide 93–103, 135, 246–7
surplus-element 236, 239–40
suspense 15–29, 131–5, 146–9, 153
Suspicion (AH) 9, 20, 25, 109, 116–18, 126,
    143–9, 235, 236
symptom 238

Telotte, J.P. 259, 260
Terminator 256
The Testament of Doctor Mabuse (Fritz Lang)
    204–5, 206 n1
theatre and theatricality 73–103, 159–60,
    246–7
the Thing 46, 98, 101–2
    gaze of 248–58, 270 n56
thirdness 112, 114–16, 214–15
The Thirty-Nine Steps (AH) 3, 4, 6, 8, 9,
    12 n6, 28, 44, 47, 50, 52, 73, 79, 215
Thompson, D'Arcy W. 172
To Catch a Thief (AH) 60, 125, 268 n36
Top Secret (Zucker, Abrahams and
    Abrahams) 224
Torn Curtain (AH) 5, 219, 222, 225
transference 100–1
transgression of the Law 225–6
trauma, and fiction 130–5, 189, 217–18
The Trial (Orson Welles) 157
The Trouble with Harry (AH) 21, 126, 227
Truffaut, François (Interviews with
    Hitchcock) 31, 44, 83, 113, 130, 139,
    145, 157, 162, 178, 202, 248
truth
    stage as place of 81–2, 84
    as authenticity of subject position
        261–2

uncanny 153–4, 244
Under Capricorn (AH) 4, 12 n7, 139, 245

Vertigo (AH) 10, 12 n9, 24, 45, 52, 59,
    125–6, 228, 252–3
Viridiana (Luis Buñuel) 49
voice-over/flashback device 258–61
Vorstellungs-Repräsentanz 238–40, 244,
    268 n37
voyeurism 164, 170–6
    see also the gaze

Weir, Peter, 98–102
Weis, Elizabeth 3
    The Silent Scream 245
Welles, Orson 157, 206 n1, 259
When a Stranger Calls (Fred Walton) 251

INDEX

Wittgenstein, Ludwig 257
The Wizard of Oz 234
Wood, Robin 266 n25
The Wrong Man (AH) 25, 125, 162, 185–93,
    211–19 *passim*, 235, 271 n64

Young and Innocent (AH) 4, 9, 12 n6, 25, 28,
    73

Zecca 16
Žižek, Slavoj 40, 114